Quality of Protection
Security Measurements and Metrics

Advances in Information Security

Sushil Jajodia

Consulting Editor
Center for Secure Information Systems
George Mason University
Fairfax, VA 22030-4444
email: jajodia@gmu.edu

The goals of the Springer International Series on ADVANCES IN INFORMATION SECURITY are, one, to establish the state of the art of, and set the course for future research in information security and, two, to serve as a central reference source for advanced and timely topics in information security research and development. The scope of this series includes all aspects of computer and network security and related areas such as fault tolerance and software assurance.

ADVANCES IN INFORMATION SECURITY aims to publish thorough and cohesive overviews of specific topics in information security, as well as works that are larger in scope or that contain more detailed background information than can be accommodated in shorter survey articles. The series also serves as a forum for topics that may not have reached a level of maturity to warrant a comprehensive textbook treatment.

Researchers, as well as developers, are encouraged to contact Professor Sushil Jajodia with ideas for books under this series.

Additional titles in the series:

UNDERSTANDING INTRUSION DETECTION THROUGH VISUALIZATION by Stefan Axelsson; ISBN-10: 0-387-27634-3

COMPUTER VIRUSES AND MALWARE by John Aycock; ISBN-10: 0-387-30236-0

HOP INTEGRITY IN THE INTERNET by Chin-Tser Huang and Mohamed G. Gouda; ISBN-10: 0-387-22426-3

CRYPTOGRAPHICS: Exploiting Graphics Cards For Security by Debra Cook and Angelos Keromytis; ISBN: 0-387-34189-7

PRIVACY PRESERVING DATA MINING by Jaideep Vaidya, Chris Clifton and Michael Zhu; ISBN-10: 0-387- 25886-8

BIOMETRIC USER AUTHENTICATION FOR IT SECURITY: From Fundamentals to Handwriting by Claus Vielhauer; ISBN-10: 0-387-26194-X

IMPACTS AND RISK ASSESSMENT OF TECHNOLOGY FOR INTERNET SECURITY:Enabled Information Small-Medium Enterprises (TEISMES) by Charles A. Shoniregun; ISBN-10: 0-387-24343-7

SECURITY IN E-LEARNING by Edgar R. Weippl; ISBN: 0-387-24341-0

IMAGE AND VIDEO ENCRYPTION: From Digital Rights Management to Secured Personal Communication by Andreas Uhl and Andreas Pommer; ISBN: 0-387-23402-0

INTRUSION DETECTION AND CORRELATION: Challenges and Solutions by Christopher Kruegel, Fredrik Valeur and Giovanni Vigna; ISBN: 0-387-23398-9

THE AUSTIN PROTOCOL COMPILER by Tommy M. McGuire and Mohamed G. Gouda; ISBN: 0-387-23227-3

Additional information about this series can be obtained from
http://www.springer.com

Quality of Protection
Security Measurements and Metrics

edited by

Dieter Gollmann
TU Hamburg-Harburg, Germany

Fabio Massacci
University of Trento, Italy

Artsiom Yautsiukhin
University of Trento, Italy

 Springer

Dieter Gollmann
TU Hamburg-Harburg
Institute Security in Distributed
Applications
Harburger Schloßstraße 20
21079 Hamburg
GERMANY
diego@tu-harburg.de

Fabio Massacci
University of Trento
Dipartimento Informatica e
Telecomunicazioni (DIT)
Via Sommarive, 14
38050 TRENTO
ITALY
Fabio.Massacci@unitn.it

Artsiom Yautsiukhin
University of Trento
Dipartimento Informatica e
Telecomunicazioni (DIT)
Via Sommarive, 14
38050 TRENTO
ITALY
evtiukhi@dit.unitn.it

Quality of Protection: Security Measurements and Metrics
edited by Dieter Gollmann , Fabio Massacci, and Artsiom Yautsiukhin

ISBN 978-1-4419-3965-4   e-ISBN 978-0-387-36584-8

Printed on acid-free paper.

Printed in the United States of America.

9 8 7 6 5 4 3 2 1

springer.com

Table of Contents

vi

Preface

Information Security in Industry has matured in the last few decades. Standards such as ISO17799, the Common Criteria, a number of industrial certification and risk analysis methodologies have raised the bar on what is considered a good security solution from a business perspective.

Yet, if we compare Information Security with Networking or Empirical Software Engineering we find a major difference. Networking research has introduced concepts such as Quality of Service and Service Level Agreements. Conferences and Journals are frequently devoted to performance evaluation, QoS and SLAs. Empirical Software Engineering has made similar advances. Notions such as software metrics and measurements are well established. Processes to measure the quality and reliability of software exist and are appreciated in industry.

Security looks different. Even a fairly sophisticated standard such as ISO17799 has an intrinsically qualitative nature. Notions such as Security Metrics, Quality of Protection (QoP) or Protection Level Agreement (PLA) have surfaced in the literature but still have a qualitative flavor. The "QoP field" in WS-Security is just a data field to specify a cryptographic algorithm. Indeed, neither ISO17799 nor ISO15408 (the Common Criteria) addresses QoP sufficiently. ISO17799 is a management standard, not directly concerned with the actual quality of protection achieved; ISO15408 is instead a product assessment standard and yet does not answer the question of how a user of a product assessed by it can achieve a high QoP within his/her operational environment. Both standards cover just one aspect of an effective QoP and even the combination of both would not address the aspect sufficiently. "Best practice" standards, such as the baseline protection standard published by many governments agencies, also belong to the category of standards that are useful, but not sufficient, for achieving a good QoP.

Security is different also in another respect. A very large proportion of recorded security incidents has a non-IT cause. Hence, while the networking and software communities may concentrate on technical features (networks and software), security requires a much wider notion of "system", including users, work processes, organizational structures in addition to the IT infrastructure.

This collection of essays is a first attempt to discuss how security research can progress towards a notion of Quality of Protection in Security comparable to the notion of Quality of Service in Networking, Software Reliability, or Software Measurements and Metrics in Empirical Software Engineering. They are first step towards the establishment of scientific and technical methodologies for evaluating security solutions and security patterns in *Security Engineering*.

The collection is started by a short survey by A. Atzeni and A. Lioy: Why should we adopt a security metric, and how can it be used to guarantee an high level Quality of Protection? G. Karjoth and his co-authors from IBM Research offers also a motivating scenario from industry based on the need of providing service-oriented assurance and claim that the only way to provide a comprehensive security is indeed to provide an explicitly assurance as a protection level agreement.

The second part of the book is devoted to the issue of measurements and how one can use models and techniques from reliability and related fields to capture security issues. In the first paper A. Ozment discusses the adequacy of reliability statistics for capturing the trends in software vulnerabilities, whereas S. Gokhale and R. Mullen advocate the usage of a lognormal model that can explains the relations between software defects and the overall QoP of a product while M. McQueen and his co-authors suggest a variant of the well known Mean-Time-To-Failure reliability metric in the form of the Time-to-compromise model to estimate cyber risks related to QoP. Another model based on risk analysis is also proposed by D. Balzarotti, M. Monga, and S. Sicari. Finally E. Alata and his co-authors report the results of the analysis of a large data gathering experiment based on honeypots.

Quantitative formal security models are discussed at length in the third part of the book. S. Foley and his co-authors presents a modification of the classical Multilevel Security model that allows for quantitative and not just qualitative notions of security levels. J. Rosseboe and her co-authors proposes a challenging conceptual model for service availability from a telecommunication perspective while V. Casola and her co-authors proposed a SLA methodology for service oriented architectures. The paper by I. Cervesato concludes the section with a carefully constructed model for quantitative security analysis based on logic.

Metrics for anonymity and confidentiality are discussed in the last section of the book by D. Kesdogan, L. Pimenidis and T. Koelsh both from a theoretical and an experimentaland perspective. R. Lundin and her co-authors suggest to use guesswork as a measure for confidentiality whereas E. Damiani and his co-authors discuss a comprehensive model for measuring inference exposure in outsourced (yet encrypted) databases

The essays collected in this paper were presented at the Quality of Protection Workshop held in Milano and co-located with the European Symposium on research in security and privacy (ESORICS'05) and the 11th IEEE International Software Metrics Symposium (METRICS'05), were Helmut Kurth from ATSEC gave a stimulating invited presentation.

The papers were carefully selected by the program committee (only 15 out of 28 submitted papers were accepted for presentation) and were further revised by the authors after the discussion at the workshop.

Acknowledgements

The support of Pierangela Samarati and the ESORICS organizers have been essential for the organization of the QoP workshop and for making it a success. Artsiom Yautsiukhin's help in the preparation of the proceedings was invaluable.

The work of Fabio Massacci has been partly supported by the PAT-MOSTRO project and the project FP6-FET-IP-SENSORIA and the FP6-IST-IP-SERENITY.

March 2006

Dieter Gollmann (PC-Chair)
Fabio Massacci (PC Chair)

Conference Organization

Programme Chairs

Dieter Gollmann (PC-Chair)
Fabio Massacci (PC Chair)

Programme Committee

Alessandro Acquisti
Matt Bishop
Yves Deswarte
Paolo Donzelli
Gerhard Eschelbeck
Erland Jonsson
Audun Jsang
Svein Johan Knapskog
Helmut Kurth
Bev Littlewood
Fabio Martinelli
Roy Maxion
Flemming Nielson
Mario Piattini
Lorenzo Strigini
Ketil Stlen
Edgar Weippl
Artsiom Yautsiukhin
Marvin Zelkowitz

Local Organization

Fabio Massacci
Artsiom Yautsiukhin

External Reviewers

Mohamed Kaniche
Gabriele Lenzini
Mass Soldal Lund
Marinella Petrocchi
Atle Refsdal
Fredrik Seehusen

Why to adopt a security metric? A brief survey *

Andrea Atzeni and Antonio Lioy

Politecnico di Torino
Dip di Automatica ed Informatica
Torino(Italy)
{shocked, lioy} @ polito.it

Abstract. No doubt that computer security is a hot topic nowadays: given the importance of computer-assisted activities, protection of computer system is of the utmost importance. However we have insofar failed to evaluate the actual security level of a system and thus to justify (either in technical or economical terms) the investments in security. This paper highlights the motivations to improve security measurement techniques, analyses the existing approaches, and discusses whether their are appropriate or some new directions should be explored.

Keywords: security metric, computer system security

1 Introduction

Intuitively, security evaluation of computer systems is an important task. But why is it so important? Why is it so urgent and why so many efforts are devoted to this aim? Obviously, it is so important because *electronic machines* surround us everytime and everywhere: for example, when we make a call, when we edit a document, when we write an e-mail, or when we schedule a meeting with our Personal Digital Assistant. So, in a certain way, computer systems bear on our life the same influence that atmospheric conditions and wild animals bore on our ancestors. Undeniably, computers surround us pervasively, and they will much more spread in the future, as last decades permit us to foresee.

Measurement is the way by which humans understand with more precision the rational world. *We measure to reveal a condition and possibly alert the user. We also measure to quantify the magnitude of phenomena. Probably most importantly, we measure to control processes* [1]. Paraphrasing Lord Kelvin, *when you can measure what you are speaking about and express it in numbers, you know something about it* [2]. Starting from this base, we will explore the scientific literature to gain more insight to the motivation of measuring the security of a computer system, recalling that measurement and metric adoption is almost always a tool to improve and manage developing process [3]. The rest of the paper is organised in following manner. Section 2 briefly describes general concepts related to metric and measurement systems, sections 3, 4 and 5 examine three main motivations justifying the improvement of security measures, respectively efficiency, economical gain and social management. Section 6 explores some

* This work is part of the POSITIF project, funded by the EC under contract IST-2002-002314.

actual work developed on measurement tools in security. This topic permits to understand if spending an effort in the definition of a security metric is worthwhile or not. Conclusions follow in section 7.

2   What is a measure

To understand the importance of measuring a system, it is first necessary to understand what a measure is. A measure is the result of a measurement, i.e. a process aiming to acquire quantitative or qualitative values of real world attributes. A "real-world attribute" is any property of an abstract or concrete existing entity. For example, my clock is an entity, and one attribute is its colour, which could be expressed in qualitative term (it is black) or in quantitative term (its Red-Green-Blue hexadecimal component values are 06-03-03).

A measurement system should exhibit some properties in order to be effective and useful:

- **Clarity** A measure should be easy to interpret, at least in its operative context. A measure without clear meaning will lead to discussions and different beliefs in the best case, to wrong conclusions in the worst. In both cases, the usefulness of the measure is reduced.
- **Objectiveness** The measure should not be influenced by the measurer will, or beliefs, or actual feeling. Otherwise, its value will retain the correct sense only for the original measurer, and the measure would lose in generality.
- **Repeatability** If repeated in the same context, with exactly the same conditions, the measure should return the same result. If this is not the case, as the uncertainty in the value increases so the measurement's usefulness may decrease, and its treatment may become harder.
- **Easiness** The measure of an attribute should raise knowledge about the entity itself, sometimes with the purpose of improving the usefulness of the entity. However, if the measure is too difficult to be performed, or simply impossible to accomplish, the knowledge's gain is not sufficient to motivate the measurement.
- **Succinctness** Only important parameters should be considered, letting aside aspects not important to the definition and/or the comprehension of the entity under measurement. Such property aims to reduce both measure's complexity and uncertainty. In a few words, "don't miss the forest for the trees".

These properties are always desirable, but they are very difficult to achieve when dealing with measure of complex quantities – such as security (or goodness or any other not easily definable entity). Therefore, as the simple existence of statistics proves, many attempts successfully treat measures not clearly understood or prone to relevant uncertainty.

After this brief discussion of the desirable properties, we may now face the paper's main question: *why would the adoption of a security metric be a profitable enhancement?*

3   Efficiency

A natural answer to the paper's question is *because to work without measure is not efficient*, that is, the ratio of output to input of a system may be improved by employing better metrics. Blakley [4] claims that the *traditional approach to information security has failed*, and this is due to a number of reasons, that can be resumed by the tremendous complexity of large computer systems. Composing a large, secure system from little and simple secure components is a daunting purpose, due to the difficulty of the composition, rather than to building the single components, which may be easy. On the other hand, starting directly with the construction of huge secure system is worse. As previously stated, this is not surprising, because the complexity of general-purpose system permits billions of different operation types, hence it is quite difficult to foresee each of them in different possible scenarios. However, in spite of the problem difficulty, measurement systems can greatly help. As stated by Bush et al. [5] *the better one understands a phenomenon, the more concisely the phenomenon can be described*, so description's efficiency improves. In fact, the simple act to measure can improve the efficiency, we could just recall the axiom, circulating in software engineering field, *when performance is measured, it improves* [6]

A metric is not only important for its own sake, but as part of a more wide schema. The measures permit to acquire knowledge and improve the system. As in the conceptual schema of Fig. 1, the *acquisitors* are means to gain knowledge of the external world, i.e. to measure some attributes. These acquisitors are the focus of the measurement's system definition, they are the ones that should exhibit properties of "good measure". The remaining part of the figure refers to the *treatment system* (for data manipulation to extract meaning) and *feedback system* (for the desirable feedback to the system under measurement, in terms of improving changes). It is noticeable that all the other system parts profit from a "good" measurement system.

If embedded in an overall evaluation schema, the power of the measurement can inspire awe. In the ongoing European project POSITIF [7] a holistic approach is proposed to face the security concern, restricted to the computer network environment.

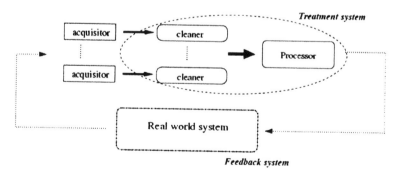

Fig. 1. The righteous improving schema

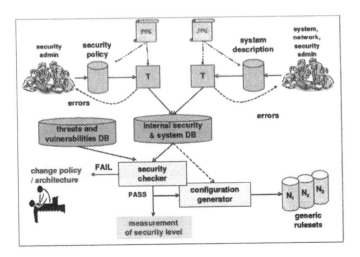

Fig. 2. The Positif framework

In the POSITIF framework (depicted in Fig. 2) the network will be described in formal terms by a formal *system description language*, the desired security level will be described by a formal *policy description language* and the security evaluation will be performed by a *security checker*, capable of evaluating the actual network security level.

4   Economical motivations

Without the conscious decision to agree on a way of measuring, cooperative activity could hardly take place. With it, marketplaces and increasingly sophisticated economies can develop, matching barter, cash, or credit to whatever is owned by one person and desired by another [8]

In our current society, economical reasons are the most common motivation for human actions[1], thus, many researches approach the metric definition problem from an economical perspective. An issue in metric establishment is that security is not described in "comprehensible terms" with respect to a business expert [4], and even more for "normal computer users". This holds a great difference to other field, like medicine (for example, the effect of smoking on a human body is much more clear, also in "monetary" terms). This issue arises in security due to the difficulty of the evaluation of the benefits of adopting a security technology, which are hard to assess. It is difficult to know beforehand the impact of a security change, to compare alternative designs and

---

[1] We are really afraid that many people would agree upon this statement … Anyway we don't want to linger in moral judgements in this (scientific) paper (and, however, other wide motivations, such as military supremacy, often are also worse).

to make the right choice with poorly-objective available data [9]. Furthermore, without an economical evaluation framework, the companies' tendency may be to not share security information, embracing a greedy strategy of short-period gain [10].

Another urgent point is the dramatical increment in the last few years of the attack frequency. Long ago, in the early Internet stage, only universities and "good guys" shared information by wide area networks, so security concerns has been far remoted from Internet developer's minds for long time[2]. When Internet spread its influence and became commonplace to the majority of computer users, also "bad guys" came into play, and security threats multiplied as well. At the same time, the company's economic reliance on information and informatics grows more and more [11] and hence Internet (in)security has become an economic concern.

Nowadays, cyber-attacks cause huge losses. For example, a survey [12] estimates that *the stock price impact of cyber-attacks show that identified target firms suffer losses of 1%-5% in the days after an attack. For the average New York Stock Exchange corporation, price drops of these magnitudes translate into shareholder losses of between $50 million and $200 million.* The same survey also claims a worldwide overall loss, for all attack types, of about $226 billion[3]. However, the fact remains: attacks on information systems influence the stock market, the extent of which depends on the firm's business type and on the attack type. Some partially contradictory studies exist on the topic, e.g. [13–16], summarized by [12]. The apparent trend is, in general, a loss in the short time period, and a smaller loss in the medium-long range. The extent of such losses is surely related to the type of company, for example B2C companies, such as Amazon and eBay, almost completely relying on Internet technology, can suffer very wide financial losses, as demonstrated in June 1999 when eBay's site was unavailable for 22 hours and the stock lost twenty-five percent of its value [17]. Possibly, the type of attack is an influencing factor, in particular attacks impacting confidentiality seem to cause a greater damage than others [14], but such result is probably related to the company type.

Other researches and surveys highlight the overall financial impact of virus and worm diffusion, and general economic damage imputable to any kind of cyber-attack. Costs are always many billion dollars. Moreover, cyber attacks can influence cost in more subtle terms, for example diminishing the adoption of informative infrastructure, hence decreasing the achievable productivity.

All these menaces are reduced by better security tools, and a meaningful and effective measurement system is propaedeutic to any security improvement .

5   National security motivations

Domination and leadership are one of the earliest and strongest motivations for knowledge acquisition among human beings. The capability to measure security enables strategic plans and appropriate counteracts to enemy's actions. Computer system attacks, depending on motivations, may be a concern of national and international rel-

---

[2] But for availability issues, that were studied since the very beginning of Internet development.

[3] The survey also states that *the reliability of these estimates is often challenged; the underlying methodology is basically anecdotal.*

evance. Since metaphors and similitudes are a way to *give maximum meaning with a minimum of words* [18], they often illuminate on the real meaning of a concept in a particular context. Words like *cyber-terrorism* or *cyber-war*, used in many government and police documents, point out the great importance informatics attacks hold in such environments. We can just notice that rumours report that even the (in)famous head-terrorist Osama-Bin-Laden spread orders and informations to his followers by means of Internet and steganographic techniques [19]. Of course, a security measure able to measure both the attacking techniques and also the defending countermeasures, in a comparable fashion, would be of great help to understand if terrorists can by-pass the defences or if instead the situation is relatively safe.

A series of yearly USA CSI-FBI surveys gather data by interviewing a large number of computer security practitioners in U.S. corporations, government agencies, financial institutions, medical institutions and universities. Investigation concerns include, among others, the way organisations evaluate the performance of their investments in computer security, the portion of the IT budget devoted to computer security, the security training needs of organisations, the level of organisational spending on security investments, the impact of outsourcing on computer security activities. The most recent surveys [20] exhibit some good news, such as the decrease of financial losses related to security breaches, and the extensive adoption of security audits. On the other hands, virus and denial of service attacks increase to a value of $55 million, and the sharing of intrusion information is in decline, due to the consequent bad publicity. However, the report does not highlight clear trends in computer crime and, by the way, its samples are probably not chosen in a statistically sound fashion [12]. These facts point out one more time the need of useful metrics to determine security and the consequence of security action. Such consequences should be determined both to analyse business interaction and to evaluate effectiveness of countermeasures.

6   Proposed solutions

The purpose of this section is to illustrate the proposes actually in the arena, in order to judge the opportunity to adopt or not a security metrics.

First of all, an advice always valid when dealing with measures and metrics is to *give meaning to measurement*, that is, to follow the principles explained in section 2, and some other practical principles, like visibility of the measure (the results should be close to the end-user), tail-to-the-audience (the results should be adapted to the end-user, for example eliminating non-relevant data), traceability (the tools and measures employed should refer to an explaining base, for example, the needed knowledge base to calibrate a sensor) [21]

The way to improve the world can be economic and/or technical, and it may come from one or more of the approaches considered in the next subsections.

6.1   Technical solutions

Several approaches to establish a technical security evaluation have been proposed. Maybe the most promising ones involve statistical research. The idea is the establishment of a model capable of describing system behaviour. Starting from such a description, the aspired result is the acquisition of further knowledge on the (simulated) system, and hopefully the forecast of the system security evolution. This modus operandi mainly stems from the dependability field, not surprisingly however, since dependability and security share many common points, and security or dependability are sometimes considered one as a subset of the other, as expressed in [22]. An excellent paper [23] surveys many methodologies developed.

Reliability block diagrams, usually adopted in large network analysis [24, 25], represent a system as composed by many interconnected components. The components are modelled with statistical properties, like mean-time-between-failure, and the system behaviour is simulated starting from single-component characteristics and properties of the component linking connection.

Fault trees are acyclic graphs (trees), in which the root is the system of interest, leaves are single component and inner nodes, that is nodes between the root and the leaves, are "logic gates", able to model the failure flow from the leaves to the root. If a flow from leaves to root is established, then a failure occurs. These systems are well understood and general enough to be applied in *hardware, software and humanware in complex computer-based systems* [26].

Attack trees are a natural security adaptation of fault trees, where a system failure (i.e. the root of the tree) is a security breach, the leaves are the menaces to which the system is exposed, and the flows between leaves and root are the possible ways of exploiting the basic weaknesses. The first mention of attack trees is in the Schneier's milestone book *Secrets and Lies: Digital Security in a Networked World* [27].

Other modelling tools include model checking, in which the system is formally depicted by its possible operative states, and the evaluation is based on reachability analysis of the state space, and stochastic representation of the system evolution by Markov chains, as pointed out by Dacier's notable work during his PhD studies and later [28–31].

We believe that several of these approaches are very promising, as witnessed by their many successful applications to the dependability field. At the present time the problem is the lack of a formal and validated model of security behaviour, which in rough words could be resumed by a challenging issue of statistical analysis: the study of non-independent statistical variables.

6.2   US Government solutions

Governments, first among all that of the United States of America, devote considerable efforts to analyse and implement efficient metrics and measurement systems. The National Institute of Standards and Technologies (NIST) [32] is the official standardisation organism in the USA, and its CSD division is devoted to computer security standardisation [33]. Inside CSD, three sections are involved in system evaluation and certification, both mansions strictly related with measurement; these sections are:

– Federal Information System Management Act (FISMA) implementation program
– Security Testing
– Security Management and Guidance

FISMA is the emanation of the US Congress that highlights the risks of aggressive cyber attacks at the heart of critical infrastructures, and that urges countermeasures in order to prevent such possibilities from becoming real. The FISMA implementation project is a NIST's CSD effort aiming at promoting standards and guidelines to reach goals like security categorisation of information and information systems, selection of appropriate security controls for information systems, verification of security control effectiveness and determination of information system vulnerabilities, operational authorisation for processing (security accreditation) of information systems, in order to make available more consistent, comparable, and repeatable evaluations of security controls applied to information systems, a better understanding of enterprise-wide mission risks resulting from the operation of information systems, more complete, reliable, and trustworthy information for authorising officials, facilitating more informed security accreditation decisions, or, synthetically, more secure information systems within federal agencies, which composes the critical computer infrastructure of the United States [34]. Roughly speaking, almost all activities relate to qualitative or quantitative measurements.

The Security Testing Unit approaches the problem of developing, managing and promoting assessment tools as means of secure system development. Under this Unit fall partnerships promoting the dissemination and use of evaluated IT products and systems and the growth of such products in U.S.A., like National Information Assurance Partnership [35] or Trust Technology Assessment Program [36]. Other aspects involve the development of an automatic testing toolset, in order to improve the economics of security functional testing [37], or the development and dissemination of cryptographic-modules validation program [38] against FIPS 140-2 Security Requirements for Cryptographic Modules [39].

The Security Management and Guidance Unit mainly gathers standards, best practices and guidelines adopted inside federal US agencies [40] aiming to export virtuous behaviour or to discuss and improve possible weak practices. Moreover, this division emits or collects publications related to all system security aspects, from system evaluation to information acquisition by means of questionnaires [41].

Other CSD duties include guidance to embed security development into the system life-cycle [42], to adhere to federal security requirements for federal agencies, a.k.a policies [43], helping program for security management [44], and economical framework evaluation method for IT security investment [45] . Also a software tool helping towards automating security self-assessment is freely available from the web site [46]

6.3 Economical solutions

Blakley [4] proposes the "monetisation" of security actions. In such a way, information loss and product effectiveness will be available in monetary terms, and may possibly become a usual insurance and trade instruments. He remarks how the publication of such monetary information would create an *effective information security market* and permit to allocate capitals in the right manner, and would stop the rewarding of ineffective solutions. However, such a solution appears really hard to achieve. Blakley's suggestion is to initially accept limited liabilities for security products, which will be adjusted by the market with its usual demand-offer mechanism. Even if Blakley's position may make sense, a long and hard work appears essential to correctly price security.

Butler proposed an intriguing cost-benefit analysis, called Security Attribute Evaluation Method (SAEM) able to *bridge the communication gap between security managers and information technology (IT) managers* [9], that is, in simple term, to make clear the benefit and the cost of a security solution to a non-security adept. SAEM method involves four steps: 1) a security technology benefit assessment, 2) an evaluation of the effect of security technologies in mitigating risks, 3) a coverage assessment and 4) a cost analysis. Of course, the hard part is not to state but to accomplish such tasks. The first point is accomplished by supervised and extensive interviews of IT and security managers. The second point is achieved through statistical data, describing the frequency and the outcome of threats. The last two points can be developed in parallel, and relate to the evaluation of how large is the coverage of the countermeasure and what is its relative cost. Many problems arise with such evaluation systems. The initial data acquired in the first phase are not objective, so all the subsequent phases are potentially influenced by such errors. Moreover, the statistical data required for the second phase may be not available. With regard to this point, Butler proposes the multi-attribute analysis, a useful technique able to treat uncertainty when many attributes are involved. However, much of the multi-attribute approach is based on human subjective choices, hence the final result is often useful, but rarely objective.

Gordon et al [10] studied the topic of sharing security-breach information. Based on previous literature and on the experience of Trade Associations (TAs), Information Sharing Analysis Centres (ISACs)[4] and Research Join Ventures (RJVs), they conduct a deep analysis of pros and cons for information sharing, stating that the combination of literature regarding TAs and RJVs *provides theoretical underpinnings to develop a model for examining information sharing related to security breaches*. The work is very interesting, but not conclusive, leading to suggest further research for the development of such a model. An investment security model was carried out in a more recent work [11]. Many are the simplifying assumptions, nevertheless the model retains a sound economical sense, capable of evaluating the best trade-off between cost of security breaches and benefit of threat reduction.

7   Conclusion

Security is a complex matter, neither deeply understood nor easily measurable, therefore, in order to better understand and evaluate it, the actual measurement system has to improve and possibly new measurement schemes have to come into play. From the economical perspective, the huge amount of money loss is a natural engine towards improvement, therefore many economical researches are going toward some sort of econometric models, as shown by the last 5-6 years of literature. Unluckily, these studies are not at the present time conclusive nor widely proven, hence further studies and

---

[4] ISACs are industrial based organisation, with federal participation and assistance, aiming to information sharing, for example offering confidential venue for sharing security vulnerabilities and solutions

researches are welcome. In spite of this, we believe the scenario to be promising and fruits near to be borne.

As said, security is a complex matter, but this seems to stimulate a vast enflowering of studies, improving the day-by-day knowledge on the topic and the capability of structured evaluation, as pointed out by the cited papers. This should not come as surprise, since security is both a matter of civilian concern and government concern; so, it is natural that stimulating action is taken by more sensitive states (like the USA).

Perhaps, a problem of the past approaches was a too stringent focus on the evaluation issue. Instead, we believe that in order to work out practically usable solutions, the problem has to be approached in a more holistic way, formalising the goal to be achieved, formalising the properties of the system, and then using formal and automatic tools to evaluate the security. Positive side-effects, letting aside the automation of the evaluation, should be highly customisable results, precisely suitable for the actual evaluated system.

References

1. K. Fowler and J. Schmalzel. Why do we care about measurement? *Instrumentation & Measurement Magazine, IEEE*, 7(1):38–46, March 2004.
2. William Thompson. Popular lectures and addresses, 1891-1894.
3. KnowledgeRoundtable. Metrics. http://www.knowledge-roundtable.com/app/content/knowledgesource/section/149.
4. B. Blakley. The measure of information security is dollars. In *The First Workshop on Economics and Information Security, Berkeley (CA, USA)*, 16-17 May 2002.
5. S.F. Bush and S.C. Evans. Complexity based information assurance. Technical report, General Electrics corporate research and development, October 2001.
6. S.J. Keene. Cost effective software quality. In *Proceedings of Annual Reliability and Maintainability Symposium, Orlando (FL, USA)*, pages 433–437, 29-31 January 1991.
7. Sixth Framework Programme IST-2002-002314. Policy-based security tools and framework. [Online] http://www.positif.org/.
8. A. Linklate. *Measuring America*. Walker & company, 2002.
9. S. A. Butler. Security attribute evaluation method, a cost-benefit approach. In *Proceedings of ICSE2002 International Conference on Software Engineering, Orlando (Florida, USA)*, pages 232–240, 19-25 May 2002.
10. L. A. Gordon, M. P. Loeb, and W.Lucyshyn. An economics perspective on the sharing of information related to security breaches: concepts and empirical evidence. In *The First Workshop on Economics and Information Security, Berkeley (CA, USA)*, 16-17 May 2002.
11. L. A. Gordon and M. P. Loeb. The economics of information security investment. *ACM Transactions on Information and System Security*, 5(4):438–457, 2002.
12. B. Cashell, W. D. Jackson, M. Jickling, and B. Webel. The economic impact of cyber attacks. Technical Report RL32331, U.S.A. Government and Finance Division, 1 April 2004.
13. H. Cavusoglu, B. Mishra, and S. Raghunathan. The effect of internet security breach announcements on market value: Capital market reactions for breached firms and internet security developers. *International Journal of Electronic Commerce*, 9(1):69, Fall 2004.
14. M.P. Loeb Campbell K, L.A. Gordon and L. Zhou. The economic cost of publicly announced information security breaches: Empirical evidence from the stock market. *Journal of Computer Security*, 11(3):431–448, 2003.

15. M. Ettredge and V. J. Richardson. Assessing the risk in e-commerce. In *Proceedings of the 35th Hawaii International Conference on System Sciences, Big Island (Hawaii)*, page 11, 7-10 January 2002.

16. A. Garg, J. Curtis, and H. Halper. Quantifying the financial impact of it security breaches. *Information Management & Computer Security*, 11(2):74–83, 2003.

17. S. Glover, S. Liddle, and D. Prawitt. *Ebusiness: principles & strategies for accountants.* Prentice Hall, 2001.

18. OnlineWritingLab. Using metaphors in creative writing - why use metaphors? http://owl.english.purdue.edu/handouts/general/gl_metaphor.html.

19. P. Swami. Failed intelligence. *Frontline*, 18, 7 December 2001.

20. L. A. Gordon, M. P. Loeb, W.Lucyshyn, and R. Richardson. Ninth CSI/FBI computer crime and security survey. Technical Report RL32331, C.S.I. Computer Security Institute, 2004.

21. K. Fowler. Giving meaning to measurement. *Instrumentation & Measurement Magazine, IEEE*, 4(3):41–45, September 2001.

22. A. Avizienis, J. Laprie, and B. Randell. Fundamental concepts of dependability. Technical Report N01145, LAAS-CNRS, April 2001.

23. D.M. Nicol, W.H. Sanders, and K.S. Trivedi. Model-based evaluation: from dependability to security. *IEEE Transactions on Dependable and Secure Computing*, 1(1):48–65, Jan.-March 2004.

24. M. Sahinoglu, C.V. Ramamoorthy, A.E. Smith, and B. Dengiz. A reliability block diagramming tool to describe networks. In *Proceedings of Reliability and Maintainability Annual Symposium, Los Angeles (CA, USA)*, pages 141–145, 26–29 January 2004.

25. W. Wang, J.M. Loman, R.G. Arno, P. Vassiliou, E.R. Furlong, and D. Ogden. Reliability block diagram simulation techniques applied to the ieee std. 493 standard network. *IEEE Transactions on Industry Applications*, 40(3):887–895, May-June 2004.

26. L.L. Pullum and J.B. Dugan. Fault tree models for the analysis of complex computer-based systems. In *Proceedings of Reliability and Maintainability Symposium, 'International Symposium on Product Quality and Integrity', Las Vegas (NV, USA)*, pages 200–207, 22–25 January 1996.

27. B. Schneier. *Secrets and Lies: Digital Security in a Networked World.* John Wiley & Sons, 2000.

28. M. Dacier. *Towards Quantitative Evaluation of Computer Security.* PhD thesis, Institute National Politechnique de Toulose, 1994.

29. M. Dacier and Y. Deswarte. The privilege graph: an extension to the typed access matrix model. In D. Gollman, editor, *European Symposium in Computer Security (ESORICS 94), (Brighton, UK), Lecture Notes in Computer Science, 875*, pages 319–334. Springer Verlag, 1994.

30. M. Dacier, Y. Deswarte, and M. Kaaniche. Models and tools for quantitative assessment of operational security. In *12th International Information Security Conference (IFIP/SEC 96), Samos (Greece)*, pages 177–186. Chapman & Hall, 1996.

31. M. Dacier, Y. Deswarte, and M. Kaaniche. Quantitative assessment of operational security: Models and tools, 1996.

32. National institute of standards and technologies. http://www.nist.gov/.

33. National institute of standards and technologies - computer security division. http://csrc.nist.gov/.

34. National institute of standards and technologies - security certification index. http://csrc.nist.gov/sec-cert/index.html.

35. National information assurance partnership. http://niap.nist.gov/.

36. Trust technology assessment program. http://csrc.nist.gov/ttap/.

37. NIST - automatic functional testing. http://csrc.nist.gov/auto-func-test/index.html.

38. Cryptographic-modules validation program. http://csrc.nist.gov/cryptval/.
39. Federal information processing standard 140-2. http://csrc.nist.gov/cryptval/140-2.htm.
40. Federal agencies security practice. http://csrc.nist.gov/fasp/index.html.
41. Computer security research center - pubblications. http://csrc.nist.gov/publications/.
42. NIST - system development life cycle. http://csrc.nist.gov/SDLCinfosec/index.html.
43. NIST - federal agencies policies. http://csrc.nist.gov/policies/index.html.
44. Program review for information security management assistance (PRISMA). http://prisma.nist.gov/.
45. Return on security investment and IT security capital investment planning. http://csrc.nist.gov/roi/index.html.
46. NIST - software assessment tool. http://csrc.nist.gov/asset/index.html.

Service-oriented Assurance –
Comprehensive Security by Explicit Assurances

Günter Karjoth, Birgit Pfitzmann, Matthias Schunter, Michael Waidner

IBM Research, Zurich Research Laboratory
Säumerstrasse 4, 8803 Rüschlikon, Switzerland
{gka,bpf,mts,wmi}@zurich.ibm.com

Abstract. Flexibility to adapt to changing business needs is a core requirement of today's enterprises. This is addressed by decomposing business processes into services that can be provided by scalable service-oriented architectures. Service-oriented architectures enable requesters to dynamically discover and use sub-services. Today, service selection does not consider security. In this paper, we introduce the concept of Service-Oriented Assurance (SOAS), in which services articulate their offered security assurances as well as assess the security of their sub-services. Products and services with well-specified and verifiable assurances provide guarantees about their security properties. Consequently, SOAS enables discovery of sub-services with the "right" level of security. Applied to business installations, it enables enterprises to perform a well-founded security/price trade-off for the services used in their business processes.

1 Introduction

Enterprises struggle to increase their flexibility to adapt to changing business needs. Service-oriented architectures address this challenge by decomposing enterprises into loosely coupled services, which are hosted on platforms that can adapt to changing load and performance requirements [2]. This trend is reflected by the growth of value networks, in which enterprises specialize on their core competencies and interconnect these critical services to provide a better overall service to their customers.

Whereas current research focuses on how to integrate the business processes of these value networks, security will be a major obstacle to their wide-spread adoption. Cross-enterprise security is still addressed by long-lasting trust relationships, contracts, and manual audits. Emerging service-oriented architectures and flexible usage patterns are slowly invalidating this static closed-world approach. There exists no approach that guarantees overall security while permitting the flexibility required today.

In this paper, we propose a new concept called "Service-oriented Assurance" (SOAS) that enables providers to advertise their security, allows customers to monitor the actual security of a service, and provides well-defined recourse for violations of promised security features. SOAS provides a framework to express and validate assurances. An *assurance* is essentially a statement about the properties of a component or service, typically made by the producer of the component or the provider of the service. Besides the specification of the security properties of the component, it adds a definition of how these properties are to be measured and by whom, and a recourse for the case that the promised property does not hold. *Assurance verification* is done by determining the existence or absence of the above properties. Enterprises can then link the required level of security of their IT systems and their business requirements, namely, the level of risk that the enterprise is willing to accept. In conclusion, SOAS empowers enterprises to provide security in dynamic service-oriented architectures while automatically procuring services that offer the right level of security.

This paper first presents the taxonomy concepts of SOAS, the use of SOAS for Web Services, and a basic architecture for monitoring assurances (§2). Next, it describes the actual use of SOAS (§3) and illustrates the concept of assurances by means of some example scenarios, putting particular emphasis on the separation of the assurance from the security mechanisms that achieve the assured property (§4). Finally, it discusses related work (§5) and concludes (§6).

2   Service-oriented Assurance

SOAS is a new paradigm defining security as an integral part of service-oriented architectures. It enables services to formalize and advertise their security assurances. Based on these declarations, services can address the core challenges of secure and flexible service composition:

– What are the security properties of a given service?
– How can the actual security be measured?
– What are the assumptions, failure possibilities, and dependencies of a given service?
– What evidence can be given that a service will or does indeed meet its security promise?
– Which remedies will be taken if a service does not provide the promised security?

In the remainder of this section, we outline the use of SOAS for Web Services, the taxonomy concepts of SOAS, and a basic architecture for monitoring SOAS assurances.

2.1   From Service Level Agreements to SOAS

Web Services are the preferred way of describing services in a service-oriented architecture. If a component needs a certain service, it discovers potential providers via directories and brokers, e.g., using UDDI, WSDL, and WS-Resource descriptions, and then engages with a specific service provider. In particular in cross-domain scenarios, this engagement is governed by a Service Level Agreement (SLA), e.g., expressed in WS-Agreement, which summarizes the requester's and provider's agreement on what the service is supposed to do. An SLA defines the quality of service, how and by whom that quality is measured, and what has to happen if the service quality is insufficient. Today SLAs are often implicit (in particular for services within one organization) and in most cases fairly static and pre-negotiated. But this is expected to change – in the future service providers will be selected more dynamically and hence SLAs will be more pervasive and negotiated in real time. This negotiation will become part of the overall process and of the overall Web Services stack.

Service-oriented Assurance adds security to this picture: Before two components engage in a service, they provide each other with assurances, i.e., security guarantees, as part of the SLA negotiation process. Examples are promises to provide certain process or data isolation, to comply with a regulation, or to accept a certain risk, or also statements of identity, etc., together with arguments why these properties hold, such as certificates for Common Criteria security evaluations, hardware-based integrity statements, or identity certificates and digital signatures.

Depending on how the SLA defines the manner in which security quality is measured, components may gather evidence during operation, i.e., information that documents and maybe even proves the state of transactions or the security posture of the component. This information can be security alarms, entries in log files, authenticated messages received from other components, hardware-based integrity measurements, etc. If something goes wrong, this information becomes the basis for fault diagnosis and forensics. Once a problem has been identified, the assurances will point to the components responsible for solving the problem and for covering damages. This is particularly important in a cross-domain scenario involving different organizations, where the result may be an actual financial recourse.

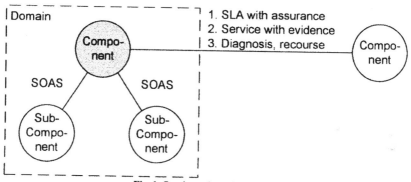

Fig. 1. Service-oriented Assurance

Figure 1 summarizes the use of assurances. We mainly consider the gray component on the left, e.g., a business process. It uses the service of another component (process), which may be in another domain, and of local sub-components. In a service-oriented architecture, there is no great difference between these two uses, except that there is by necessity a stronger dependency on some local components, e.g., the underlying operating system. In a first step, the processes negotiate an SLA with assurances. This is done in the context of the processes' own service assurances to their users. Secondly, during normal service, both processes may gather evidence of their own correct operation and of the operation of their partner; some of this evidence may be exchanged explicitly. In case of problems, diagnosis and forensics should be possible based on the evidence gathered, and the SLA will provide procedures for a potential cross-domain recourse.

2.2   High-level Model

To enable the formalization of statements that express the security promised for a given service, SOAS defines a model as shown in Figure 2. In theoretical terms, this is in essence a meta-model of service descriptions.[1] Note that SOAS only formalizes the structure of security statements and that properties must not necessarily be expressed in a formal way; they may simply denote a certification such as a security label like EAL-4 or a privacy seal like TRUSTe having a precise meaning given from outside the SOAS model. The figure is drawn in UML, a widely used graphical design language.

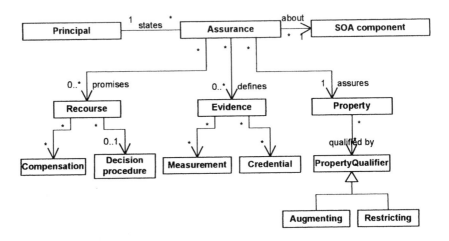

Fig. 2. Assurances on SOA components

The security of a SOA component is established by the properties it is expected to implement. Thus, declaring (security) *properties* is the foundation of the SOAS model. Properties of SOA components can be written texts (like contracts) but will often be machine-readable to enable automation and comparison beyond equality tests. Simple properties may define the I/O syntax of a service by, e.g., promising to adhere to a WSDL schema. Properties may also make statements about the actual behavior of a service stating, for example, the privacy of personal data. More examples are given in §4. This can be done using formal specifications or textual descriptions of the expected services.

Properties either hold unconditionally or are qualified. A *qualifier* augments or restricts a given property. In an augmenting qualifier such as availability or performance,

---

[1] A meta model of SOA exists in [1], but it does not classify service descriptions or service properties. Given a meta model, corresponding models can be serialized either automatically, i.e., a "language" is defined implicitly by the UML model, or manually, e.g., into extensions of existing Web Services specification languages.

the resulting qualified property always implies the original property. Restricting qualifiers are key to modeling security. Typically they express environmental assumptions needed, e.g., a trust model specifying entities that are assumed to be correct, failure probabilities, or validation methods.

An *assurance* is a statement about a property of a *SOA component* or service, made by a *principal* such as the producer of the component or the provider of the service. Assurances define the evidence the component has to deliver to show it indeed provides the desired properties, and a specification of recourse if the component fails to provide these properties.

Evidence describes the information provided by the service to support the assurance, typically by enhancing the credibility of other elements. Mostly provided in the form of credentials, evidence may corroborate that the principal builds good components by customer references or a formal certification. Or it may corroborate the component properties, e.g., by supplying a certificate of a claimed Common Criteria evaluation or by describing the procedure used for determining the mean time between failures. Or it may corroborate a recourse, e.g., by showing that the principal has reserved funds. Evidence also defines how the property can be measured and by whom. For instance, it can be the retrieval of a log file by the service provider, a third-party audit, or a measurement signed by secure hardware included in the platform [11].

A *recourse* consists of a decision procedure and possible compensations. For dispute resolution, agreement on the interpretation of the measurement is essential to enable the parties to agree whether a property is fulfilled. A *decision procedure* provides instructions on how to deal with cases where, for example, some properties are not immediately measurable because, for instance, probabilities depend on how long one measures, or secrecy violations may not be noticed at once. If neither party fully trusts the other's measurements, the decision procedure may require that both sides measure in parallel or may even state that in case of conflicts additional proofs are provided by third parties [5].

Whenever the stated security property does not hold or can no longer be guaranteed, a *compensation* states a penalty, e.g., a sum of money, or defines a remediation process that re-instates security and is considered to be sufficient to satisfy the property. Whereas a penalty does not necessarily require the assurance to be re-established, remediation on the other hand is a well-defined process how a violation can be removed and how the system is guaranteed to reach a state that provides the given assurance. An example of the latter is the property of absence of viruses. The provider can guarantee that once a virus is discovered during a regular check, the virus is removed within 1 h and integrity of the installation is re-verified.

2.3 Monitoring Security Properties

Besides giving *explicit security assurances* as outlined above, SOAS must also support the *verifiability* of these assurances. Whereas the first challenge requires a language for specifying the assurances to be included into SLAs, verifiability of these assurances may be achieved by providing measurements supporting the evidence in the stated properties. Figure 3 outlines possible interactions between measurement components of a SOAS-enabled service. The interactions are structured into two phases. Before actually providing a service, the provider and requester agree on the Security SLA that describes the desired security. Once an agreement is reached, the service will be provided and its security can be monitored. Depending on the trust model, an optional observer can act as a referee to decide whether the properties are indeed met.

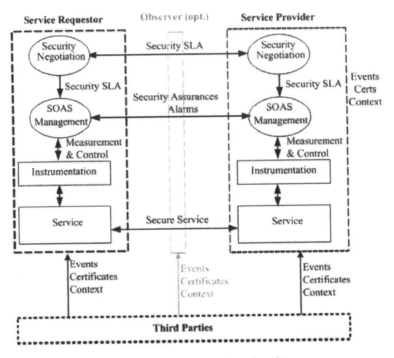

Fig. 3. Run-time monitoring of Service-oriented Assurance

To enable security monitoring, both the service and the client are instrumented. This instrumentation measures the security parameters of the service, input to a SOAS Management component verifying the given security assurance.

2.4   Types of Security Evidence

For assessing the security properties, data from various sources are needed. Both parties may evaluate system states – including security policies in place – and events that are provided through instrumentation as well as certificates, and other context from third parties. Examples are certificates of acceptable software as well as events that represent newly discovered vulnerabilities of the installed code base.

In principle, we distinguish three main types of security measurements depending on the time period addressed:

- An *audit log* makes it possible to verify whether a system has provided the assurance in the past. Examples include log files of past virus scans, an execution history listing the executables loaded in memory [11], and access records for confidential data.
- The current *state* enables one to prove statements about a given moment in time. This can include ownership proofs about the provider implemented by certificates or the absence of a virus at this point by a virus scan.
- Convincing a verifier that certain *policies* are enforced enables a system to indicate that a security property is likely to hold in the future. Examples are training programs, access-control policies, and policies for re-mediating specific failures.

Depending on the trust model, additional evidence may be needed to convince the verifier that the given data is accurate. In particular for policies, it is essential to convince the verifier that they will not be replaced with inappropriate ones. A similar challenge exists for state and audit logs. If the verifier does not trust the systems providing the service, additional evidence such as audits at random times may be needed. Furthermore, evidence of insecurity may turn up in various ways, e.g., by finding confidential data on the Internet or via whistle blowers.

Properties and thus their measurements may be qualitative or quantitative. Whereas the former simply determine whether a property holds, the latter measurements determine how strong the property is. Quantitative security is not yet common-place but there are example properties such as quantitative information flow or measures like the number of known vulnerabilities and k-anonymity.

3   Applying SOAS

To gain security addressed consistently and naturally at the right places, SOAS should be integrated in the overall software architectures and tooling. However, SOAS can to some extent also be retrofitted to legacy systems by documenting and exposing their known security properties and publishing corresponding security assurances. This explicit expression of security enables service selectors to consider security as a criterion for service selection, which in turn creates a reward for security. This reward will enable appropriate economic mechanisms that lead to the highest levels of security where this is most beneficial, and allows security to increase in economically cost-effective steps.

To implement fine-grained assurance statements, security assurances must be propagated and implemented along the software stack. As a consequence, software components would either implement their own security mechanisms (e.g., a banking application using one-time passwords), use security mechanisms from lower layers (e.g., SSL encryption), or use a security infrastructure for transparent protection (e.g., anti-virus or isolation services).

Propagating explicit assurances of components requires explicit exposure of assumptions as well as a more active security management in each component. Accordingly, components need to identify their assurances based on the assurances offered by sub-components. Another important aspect is that in order to enable its use in an open environment where not all components trust each other, SOAS creates an incentive that components enable verifiability of their security properties. This means that components can produce evidence that the claimed properties are actually true. A (simple) example is ownership: A service can use attribute certificates to prove that it is owned by a certain entity. This enables higher-layer services to measure and validate the assurances provided by lower-layer services. More complex scenarios include components that guarantee to report their security status honestly based on a well-defined measurement method.

Another important application of SOAS is to use security assurances to select appropriate services and to compose services. Once sub-components declare their service guarantees, services can factor security into the decision which sub-service to select. Loosely speaking, SOAS enables a service to discover the sub-service with the right level of security and the best cost/risk trade-off. Based on the assured security properties including potential qualifiers, a service may decide which tasks to entrust to each particular service. If a sub-service does not provide the full guarantees that are needed, a service can decide to augment the guarantees, e.g., by running replicas or obtaining additional recourses that remedy the losses in case of failure.

4   Example: Security of an Outsourced Business Process

In this section we illustrate the concept of assurances based on a larger example where a bank outsources a business process to an external provider. We first identify the overall assurances and then elaborate on two specific properties.

4.1   Overall Security Agreement

The overall goal is to manage the security of a business process by identifying and verifying the security properties of its sub-processes. In practice, this initial usage of SOAS is possible without automatic verifiability of the security properties. Instead, assurance can be achieved by signed statements of the service provider containing sufficient compensation in case well-defined security measurements indicate that the promised security cannot be or has not been achieved.

Let us consider a bank that outsources a sub-process such as payment processing to an outsourcing company. As is currently done, the bank and the outsourcing provider establish a service-level agreement for the outsourced process. This SLA defines the actual service as well as key performance indicators such as availability and throughput. This SLA can be negotiated and fixed using WS-Agreement. It will also define the WSDL interfaces to the service.

Because the sub-process is critical to the business of the bank, security requirements have to be added. Using SOAS, the bank and the outsourcing provider agree upon the actual security to be provided by the sub-process, how it is measured, and what compensation will be offered in case of failure. These security guarantees may cover different aspects of the outsourcing infrastructure and can be structured into distinct properties:

Basic integrity properties. The provider assures integrity properties on the input and the output data. In addition, it may state that input data of any kind will not lead to buffer overflows.

User management. The provider defines how users are authenticated and how access to the sub-process is restricted to the appropriate applications in the bank.

Basic infrastructure. The provider defines which availability is guaranteed and how it will be achieved, e.g., by replication, backups, and disaster recovery measures.

Isolation. The provider guarantees that this business process is completely isolated from other business. In particular, isolation holds even if processes are executed on behalf of other banks.

Application quality control. The provider defines how applications are tested and how quality is achieved. In particular, the provider guarantees that only applications that have passed a well-defined test-suite will be used to provide the service.

Security policies. The provider guarantees that the process is managed according to well-defined security policies. These policies include staff education, proper security zoning and boundary control, as well as emergency response for the corresponding services. The security policies also include virus protection and intrusion detection and response measurements.

All these properties are declared using signed statements. Because they are difficult to be verified automatically, validation can still be achieved by external auditors or audit teams from the bank or from the provider. Once the provider fails to comply, appropriate recourses from the initial assurance are used to remedy or compensate a failure.

4.2   Security Management – Customer Isolation

In an outsourcing environment, data owned by different customers must be isolated; i.e., no information may flow between customers except through well-defined business processes. This causes no problem in today's outsourcing environment, where most resources and applications are dedicated to one customer. In the case of shared applications or resources, however, they must be certified to provide appropriate isolation. As a consequence, a property promised may be that "there is no information flow between all services of this customer and any service provided to another customer".

To securely implement above guarantees, the provider either has to provide dedicated resources for each customer or to guarantee that no shared resource leaks any information between customers. This guarantee for shared applications can be done by means of an evaluation and certification. An alternative is the provision of virtualized resources (such as logical partitions) that are dedicated to each customer, enabling different customers to share one machine but still providing guaranteed separation. However, as it is hard to analyze whether a shared application allows information flow or not, both parties may have to accept some level of risk.

Depending on the trust the bank puts into the provider, the actual mechanisms that are used as well as their verifiability will differ. One way to provide assurance is to provide a signed statement of the provider or an auditor. If the trust in the provider or the auditor was unjustified, the customer may notice a violation only if the undesired information flow has visible effects, e.g., secret data clearly being used by competitors. For these cases, there must be compensation. The decision procedure may be aided by watermarking techniques. However, mechanisms where the service provider is trusted to notify someone of security violations are known and can be effective, as the experience with the California Senate Bill No. 1386 shows.[2]

Property qualifiers can be used to define limitations of virtualization including the requirement that certain services be not virtualized, virtualized on a dedicated resource, or hosted on machines satisfying certain criteria such as physical security protection or location [3]. An example of the latter are the concerns that Canadian personal data will fall under the US Patriot Act once they are hosted on machines that are physically in the USA [9].

4.3   Security Management – Virus Protection

Service users require that machines hosting critical services follow basic security guidelines. The property that is promised by a service is that the machine providing a service is managed according to well-known security guidelines. Such guidelines usually require sound patch management, firewalls, and appropriate virus protection.

Assurance of appropriate virus protection, for example, can be implemented in different ways. Using certification and recourse, the service provider promises to manage the machines according to the guidelines and certifies this including recourse. As virus attacks are usually quite visible by loss of availability, the bank may not require specific measurements in the assurance if the recourse is sufficient to cover potential losses. Alternatively, sound virus protection may be indicated by means of an audit trail of recent virus scans to convince a verifier that no virus activity was detected while a given service was being provided. Moreover, assurance for this property can be provided by means of integrity-based computing (IBC) mechanisms. For virus protection, IBC can prove at regular intervals that a virus scanner has been resident in memory and not been invalidated.

5   Related Work

Several models and languages formalize agreements (contracts) on electronic services [5, 12, 13], covering agreement specification as well as system architecture. However, they mainly focus on specific aspects of services. For example, WSLA is a language for the specification of quality-of-service agreements for Web services. Besides providing a type system for SLA artifacts, WSLA identifies the contractual parties, specifies the characteristics of the service and its observable parameters, and defines the guarantees and constraints that may be imposed on the SLA parameters [5].

WS-Agreement is a standardization effort defining an agreement format, an agreement establishment protocol, and a runtime agreement monitoring interface. Agreement terms represent contractual obligations, including specific guarantees given [6]. Guarantee terms specify service level objectives, a qualifying condition under which objectives are to be met, and a business value giving the importance of meeting these objectives.

---

[2] Summaries of incidents cataloged on PIPEDA and Canadian Privacy Law can be found at www.privacylawyer.ca/blog/2005/02/summaries-of-incidents-cataloged-on.html.

The Composite Assurance Mapping Language (CAML) provides a notation for claim trees for the assurance arguments related to enterprise security objectives, providing causalities, relationships, vulnerabilities, threats, and other system- and environment-related issues [7]. A CAML specification hierarchically refines security claims about the system into sub-claims that, eventually, are linked with the evidence that a claim is satisfied. Refinement is supported by the general strategy, assumptions, and dependencies, justifying reasons, and contextual models.

Security properties of components can be measured and verified by using products such as Symantec Enterprise Security Manager or IBM Tivoli Security Compliance Manager[3] (SCM). SCM gathers information from multiple computer systems, such as registry and application information, analyzes the data, and produces reports to reveal adherence to security policies. Collectors retrieve specific data by reading files or running an executable program. Data collected on client systems is stored in a database on the server. Conditions are expressed as SQL statements that analyze data from the database tables to provide a list of client machines violating the conditions.

Also trusted computing allows one to verify the integrity of a platform (attestation), whereby secure boot and strong isolation guarantee integrity. Remote attestation authenticates software to remote parties. However, attestation based only on the configuration of software and hardware components entails the problem of managing the multitude of possible configurations, system updates, and backups [4, 8, 10]. A trusted virtual machine, as for example proposed by Haldar et al [4], can execute platform-independent code to attest programs, thus certifying various properties of code running under it by explicitly deriving or enforcing them. SOAS assurances may provide the language to express these properties and the way they should be verified.

6 Conclusion

Service-oriented Assurance enables products and services to provide well-specified security guarantees, which can be monitored and validated. These assurances enable enterprises to select services that offer the right level of security. Our example illustrates that it is feasible to specify important security properties in a vendor-agnostic and platform-independent way. As a consequence, we believe that SOAS is the logical future of security in service-oriented architectures.

Our proposal is only a first step in this direction. Further work is required in the formalization of a broad range of specific security properties and on assurance verification as well as on service composition. There is still a long way to go before security risks are comprehensively managed and become normal economic factors on the business layer. Nevertheless, we have demonstrated a framework that shows how the objectives stated above can be achieved and that first meaningful ways exist to instantiate this framework based on current software and hardware capabilities.

---

[3] http://publib.boulder.ibm.com/tividd/td/IBMTivoliSecurity
ComplianceManager5.1.html

Acknowledgments

We want to thank Bob Blakley, Tom Corbi, Bruce Harreld, Linda Henry, Anthony Nadalin, Nataraj Nagaratnam, Chris O'Connor, Charles Palmer, Ronald Perez, and Andreas Wespi for interesting feedback.

References

1. L. Baresi, R. Heckel, S. Thöne, and D. Varró. Modeling and Validation of Service-Oriented Architectures: Application vs. Style. In *ESEC/FSE'03*, pages 68–77. ACM Press, 2003.
2. T. Erl. *Service-Oriented Architecture: Concepts, Technology, and Design*. Prentice Hall PTR, 2005.
3. J. L. Griffin, T. Jaeger, R. Perez, R. Sailer, L. van Doorn, and R. Cáceres. Trusted Virtual Domains: Toward secure distributed services. In *Workshop on Hot Topics in System Dependability*, 2005.
4. V. Haldar, D. Chandra, and M. Franz. Semantic remote attestation: A virtual machine directed approach to trusted computing. In *USENIX Virtual Machine Research and Technology Symposium*, pages 29–41, 2004.
5. A. Keller and H. Ludwig. The WSLA framework: Specifying and monitoring service level agreements for web services. *Journal of Network and Systems Management, Special Issue on E-Business Management*, 11(1), Mar. 2003. Plenum Publishing Corporation.
6. H. Ludwig, A. Dan, and R. Kearney. Cremona: an architecture and library for creation and monitoring of WS-agreements. In *2nd International Conference on Service Oriented Computing (ICSOC '04)*, pages 65–74. ACM Press, 2004.
7. J. S. Park, B. Montrose, and J. N. Froscher. Tools for information assurance arguments. In *DARPA Information Survivability Conference and Exposition II (DISCEX'01)*, volume 1, pages 287–296, 2001.
8. J. Poritz, M. Schunter, E.V. Herreweghen, and M. Waidner. Property attestation — scalable and privacy-friendly security assessment of peer computers. IBM Research Report RZ 3548, 2004.
9. Public Sector Outsourcing, Information & Privacy Commissioner for British Columbia. Privacy and the USA Patriot Act - Implications for British Columbia. www.oipcbc.org/sector_public/usa_patriot_act/pdfs/report/privacy-final.pdf, Oct. 2004.
10. A.-R. Sadeghi and C. Stüble. Property-based attestation for computing platforms: Caring about policies, not mechanisms. In *New Security Paradigm Workshop 2004*, pages 67–77. ACM Press, 2005.
11. R. Sailer, T. Jaeger, X. Zhang, and L. van Doorn. Attestation-based policy enforcement for remote access. In *11th ACM Conference on Computer and Communications Security*, pages 308–317. ACM Press, 2004.
12. J. Skene, D. Lamanna, and W. Emmerich. Precise service level agreements. In *26th Int. Conference on Software Engineering*, pages 179–188. IEEE Computer Society Press, 2004.
13. V. Tosci, B. Pagurek, and K. Patel. WSOL – a language for the formal specification of classes of service for web services. In *International Conference on Web Services (ICWS'03)*, pages 375–381. CSRA Press, 2003.

Software Security Growth Modeling: Examining Vulnerabilities with Reliability Growth Models

Andy Ozment*

Computer Security Group
Computer Laboratory, University of Cambridge

Abstract. The software engineering tools historically used to examine faults can also be used to examine vulnerabilities and the rate at which they are discovered. I discuss the challenges of the collection process and compare two sets of vulnerability characterization criteria. I collected fifty-four months of vulnerability data for OpenBSD 2.2 and applied seven reliability growth models to the two data sets. These models only passed applicability tests for the data set that omits dependent data points. Musa's Logarithmic model has the best one-step-ahead predictive accuracy of the three acceptably accurate models for that data set. It estimated that fifty-four months after OpenBSD 2.2's release, the mean time to vulnerability discovery for OpenBSD 2.2 was 42.5 days and that 58.4% of the vulnerabilities it contains had been found. However, a trend analysis cannot rule out the possibility that there is no trend at all in the rate of vulnerability detection, and this result casts doubts on the accuracy of the reliability growth models. The lack of a clear decreasing trend in that analysis highlights one of the challenges of using reliability growth models on vulnerability data: it may be a true reflection of the system or it may be caused by the changes over time in the effort invested in vulnerability detection.

1 Introduction

Most commercial software suffers from significant design and implementation security vulnerabilities. This lack of security can be traced to two primary factors: complexity and motivation. Software developers push to create ever more complex products and work constantly on the boundary of manageable complexity. However, even taking this difficulty into account, most software contains security flaws that its creators were readily capable of preventing. The second cause of software insecurity is motivation: although vendors are capable of creating more secure software, the economics of the software industry provide them with little incentive. Consumers generally reward vendors for adding features and for being first to market. These two motivations are in direct tension with the goal of writing more secure software, which requires time consuming testing and a focus on simplicity. Nonetheless, the problems of software

* This work was funded by a Marshall Scholarship and a United Kingdom Overseas Research Student Award.

insecurity, viruses, and worms are frequently in the headlines; why does the potential damage to vendors' reputations not motivate them to invest in more secure software?

Vendors' lack of motivation is readily explained: the software market is a 'market for lemons' [1]. In a Nobel prize-winning work, economist George Akerlof employed the used car market as a metaphor for a market with asymmetric information [2]. In his model, buyers cannot ascertain the quality of the used cars on the market, and as a result they are unwilling to pay a premium to obtain a higher quality car. After all, why pay more for quality when you are uncertain of obtaining it? Owners of high quality cars thus become unwilling to sell them, because they cannot obtain a reasonable premium.

The software market suffers from the same asymmetry of information. Vendors may have some intuition as to the security of their products, but buyers have no reason to trust the vendors' assertions. Worse, even the vendor is unlikely to have a truly accurate picture of its software's security. As a result, buyers have no reason to pay the premium required to obtain more secure software, and vendors are disinclined to invest in securing their products.

An effective means of measuring software security could decrease the asymmetry of information and ameliorate the 'market for lemons' effect. Unfortunately, the current measures of security are a consideration of the process by which the product was made, a superficial security review of the product, or a gross consideration of its vulnerability history. In addition to being imprecise, none of these techniques are consistently reliable or particularly useful in cross-product comparison.

However, in a related domain, software engineers have invested a great deal of effort in the measurement and prediction of quality. These efforts have largely focused on three areas [3]:

1. Estimating the total number of faults in a system
2. Estimating the time-to-failure of the system
3. Quantifying the impact of design and implementation methodologies

This work has often utilized the study of faults (defects) identified during the testing and post-release lifespan of the software.

There exists a security corollary to the study of faults: the study of vulnerabilities. This work examines the feasibility of applying software *reliability* growth models to vulnerability data, which I refer to as software *security* growth modeling. Security growth modeling has the potential to provide useful predictions or metrics of security. Security growth models can produce useful and readily understandable results like the mean time to the next failure or the total estimated number of vulnerabilities in that product. These results could be used as both relative measures (with respect to competing products) and absolute measures (with respect to a desired level of assurance). However, these models are necessarily applied to noisy data and are highly dependent upon the vulnerability hunting environment. Nonetheless, security growth modeling may provide useful quantitative insight to supplement the current approaches to assessing software security.

The next section provides an overview of reliability growth modeling and previous work. Section 3 describes the data collection challenge that is the most significant barrier to the adoption of security growth modeling. It also describes the two perspectives on vulnerability characterization that are examined here: failure and flaw. Next, in Sect.

4, I apply traditional reliability growth models to both perspectives of the same data set, and I discuss the results of this effort. In Sect. 4.3, I emphasize the need for data normalization. Section 5 highlights areas of potential future work.

2 Reliability Growth Modeling

Reliability growth models are based upon the assumption that the reliability of a program is a function of the number of faults that it contains. Such models "apply statistical techniques to the observed failures during software testing and operation to forecast the product's reliability" [4, p. 6]. As faults are identified and removed, the system will fail less frequently and hence be more reliable. These models can thus be utilized to estimate characteristics about the number of faults remaining in the system and when those faults may cause failures. They are useful for scheduling testing and for ensuring that a product meets its reliability requirements.

Unfortunately, applying reliability growth models to vulnerabilities rather than faults is impeded by a significant problem: the lack of high-quality data. The literature on reliability growth models generally assumes that they have been applied during pre-release testing and in settings where the collection of failure data was an integral part of the testing environment. Vulnerabilities are extremely unlikely to be identified as such in that stage of software development: if they are found at all, they will probably be perceived simply as faults. As a result, vulnerabilities are most often identified after the product is released—when the collection of precise data is much more difficult.

In order to be effective, reliability growth models require that the environment from which the data is obtained (usually the testing environment) must be equivalent to the environment in which the software will be utilized after deployment [5]. However, many vulnerabilities rely upon the adversary intentionally inputting abnormal data—data outside the bounds of a normal operational profile. Nonetheless, over a long period of time and the wide range of real world environments, it can be considered that the operational profile includes *all* possible input. This perspective justifies the application of these models to vulnerabilities, but it does imply that vulnerabilities may be identified more slowly than faults would be identified.

These models also require that time be normalized for testing effort. If program execution time is utilized, this assumption is readily satisfied. However, if calendar time is used then it should be normalized for the number of testers participating, work days, holidays, *etc.* This assumption has strong implications for the usage of vulnerability data and is discussed in Sect. 4.3.

2.1 Previous Work

The ideal security metric would enable the measurement of both a product's changing security over time and its security relative to other products. Stuart Schechter noted that software producers can use a market for vulnerabilities to establish that a vulnerability in their own program is more expensive than one in a competitor's program; the vendor can thus credibly argue that its software is more secure than that of the competitor [6], [7]. I argued that a vulnerability market can be better designed as an auction; the large body of work on auction theory can then be used to optimize it [8]. Several organizations are now actively purchasing vulnerabilities, so these proposals are not unfeasible. Unfortunately, the current purchasers of vulnerabilities are not sharing pricing information, and there is no broad movement towards an open market or auction. Until such an entity or entities arise, other means of measuring software security are necessary.

Eric Rescorla has previously applied reliability growth models to post-release vulnerability data from the ICAT database [9]. In general, he found no clear trend of security growth, and he questions the social utility of publicly disclosing vulnerabilities.

However, the ICAT database is not focused on vulnerability age; as a result, it may not report all of the out-of-date versions of a program to which a vulnerability applies. This aspect of the database limits the accuracy of Rescorla's work. In previous work, I utilized a data set with full vulnerability birth and death data to challenge Rescorla's results and argue that a trend towards security growth could not yet be ruled out [10]. However, that work focused on the social utility question posed by Rescorla and the data collection process used was not well described. In particular, this process requires decisions and utilizes assumptions that have a significant bearing on the results of the analysis. This work assess two different approaches to data characterization and considers the more broad use of reliability growth models as one tool for evaluating software security.

3   Collection Technique for this Data Set

OpenBSD was selected for this study because its developers emphasize secure programming and code audit; furthermore, its entire source code and every change that has been made to it are readily accessible via internet CVS (a version control system). Version 2.2 was selected as the starting point for the data set because vulnerabilities were fixed silently in the prior two versions; this analysis relies upon the careful documentation of all vulnerabilities identified. The data set was created through the following process:

1. A list of vulnerabilities was compiled from the OpenBSD web page and the most prominent public vulnerability databases: ICAT, Bugtraq, OSVDB, and ISS X-Force.
2. The source code was examined to identify the date on which the vulnerability was repaired (the vulnerability's 'death' date).[1]
3. Prior versions of the source code were then examined until the date on which the vulnerability was introduced into the software could be identified (the vulnerability's 'birth' date).
4. Vulnerabilities were then grouped according to the version in which they were introduced. For this work, only vulnerabilities that were introduced prior to the release of version 2.2 were considered.

Although the process described above seems precise, the reality is that the data is complex and is not always readily categorizable. The most significant challenges in characterizing the vulnerabilities dealt with inclusion and uniqueness.

---

[1] If the fix was itself faulty, the date of the first effort is used rather than that of the last effort. This simplification is in accordance with most models' assumptions that flaws are fixed instantly and without introducing new flaws.

3.1 Inclusion

The vulnerability sources listed above included vulnerabilities that affected only specific hardware platforms or particular localizations. In the interest of universality and simplicity, vulnerabilities were included only if they were location and platform neutral (however, those specific to Intel 386 were also included, under the assumption that this platform is the most common).

In addition, the OpenBSD security page lists vulnerabilities whose inclusion stretches the definition of a vulnerability. For example, the patch description for one vulnerability listed on the OpenBSD security page is: "Improve xlock(1)'s authentication by authenticating via a pipe in an early forked process. No known vulnerability exists, this is just a precautionary patch" [11]. Although the OpenBSD security philosophy is commendable (and was the motivation for its selection as the software to model), including vulnerabilities like these has a negative impact on the models' assessment of OpenBSD's security. One way of resolving this dilemma is to include only vulnerabilities of a clearly specified and easily tested severity: e.g. remote root vulnerabilities. Unfortunately, assessing the risk of a potential vulnerability is enormously time consuming and risk prone. For the purposes of this analysis, no vulnerability was excluded for being unlikely or debatable. The results are thus potentially negatively biased: OpenBSD 2.2 will appear less secure than it actually is.

A similar question is posed by vulnerabilities for which the default configuration of OpenBSD is *not* vulnerable. Should those be counted? A default configuration in which most services are disabled is another commendable aspect of OpenBSD's security policy; however, in practice, many of those services will be enabled by the users. As a result, such vulnerabilities were also included in this analysis. As with the previous decision, the results are thus potentially negatively biased.

3.2 Uniqueness, or Flaw *vs.* Failure

The most difficult task was deciding upon uniqueness: whether a patch or group of patches repaired one vulnerability or multiple vulnerabilities.

OpenBSD includes some software that is maintained by third parties (*e.g.* sendmail). Those third parties often released a new version of their software that contained fixes for multiple (previously secret) security flaws. One solution is to simply count such a 'bundle' patch as repairing only one vulnerability and use the birth date of the youngest vulnerability. However, this solution will result in a positive bias and hence an inflated perception of security for the product: the models will indicate fewer vulnerabilities than actually exist and a more rapid trend towards depletion. Conversely, counting each individual security flaw in the bundle patch as a vulnerability will cause the death date of those vulnerabilities to be recorded as later than it should be: they were actually identified and repaired at some unknown date prior to the release of the bundle patch. That solution would thus bias the model away from depletion and result in an overly negative measure of security.

Similarly, individuals may find multiple related security flaws at once: either by discovering a number of security flaws of one type or by discovering a poor quality section of the code base. Often these related security flaws are remediated in the same patch; should they be considered as individual vulnerabilities or as a single, combined vulnerability?

The question of whether to consider these bundled/related security flaws as unique vulnerabilities or as a single combined vulnerability has a significant impact on the analysis. In a theoretical sense, counting them as unique is equivalent to performing the security growth modeling on *flaw* discovery data: such a data set would include dependent data points. From this perspective, each flaw is considered to be a separate vulnerability. Counting them instead as a single vulnerability is the theoretical equivalent to performing security growth modeling on *failure* data, in which every data point is independent of the others. From this perspective, a single failure initiated the discovery of multiple related security flaws. Traditionally, reliability growth models have used the times of system *failure* as their input data and require that the data points be independent.

The approach chosen has a significant impact on the analysis. In this work, the data were analyzed from both failure and flaw perspectives. Table 1 shows the differing vulnerability counts when each approach is used. The first row shows the number of vulnerabilities discovered per year when related and bundled vulnerabilities are grouped (the failure/independent perspective). The second row shows the number of vulnerabilities discovered per year when vulnerabilities are considered individually (the flaw/dependent perspective). For the flaw perspective, each of those unique–but possibly dependent–vulnerabilities was used as a data point, thus increasing the total number of data points considered. Note that the data for 2002 covers only the first five months of the year.

Table 1. Vulnerabilities identified in OpenBSD 2.2 from 1998-01 – 2002-05†

Perspective	1998	1999	2000	2001	*2002‡*	Total
Treated as failures (only independent data points)	19	17	17	13	2	68
Treated as flaws (dependent data points included)	24	18	22	13	2	79

† No vulnerabilities were found in December 1997, the first month that version 2.2 was available.
‡ The first five months of 2002.

4 Results

4.1 Rate of Vulnerability Detection

I analyzed both the failure- and flaw-perspective data sets with seven time-between-faults reliability growth models.[2]

The data indicate the number of days that elapsed between the identification of faults. The mean, median, and standard deviation for the failure-perspective data are:

---

[2] The SMERFS[3] reliability growth modeling tool was used to assess the models [12].

23.7, 13.5, and 28.0. For the flaw-perspective data: 19.8, 7.0, and 26.54. For both data sets, the minimum was 0 and the maximum was 126.

Three models were applied successfully to the failure-perspective data set; these three models had acceptable bias, noise, trend, and goodness-of-fit results. Table 2 shows the pertinent applicability results. For each quantitative result, that model's ranking with respect to the other two models is shown in parentheses. The first row shows bias, as determined by a μ-plot; this measure assesses the absolute predictive accuracy of the models. The noise and trend results in the second and third rows are useful primarily to ensure that the predictive accuracy indicated by the μ-plot results was not due to opposing trends of inaccuracy canceling each other out on the average. The prequential likelihood values of the three models, shown in row four, are used to assess the relative accuracy of the models with respect to each other. Overall, Musa's Logarithmic model was the most accurate and was ranked first (1).[3]

Table 2. Applicability results for models applied to the failure-perspective data

Statistic	Successful Models		
	Musa's Logarithmic	Geometric	Littlewood/Verrall (L)
Bias (μ-plot)	0.12 (1)	0.13 (2)	0.18 (3)
Noise	0.31 (1)	2.39 (2)	2.44 (3)
Trend (y-plot)	0.20 (3)	0.18 (2)	0.14 (1)
Prequential Likelihood	148.35 (1)	150.23 (2)	150.50 (3)
Overall Rank	(1)	(2)	(3)

None of the seven models were successfully applied to the flaw-perspective data. Each model applied to this data set failed one of four tests: bias, trend, noise, or goodness-of-fit. This failure is not surprising: reliability growth models require that their data points be independent: the flaw-perspective data included vulnerabilities whose discovery was clearly dependent upon the recent discovery of a similar vulnerability. As a result, it seems likely that failure-perspective analysis is a superior method of considering vulnerabilities; it has a sound theoretical basis and the attempt to model the quantitative data was much more successful with this approach. However, data filtering, regardless of the theoretical justification, is always suspect. I am gathering three more years of data in order to verify the accuracy of these results.

Table 3 displays the various estimates produced by the models successfully applied to the failure-perspective data. The intensity is the expected number of vulnerabilities per day. Rows one and two display the intensity at the first and last day of the analysis. The purification level, shown in row three, is a normalized estimate of how vulnerability-free the program is at the end of the period covered by the data set. A purification level of one would indicate a program entirely free of vulnerabilities. The purification level formula used here is undefined for infinite-failure models like Littlewood/Verrall Linear; however, alternative formulations of purification level can be

---

[3] For a more detailed explanation of the acceptability tests, see [13]

used for these models [14]. The fourth row displays the current Mean Time To Failure (MTTF), the expected number of days before the next vulnerability is identified.

Table 3. Estimates made by the successful models using the failure-perspective data set

Statistic	Successful Models		
	Musa's Logarithmic	Geometric	Littlewood/Verrall (L)
Initial Intensity	0.059	0.062	0.066
Current Intensity	0.031	0.030	0.030
Purification Level	0.584	0.505	N/A
Current MTTF	42.5	33.1	33.8

Figure 1 shows both the failure-perspective data set (left) and the flaw-perspective data set (right). For the former, the successfully fitted Musa's Logarithmic model is shown superimposed over the data set; this model was ranked as most accurate of the three successful models. For the latter data set, no models were successfully applied, so the data points alone are displayed.

Fig. 1. Time-between-fault data sets

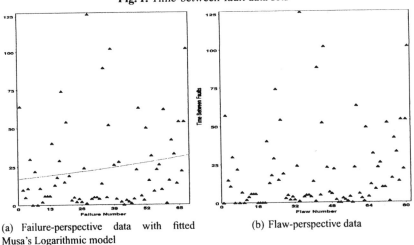

(a) Failure-perspective data with fitted Musa's Logarithmic model

(b) Flaw-perspective data

4.2 Trend Analysis

Reliability growth models assume an eventual trend in which the rate of vulnerability detection decreases over time. One way to test for such trends is through the use of a Laplace test [5]. The calculated Laplace Factors for each data set are shown in Fig. 2. Values below 0 indicate a trend towards decreasing rate of vulnerability detection. However, only values below -1.96 indicate that trend within a 95% confidence level for a two-tailed test (-1.64 for a 90% confidence level). The null hypothesis, that the data exhibits no trend, cannot be rejected for the failure-perspective data set. The flaw-perspective data set shows a more clear trend towards decreasing rate of vulnerability detection. Again, however, the null hypothesis of no trend cannot be ruled out for large periods of time. Both data sets have an initial period in which the rate of vulnerability detection increased. This initial increase is likely caused by the sudden increase in users and environments of use after the software was released; it suggests that an S-shaped reliability growth model may be most appropriate. However, none of the models with acceptable predictive accuracy were of this category.

Fig. 2. Trend Analysis

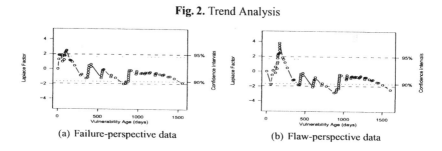

(a) Failure-perspective data   (b) Flaw-perspective data

4.3 Data Normalization

The results indicate that a decreasing rate of vulnerability detection cannot simply be assumed for this data set. Why would the rate of vulnerability detection have increased or stayed constant? One possible answer is that the effort invested in vulnerability discovery during the time period covered in this study increased: more individuals searched for vulnerabilities or those who searched grew more capable of finding vulnerabilities.

As discussed in Sect. 2, one of the underlying assumptions of all reliability growth models is that the data is normalized for effort. The data for the time necessary to find a vulnerability should ideally be the execution time; if such data is not available, the time should be the skill-equivalent person hours. Unfortunately, the data available on vulnerabilities does not include the number of individuals examining that software, much less their relative skill.

This data set thus cannot provide an accurate characterization of the 'true' security of the product (*i.e.* the number of unknown vulnerabilities in the product). The time period from which data was collected, 1997-12-01 to 2002-05-31, witnessed an explosion of interest in computer security and the identification of vulnerabilities. It thus seems likely that many more individuals were searching for vulnerabilities in 2002 than in

1997, but the data used here does not take this change into account. As a result, the the trend analysis and the estimate of the total number of vulnerabilities discussed below may not be an accurate characterization of the underlying product: they are probably conservative and thus characterizes the product as less secure than is actually the case.

The three reliability growth models in Sect. 4.1 have demonstrated acceptable predictive accuracy, but the analysis in Sect. 4.2 cannot rule out the possibility of no significant change in the rate of vulnerability detection. The successfully applied reliability growth models may be accurately characterizing the decreasing rate that appeared in the trend analysis towards the end of the study. Although this data set lacks the normalization discussed above, reliability growth models can still provide insight into the changing rate of vulnerability detection over time. At the very least, these models can describe that rate given the current vulnerability hunting environment. However, the discrepancies between the reliability growth results and the trend analysis indicate that more data is needed before a confident assessment of the system can be made.

5   Future Work

This work highlights five interesting areas for further research: normalize the data for effort, examine the return on security investment, utilize more sophisticated modeling techniques, and combine vulnerability analysis with traditional 'software metrics.'

As discussed in Sect. 4.3, the data set used is not normalized for effort: the skill of and number of individuals searching for vulnerabilities. Unfortunately, OpenBSD does not release usage figures; because it is often used as a server operating system, other available sources of usage data are also inadequate (*e.g.* the proportion of web browsing done from OpenBSD). Moreover, the number of users of a product is not necessarily a useful correlate to the number of individuals searching for vulnerabilities in the product. One area of future work is to find a proxy for effort, at least with respect to the number of individuals searching for vulnerabilities. One possible proxy is the relative numbers of individuals posting to 'full-disclosure' security lists like Bugtraq and Full Disclosure. Although finding an exact measure of effort would be prohibitively difficult, a relative measure would still be useful: *e.g.* there were twice as many individuals searching for vulnerabilities in 2000 as there were in 1998.

Another direction for this research is to examine the return on investment for secure coding practices. Do models fitted to Microsoft's post-2002 secure coding initiative indicate that it is producing results?

An additional path forward is to employ more sophisticated techniques for modeling security growth. The reliability growth literature is rich with means of improving models' accuracy. Finally, vulnerability analysis can be combined with traditional 'software metrics:' metrics that attempt to measure the size, complexity, *etc.* of a program. This line of research might lead to other fruitful measurements or predictors of security.

6   Conclusion

Software engineering provides useful tools for the analysis and potential measurement of software vulnerabilities. In this work, 54 months of vulnerability data were gathered for the OpenBSD operating system. The source code was examined to ascertain the exact dates when the vulnerability was first added to the code and when it was repaired.

The data collection process was complex, and I struggled to find rules for data characterization that covered all possible situations. For OpenBSD, collection difficulties centered around inclusion (when is a defect considered a vulnerability) and uniqueness (when do a number of defects qualify as one vulnerability and when do they qualify as multiple vulnerabilities). Two different characterization criterion were analyzed here: as expected, the reliability growth modeling was only successful when considering the data set that excluded dependent data points.

Three of the seven reliability growth models tested were found to have acceptable one-step-ahead predictive accuracy for the set of independent data points. Musa's Logarithmic model was the model ascertained to be most accurate of those three; it estimated that the mean time to failure at the end of the study is 42.5 days and 58.4% of the estimated total vulnerabilities in the product have been identified. Together, these estimates could serve as both a useful relative and absolute measure of the security of the product.

However, a trend analysis cannot rule out the possibility that vulnerabilities are being detected at a constant overall rate, which casts doubt on the results produced by the reliability growth models. If these results are a more accurate reflection of the system, the lack of a decreasing vulnerability detection rate may be due to an increase in the amount of effort invested in finding vulnerabilities during the course of the study. Reliability growth models and trend analysis are designed for data in which the amount of effort invested in finding vulnerabilities is constant. Unfortunately, no information is available on the growth in the number of individuals searching for vulnerabilities and the effort they invested; as a result, the data set cannot be normalized to take this information into account.

The results of this analysis are thus inconclusive. More data is needed before a definitive assessment can be made of the rate of vulnerability detection in OpenBSD. This problem highlights the main challenge in using software engineering tools to analyze vulnerabilities: the significant effort required in order to collect accurate data and the lack of availability of important information.

Despite these difficulties, this analysis has shown that software engineering tools can provide useful insight into software vulnerabilities. Security growth modeling, the application of reliability growth models to vulnerabilities, can build upon a long tradition of software engineering work, adapting that work as appropriate. If the technique increases in popularity, data collection could be readily incorporated into the vulnerability remediation process. Better data collection would, in turn, result in more accurate and more useful models.

References

1. Anderson, R.: Why information security is hard - an economic perspective. In: 17th Annual Computer Security Applications Conference. (2001) New Orleans, LA, USA.
2. Akerlof, G.A.: The market for 'lemons': Quality uncertainty and the market mechanism. The Quarterly Journal of Economics **84**(3) (1970) 488–500
3. Fenton, N.E., Neil, M.: A critique of software defect prediction models. IEEE Transactions on Software Engineering **25**(5) (1999) 675–689

4. AIAA/ANSI: Recommended Practice: Software Reliability. ANSI (1993) R-013-1992.
5. Lyu, M.R., ed.: Handbook of Software Reliability Engineering. McGraw-Hill (1996)
6. Schechter, S.: Quantitatively differentiating system security. In: Workshop on Economics and Information Security. (2002) Berkeley, CA, USA.
7. Schechter, S.: How to buy better testing: Using competition to get the most security and robustness for your dollar. In: Infrastructure Security Conference. (2002) Bristol, UK.
8. Ozment, A.: Bug auctions: Vulnerability markets reconsidered. In: Workshop on Economics and Information Security. (2004) Minneapolis, MN, USA.
9. Rescorla, E.: Is finding security holes a good idea? In: Workshop on Economics and Information Security. (2004) Minneapolis, Minnesota.
10. Ozment, A.: The likelihood of vulnerability rediscovery and the social utility of vulnerability hunting. In: Workshop on Economics and Information Security. (2005) Cambridge, MA, USA.
11. OpenBSD: Openbsd 2.8 errata, 014: Security fix (2000) `http://www.openbsd.org/errata28.html#xlock`.
12. Stoneburner, W.: SMERFS (statistical modeling and estimation of reliability functions for systems) (2003) `http://www.slingcode.com/smerfs/`.
13. Abdel-Ghaly, A.A., Chan, P.Y., Littlewood, B.: Evaluation of competing software reliability predictions. IEEE Trans. Softw. Eng. **12**(9) (1986) 950–967
14. Tian, J.: Integrating time domain and input domain analyses of software reliability using tree-based models. IEEE Transactions on Software Engineering **21**(12) (1995) 945–958

A Discrete Lognormal Model for Software Defects Affecting Quality of Protection

Robert E. Mullen[1] and Swapna S. Gokhale[2]

[1] Cisco Systems, USA bomullen@cisco.com
[2] University of Connecticut, USA ssg@engr.uconn.edu

Abstract. Many computer and network security crises arise because of the exploitation of software defects and are remedied only by repair. The effect of security related software defects and their occurrence rates is an important aspect of Quality of Protection (QoP). Existing arguments and evidence suggests that the distribution of occurrence rates of software defects is lognormal and that the first occurrence times of defects follows the Laplace transform of the lognormal. We extend this research to hypothesize that the distribution of occurrence counts of security related defects follows the Discrete Lognormal. We find that the observed occurrence counts for three sets of defect data relating specifically to network security are consistent with our hypothesis. This paper demonstrates how existing concepts and techniques in software reliability engineering can be applied to study the occurrence phenomenon of security related defects that impact QoP.

1 Introduction

The growing reliance of our society on the services and protections provided by software applications places a high premium on the efficient, secure, and reliable operation of these applications. Although tools and techniques are available to analyze the performance and reliability of a software application in a quantitative manner, currently the assessment of QoP afforded by a security solution is predominantly qualitative.

Many computer and network security crises arise when an existing defect in a software application is exploited. From a security perspective, software often may be the weakest link. In such situations, the only remedy is to repair the defect. In addition to being directly exploited for a security breach, a software defect may manifest itself as a field failure. In fact, the users of commercial software typically report the occurrence of field failures with the presumption of getting the underlying defects fixed so that the failures do not recur [17]. It has been reported in the literature [18], that a large number of defects encountered by customers are introduced in the process of fixing the detected defects. Repair of a defect that does not degrade QoP may lead to the introduction of a defect that does. Imperfect repair can be a major cause of unreliable software operation, reduction of QoP, and customer dissatisfaction. In summary, latent software defects that are released into the field have a two-fold impact on QoP. First, a defect may be directly exploited to cause a security breach. Second, in the process of repairing a defect that surfaces in the form of a field failure, another defect that might degrade QoP could be introduced. Because of this close relationship between security incidents and software defects, it is natural that the occurrence rates of software defects will be an important component of QoP. Understanding and analyzing the occurrence rates of software defects in general and security defects in particular may provide the basis for quantifying QoP.

In this paper we study the distribution of the occurrence counts of defects. A preliminary analysis of the field defect data collected from widely used networking software indicates that the number of occurrences of defects varies widely. Some defects manifest rarely, are never discovered, and can be considered to be corner cases, but others are pervasive and occur with high frequency. This suggests that the distribution of the occurrence counts of the defects may be highly skewed. A similar observation has been made by Adams [1] and used to devise a preventive maintenance strategy focused on the defects with the highest apparent rates. In addition to these preliminary observations made directly from the data, theoretical reasons and a variety of evidence [22] indicate that the distribution of the defect occurrence rates is lognormal.

We hypothesize that the distribution of rates is lognormal and that the distribution of the number of defect occurrences follows the Discrete-Lognormal (D-LN), also known as the Poisson-Lognormal [16] (ch. 7.11). We further hypothesize that the distribution of the number of defect occurrences of security defects also follows the D-LN. We fit the D-LN distribution to the occurrence counts of three sets of defect data relating specifically to network security and find that the hypothesis is consistent with the data. We also fit the Pareto rate distribution, a heavy-tailed alternative distribution often used in the software and network literature [10], and find that the Discrete-Pareto distribution of occurrence counts of security defects is only insignificantly inferior to the D-LN.

This paper uses the lognormal to link results from prior studies of software reliability growth, test coverage, defect failure rates, and code execution rates to the observations of security defect occurrence counts affecting QoP. It demonstrates how an important aspect of QoP, the occurrence phenomenon of security defects, may be modeled using concepts and techniques from another software discipline; namely, software reliability engineering. In that sense, it relates the software-defect-based component of QoP and its testing, maintenance, and improvement over time to the mainstream of software engineering and takes the first step towards quantifying QoP.

The layout of the paper is as follows: Section 2 provides insights as to why the occurrence count distribution is related to the lognormal. Section 3 describes the procedures used to obtain empirical data. Section 4 describes the statistical analysis of the data and discusses the results. Section 5 briefly links our research to other evidence of the lognormal in network environments. Section 6 provides the conclusions and directions for future research.

2 Lognormal Hypothesis

In this section we summarize the evidence for the lognormal distribution of event rates in software as well as its causes. We extend that research by deriving a model of the distribution of occurrence counts of software defects.

2.1   Origin of Lognormal Execution Rates

Mullen [22] suggested that the branching nature of software programs tends to generate a lognormal distribution of event rates, whether considered from the point of view of execution path, operational profile [24], or state-space.

For example, the probability of execution flowing to a given block in the code is the product of the probabilities of the conditional branches leading to that block. A large number of conditional statements guard the execution of typical code blocks; therefore. a large number of factors will be multiplied to determine the probability. The multiplicative form of the central limit theorem tells us that under general conditions the distribution of the products of those factors is asymptotically lognormal. Faulty code blocks are a random sample from that rate distribution; therefore, faults have rates that are distributed according to the lognormal. (A similar argument may be made from the perspective of an operational profile: the probability of each complex action is determined by multiplying the conditioned probabilities of its characteristics.) See [2, 9, 15] for information about the lognormal and [22] for references to alternative forms of the central limit theorem.

Bishop et al. [4] provide a specific model of the processes that lead to the lognormal distribution of block execution rates. They provide reasons and evidence that the distribution of failure rates remains lognormal even in the presence of loops and other variations in program structure.

2.2   Evidence of the Lognormal in Software

The proposed lognormal failure rate distribution has been validated previously [22] by analyzing careful studies of failure rates of faults published by IBM [1] and Boeing [25]. Bishop et al. [4] measured both the distribution of execution rates of code blocks and the distribution of failure rates of faults in the 10,000 line PREPRO application of the European Space Agency. Both were well fit by the lognormal.

Miller [20] pointed out that the mathematical transformation from a rate distribution to a first occurrence time (discovery time) distribution is equivalent to the Laplace Transform of the rate distribution. Mullen [21] derived the Lognormal software reliability growth model by approximating the Laplace Transform of the lognormal. This model was validated using Stratus Computer data and data gathered by Musa. Gokhale et al. [13] showed that the model fits code coverage growth as a function of the number of tests.

In short, key elements of the lognormal hypothesis have been confirmed in studies of more than 30 applications ranging from several thousand to several million lines of code in both test and production environments.

2.3   D-LN Hypothesis

We use the results described in Section 2.2 to motivate our derivation of an occurrence count model based on the lognormal. If the failure rates of defects follow the lognormal, the distribution of occurrence counts of those defects is the sum (integral) of Poisson distributions which in turn have a lognormal distribution of rates.

We make the following assumptions: Each defect, in a given product, against its overall operational profile, has a characteristic rate λ. Each occurrence of that defect is an event in a Poisson process with rate λ. The running time of the process is the cumulative exposure time over all users. The rate of a given defect remains unchanged until it is removed. From these assumptions it follows that the encountering of defects depends on the number of defects in the product, the distribution of those rates, the rate of use of the product over time, and the schedule of installing fixes after a defect is discovered. In our case, beyond Adams [1], we assume that fixes were not distributed and suppose that the distribution of rates of software faults is lognormal.

To say the distribution of failure rates of software faults is lognormal is to say that the logarithms of the execution rates, $\log(\lambda)$, follow the Gaussian or normal probability distribution function (pdf). For $\lambda > 0$:

$$dL(\lambda) = \frac{1}{\lambda\sigma\sqrt{2\pi}}e^{-(\log(\lambda)-\mu)^2/2\sigma^2}d\lambda \tag{1}$$

The two parameters are the mean of the log rates, μ, and the variance of the log rates, σ^2. We represent the mixture of Poisson distributions with means that follow a lognormal distribution using the notation of [16].

$$Poisson(\lambda) \bigwedge_\lambda Lognormal(\mu, \sigma) \tag{2}$$

The distribution of occurrences $DLN(i)$ is the integral of Poisson distributions, the rates of which follow a lognormal distribution. For ($i >= 0$, integer):

$$DLN(i) = \int_0^\infty Poisson(i, \lambda)\dot{d}L(\lambda) \tag{3}$$

2.4   Interpretation of Parameters

Conceptual advantages of the lognormal include the relative transparency of its parameters and the way it links various observed properties of software defects. Here we provide a brief discussion of how the parameter values are related to the characteristics of software applications.

The parameter σ makes the greatest qualitative difference and allows the lognormal its flexibility. σ, the standard deviation of the log rates, increases with increasing complexity of the software, in particular with greater depth of conditionals [4]. σ determines the ratio of the highest and the lowest occurrence rates of the defects. It determines the range over which the rates vary; the higher the σ, the higher the range of variation. If σ is zero, all defects have the same occurrence rate, leading to the exponential model [23] of software reliability growth. Values from one to three are seen more commonly. Values of four or above are unusual and carry large uncertainties [13].

The parameter μ has a simple interpretation: if rates are plotted on a log scale, changing μ merely moves the distribution to the right or left. A change in μ is obtained by changing the rates of all defects by a constant factor; for example, a system speedup or merely using different units of time. For $\mu = -2$, the median rate is $exp(-2)$ or 0.14

per year, which implies that less than half have been found by $T = 1$ year for all σ. In terms of occurrence counts, most of the defects have not occurred even once.

Changing either μ or σ, both of which relate to $\log(rate)$, does not affect the other. However changing either μ or σ affects both the mean and variance of the rates themselves [2].

The final parameter is N, the number of defects, which scales the pdf. In this paper, and in most situations, N is not a given but must be estimated in conjunction with the other parameters of the model. We can view N in a formal sense as only another number needed to fit the model, or we can view it more physically as the total number of defects, including both found and latent. If the number of latent defects is large, it is often the case that their average rate is low [3, 4]. This does not mean that they all will occur in the practical lifetime of the product – most will not – but it is possible to use a software reliability growth model to estimate how many will occur as a function of further exposure.

We expect the implications of the parameters will require additional subtlety for correct use in QoP determinations. For example, the operational profile presented by a determined adversary may be uniform during a probing phase but selectively peaked during an exploit. The value of σ used by an analyst might vary at different points in an overall calculation of risks to QoP.

3   Data Description

The data was collected in the ordinary course of recording the occurrence of software defects in two operational databases. The first is a defect tracking database that has one record for each defect. The second database uses trouble-tickets to track the occurrence of incidents at customer sites. When a customer incident is caused by a defect, a bidirectional link is established between the incident and the appropriate defect. We studied defects for which there was at least one trouble-ticket and counted the initial discovery as well as rediscoveries. In each case our queries selected defects (with at least one ticket) written within a specific year against specific body of software. Our model assumes repairs are not put into service during the interval of measurement, in the body of software measured. We have bounded our defect selections to ensure that this is approximately true. We did not further restrict the queries except as will be noted in discussions of subsets below. Each defect contains the identifiers of all trouble-tickets associated with the defect and, implicitly, its count. Some defects are duplicates of others. It would be best for our analysis if tickets attached to the duplicate defects were reassigned to the original defects; but this does not happen for 15 percent of the tickets. The average number of defects per ticket, assuming at least one, is approximately 1.4 and is not further studied here.

Table 1 shows the percentage of defects having a given number of tickets for each individual count from one to ten. Due to space limitations, cumulative percentage for the occurrence counts from 11 to 40 is reported in Table 1. However, percentages for each individual counts in the range of 11 to 40 were used for the analysis. The data is shown for three sets of defects. The first set consists of the security related defects in a large body of general purpose networking software. Orthogonal Defect Classification

(ODC) [7, 5] provides a means for the finder of a defect to record the impact of the defect. This set included only those for which the ODC Impact value "Security" was selected by the person entering the defect. In this system, a small fraction of the defects are identified as affecting security.

Table 1. Percentage of Defects with Specific Number of Tickets per Defect

Tickets per defect	ODC Security	Security Product	Security Suite
1	62.34	61.62	58.95
2	15.58	18.38	16.32
3	6.49	5.41	10.00
4	5.19	6.49	3.68
5	1.30	1.08	4.21
6	3.90	1.08	1.58
7	1.30	0.00	1.05
8	1.30	0.00	0.53
9	0.00	1.62	1.05
10	0.00	1.62	1.05
11 − 40	2.60	3.24	2.12

The second set included all software defects from a single platform that has the primary function of providing security. The third set includes all defects from a suite of security-related software products. For these last two sets, a prima facia case can be made that any defect may affect QoP. The three sets are fairly independent: an overlap of less than 10 percent occurs between the first and second sets and none with the third. Depending on perspective, defects in any of these sets could impact security directly and the QoP of a containing application. Although the defects counts are not high, the three data series provide distinct perspectives of how defects affect QoP.

Referring to the first column in Table 1, approximately 62 percent of the defects had only one ticket/defect, and fewer than 3 percent of the defects had 11 to 40 tickets per defect. A preliminary analysis of the data in column one indicates that approximately 84 percent of the defects have fewer than four tickets per defect. A relatively small percentage of defects causes a large number of incidents per defect, and a large percentage of defects causes a small number of incidents per defect.

To protect proprietary information, we did not normalize occurrence rates by the number of devices. Because some products have more than one million units, absolute error rates may be less than one millionth of what is presented here. Because $\log(10^{-6}) \approx -14$, the value of lognormal μ would be 14 lower but, σ does not change.

4   Analysis and Discussion

In this section we present the results of data analysis. We first present the alternative model, the Pareto model, which has been commonly used to fit heavy-tailed distributions. We then present the method used to fit the D-LN and Discrete-Pareto models, followed by a discussion of the comparison of the fits. We conclude the section with a discussion of how the product characteristics influence the parameters of the lognormal.

4.1 Alternative Model: Pareto Rates

The Pareto distribution is an alternative distribution that is heavy-tailed. Miller [20] noted the Pareto defect failure rate distribution, as a limit of the gamma distribution, is the basis of certain software reliability growth models. We modeled the Pareto cdf of rate λ (for $\lambda \geq k$) as:

$$N \times (1 - (\frac{k}{\lambda})^a) \tag{4}$$

where a and k are parameters of the Pareto.

4.2 Model Fitting

To approximate the integral in Section 2.3 for any given value of μ and σ, we used the LOGNORMDIST function of Microsoft Excel to determine the fraction of defects with each of 44 geometrically spaced rates from approximately 0.0001 per year to more than 200 per year. These were used to generate 44 Poisson distributions of those rates as an approximation to a continuous distribution. We summed the lognormal-weighted contribution of each of the 44 Poissons to each occurrence bucket from 0 to 40. The SOLVER function of Excel was used to find the values of the parameters of the D-LN (μ, σ, and N) that maximized the log-likelihood of the observed values. We do not have data for the number of defects with zero occurrences so we cannot use that in fitting. We constructed a defect occurrence rate distribution for the Discrete Pareto as we did for the Lognormal and fitted it in the same manner (44 weighted Poisson distributions, max log-likelihood).

We evaluate the fits using chi-square, examining the one-tail significance of deviation from both models. This test requires a minimum of approximately five counts in most buckets. The data supported only six buckets, and both models have two parameters (besides N); therefore, we have three degrees of freedom.

4.3 Model Comparison

Table 2 summarizes information about the fitted D-LN and D-Pareto in the upper sections, information relating to goodness of fit in the next, and other descriptive information at the end. We present both the actual ratio of tickets per defect and the same ratio for the fitted lognormal.

For an objective comparison, we compare the chi-square values of the Pareto and lognormal. We can do this directly because both have three parameters. The data never rejects either the Lognormal or the Pareto at the .05 level. We conclude that the data is consistent with both the lognormal and the Pareto.

In comparative terms, we see that the lognormal is a slightly better fit in one case. The differences are not significant in this data, which is unfortunately rather thin. Other research on the lognormal distribution of event rates or failure rates of software faults finds other models working well in some cases but the lognormal is a better fit in a higher number of cases - sometimes significantly better but never significantly worse [21, 22, 4, 13]. For the purposes of this paper, however, our objective is to demonstrate the applicability of software reliability engineering concepts to security defects.

4.4   Comparative Analysis of Defect Subsets

Having established the applicability of the D-LN to the distribution of occurrence counts of security defects, we want to understand how the parameters of the lognormal are affected by the nature of the software and its use. Figure 1 graphically describes the three sets of defects. According to Table 2, the ODC Impact Security defects that are embedded in the most mature product have the lowest average rate: $exp(\mu + \sigma^2)$.

Table 2. Parameters Fit and Characteristics

Parameter	ODC Security	Security Product	Security Suite
LN σ	2.63	2.40	1.75
LN μ	−5.1	−4.27	−2.23
Pareto a	0.832	0.943	1.045
Pareto k	0.057	0.111	0.187
d.f	3	3	3
LN Chi-square	0.81	5.90	3.25
LLH	−24.09	−39.28	−31.33
Pareto Chi-square	0.95	6.05	5.45
LLH	−24.11	−38.87	−32.50
Defects studied	77	185	190
Tic/Defect observed	2.60	2.48	2.31
Tic/Defect LN calc.	2.47	2.43	2.34
Mean Rate	0.193	0.249	0.497

This rate is determined from the fitted lognormal and includes contributions of all defects, not just those that have occurred. Software labeled "Security Suite" is new and has the highest number of tickets per defect. In this case, defects with higher rates are recent and have not yet been completely eliminated.

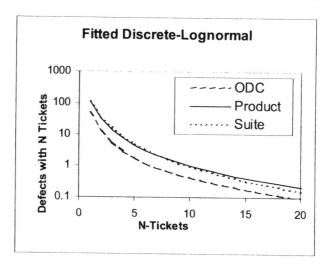

Fig. 1. Fitted curves are roughly similar inspite of differences in sources and source definitions

5 Related Research

Heavy-tailed distributions (also known as power-law distributions) have been claimed in many phenomena related to networks and software. In the Internet, these distributions have been claimed in the context of: transfer and interarrival times [26], burst sizes [6, 26], topological properties [11], sizes of files transferred over the Web [8], and Web session sizes [12]. Recently, error rates in Web servers have been observed to be heavy-tailed [14]. Statisticians have noted the lognormal can easily be confused with the Pareto [10] especially in the presence of truncated data [27].

In summary, the observation of lognormal within the operational profile of the Internet is consistent with the genesis of the lognormal outlined in Section 2.1 and in [22]. Rates (whether observed in operational profiles, state-space, or code execution) are determined by a multiplicative process and generally are lognormal. Faults, being a subset of such events, have failure rates distributed the same way, which is the basis of this paper.

We note that the lognormal is used not only for hardware reliability modeling but for risk analysis in general [19]. It arises easily in risk analysis, as in software, as the result of the multiplication of a number of random factors that may involve human decisions, technological failures, or natural or other catastrophes. Because QoP involves a considerable degree of risk analysis, we expect that the lognormal will be useful for more aspects of QoP than just modeling the effect of software security defects.

6   Summary and Future Research

In this paper we identified security defects in software as an important component of QoP and demonstrated the application of software reliability engineering concepts and techniques to QoP. We hypothesized that software security defects are like other defects in following the lognormal distribution of failure rates and we provided three sets of data supporting this hypothesis. This paper takes a significant step in linking concepts from prior studies of software reliability growth, code execution rates, test coverage, and defect failure rates to observations of defect occurrence counts of security defects. In that sense, the paper relates the software-defect-based component of QoP and its testing, maintenance, and improvement over time, to the mainstream of software engineering.

Although our security-related data is consistent with the D-LN, our present data does not rule out the Discrete Pareto. The acquisition of additional QoP-related data is the subject of future research.

7   Acknowledgments

We thank Cisco management, especially Tricia Baker and John Intintolo, for their encouragement. John asked the question that triggered this study: "Are customer-found defects corner cases?"

References

1. E. N. Adams. "Optimizing preventive service of software products". *IBM Journal of Research and Development*, 28(1):2–14, January 1984.
2. J. Aitchison and J.A.C. Brown. *The Lognormal Distribution*. Cambridge University Press, NY, 1969.
3. P. Bishop and R. Bloomfield. "A conservative theory for long-term reliability growth prediction". In *Proc. of Intl. Symposium on Software Reliability Engineering (ISSRE 96)*, White Plains, NY, 1996.
4. P. Bishop and R. Bloomfield. "Using a log-normal failure rate distribution for worst case bound reliability prediction". In *Proc. 14th International Symposium on Software Reliability Engineering (ISSRE 03)*, pages 237–245, 2003.
5. M. Butcher, H. Munro, and T. Kratschmer. "Improving software testing via ODC: Three case studies". *IBM Systems Journal*, 41(1), 2002.
6. J. Charzinski. "HTTP/TCP connection flow characteristics". *Performance Evaluation*, 42:149–162, 2000.
7. R. Chillarege. *Handbook of Software Reliability Engineering, M.R. Lyu (Eds.)*, chapter Orthogonal Defect Classification. McGraw Hill, 1996.
8. M. Crovella and M. Taqqu. *Methodology and Computing in Applied Probability*, chapter Estimating the Heavy Tail Index from Scaling Properties, pages 3–26. Chapman and Hall, 1999.
9. E. L. Crow and K. Shimizu. *Lognormal Distributions: Theory and Applications*. Marcel Dekker, New York, 1988.
10. A. Downey. "Lognormal and Pareto distributions in the Internet". *Computer Communications*, 2003.

11. M. Faloutsos, P. Faloutsos, and C. Faloutsos. "On the Power-law relationships of the Internet topology". In *Proc. of ACM SIGCOMM*, 1999.
12. A. Feldmann, A. Gilbert, W. Willinger, and T. Kurtz. "The changing nature of network traffic: Scaling phenomenon". *ACM Computer Communication Review*, pages 5–28, 1998.
13. S. Gokhale and R. Mullen. "From test count to code coverage using the lognormal". In *Proc. of 15th International Symposium on Software Reliability Engineering (ISSRE 04)*, 2004.
14. K. Goseva-Postojanova, S. Mazimdar, and A. Singh. "Empirical study of session-based workload and reliability of web-servers". In *Proc. of 15th International Symposium on Software Reliability Engineering (ISSRE 04)*, 2004.
15. N. L. Johnson, S. Kotz, and N. Balakrishnan. *Continuous Univariate Distributions*. Wiley, New York, 1994.
16. N. L. Johnson, S. Kotz, and A. Kemp. *Univariate Discrete Distributions*. Wiley, New York, 1993.
17. G. Q. Kenney. "Estimating defects in commercial software during operational use". *IEEE Trans. on Reliability*, 42(1):107–115, January 1993.
18. Y. Levende. "Reliability analysis of large software systems: Defect data modeling". *IEEE Trans. on Software Engineering*, 16(2):141–152, February 1990.
19. R.E. Megill. *Introduction to Risk Analysis*. Pennwell Books, Tulsa, OK, 1984.
20. D. R. Miller. "Exponential order statistic models of software reliability growth". Technical Report NASA Contractor Report 3909, NTIS, 1985.
21. R.E. Mullen. "The lognormal distribution of software failure rates: Application to software reliability growth modeling". In *Proc. of 9th International Symposium on Software Reliability Engineering (ISSRE 98)*, 1998.
22. R.E. Mullen. "The lognormal distribution of software failure rates: Origin and evidence". In *Proc. of 9th International Symposium on Software Reliability Engineering (ISSRE 98)*, 1998.
23. J. D. Musa. "A theory of software reliability and its application". *IEEE Trans. on Software Engineering*, SE-1(1), September 1975.
24. J. D. Musa. "The operational profile in software reliability engineering: An overview". In *Proc. of the 3rd International Symposium on Software Reliability Engineering (ISSRE 92)*, pages 140–154, 1992.
25. P.M. Nagel, F.W. Scholtz, and J.A. Skirvan. "Software reliability: Additional investigations into modeling with replicated experiments". Technical Report NASA CR-172378, NTIS, 1984.
26. V. Paxson and S. Floyd. "Wide area traffic: The failure of poisson modeling". *IEEE/ACM Trans. on Networking*, (3):244–266, 1995.
27. R. Perline. "Strong, weak and inverse power laws". *Statistical Science*, 20(1):68–88, 2005.

Time-to-Compromise Model for Cyber Risk Reduction Estimation

Miles A. McQueen, Wayne F. Boyer, Mark A. Flynn, George A. Beitel

Idaho National Laboratory, 2525 N. Fremont,
Idaho Falls, Idaho, U.S.A. 83415
{miles.mcqueen, wayne.boyer, mark.flynn, george.beitel}@inl.gov

Abstract. We propose a new model for estimating the time to compromise a system component that is visible to an attacker. The model provides an estimate of the expected value of the time-to-compromise as a function of known and visible vulnerabilities, and attacker skill level. The time-to-compromise random process model is a composite of three subprocesses associated with attacker actions aimed at the exploitation of vulnerabilities. In a case study, the model was used to aid in a risk reduction estimate between a baseline Supervisory Control and Data Acquisition (SCADA) system and the baseline system enhanced through a specific set of control system security remedial actions. For our case study, the total number of system vulnerabilities was reduced by 86% but the dominant attack path was through a component where the number of vulnerabilities was reduced by only 42% and the time-to-compromise of that component was increased by only 13% to 30% depending on attacker skill level.

1 Introduction

Control systems connected to public networks are at risk from cyber attack. Operators of these control systems need a measure of the risk associated with potential attacks to effectively manage their resources. Cyber security evaluations are traditionally qualitative in nature such that recommendations are given for remedial actions with no quantitative measure of how the recommended actions reduce the risk of a successful attack.

In April 2005 our risk analysis team was asked to perform a quantitative estimate of the risk reduction on a partial Supervisory Control and Data Acquisition (SCADA) system referred to as CS60. The baseline system had already undergone a security review, been modified to enhance security, and then been retested. For this analysis, we developed a methodology [13] for obtaining a quantitative risk reduction estimation. The methodology applies a graph theoretical approach. The methodology is briefly described by the following steps:

Step 1. Establish the system configuration.
Step 2. Identify applicable portions of the quantitative risk model.
Step 3. Identify and prioritize the security requirements of the primary target(s).
Step 4. Identify system component vulnerabilities.

Step 5. Categorize vulnerabilities on each component by compromise type.
Step 6. Estimate time-to-compromise each component.
Step 7. Generate compromise graph(s) and attack paths.
Step 8. Estimate dominant attack path(s).
Step 9. Do Steps 3–8 for baseline and enhanced system.
Step 10. Estimate risk reduction.

One could argue that all vulnerabilities should be fixed, e.g. by applying patches, thus the enhanced system should have no known vulnerabilities. We assert that a system with no known vulnerabilities continues to be at risk because of vulnerabilities that exist but are currently unknown, and we would like to measure that risk. Also, many real world systems operate with known vulnerabilities even after security upgrades. The crux of our methodology is the estimation of the time-to-compromise for each component in the system. Time-to-compromise is a measure of the effort expended by an attacker for a successful attack assuming effort is expended uniformly. We believe that as the time-to-compromise is increased, the likelihood of successful attack, and therefore risk, tends to decrease. The rest of this paper discusses the specific methods we used for step 6 of the methodology, estimating the time-to-compromise.

The estimation of time-to-compromise is particularly difficult because of the lack of reliable data. We recognize that some of the assumptions associated with our model have not been validated but we have attempted to provide justification with real data when data is available. We have used expert elicitation or have made simple assumptions when data is unavailable.

2 Related work

Researchers are testing the viability of different approaches for dealing with control system cyber security. Carlson et al. [8] describes a novel approach for applying Hidden Markov Models to an attack/defend scenario on an infrastructure system. The approach, based on sound statistical models, is flexible, but requires both detailed information about the system and significant set-up time. Madan et al. [11] apply a stochastic model to computer network system. It is used to determine steady-state availability of QoS attributes and also mean times to security failures based on probabilities of failure due to violations of different security attributes. The theory used is classic statistical stochastic modeling. Employing this type of model requires knowledge of the system in detail. Furthermore, Haimes [10] applied Hierarchical Holographic Models, event trees, and fault trees to a variety of applications, both models require specific details, are not dynamic, and rely on expert opinion.

Taylor et al. [15] provide an interesting cyber security assessment process that combines techniques from Survivability System Analysis and Probability Risk Assessment. The proposed process has some significant advantages, but seems more suitable to complete and operational systems so that costs, attack scenarios, and critical system objectives may be fully explored. Further, the process is dependent on multiple iterations of expert elicitation, which are not available in many situations.

Dacier et al. [9] suggested the use of 'privilege graphs' to analyze security. Privilege graphs require modeling of vulnerabilities at a very low level, and, for a nontrivial sized system, would involve a graph of unmanageable size. Privilege graphs are transformed into Markov chains. But the assumptions underlying Markov chains are not necessarily applicable to an intelligent adversary.

Sheyner et al. [14] describe an automated technique for generating and analyzing attack graphs. They use a model checker as the core engine to comprehensively generate every attack path sequence that could lead to an undesired system state. There is a question of scalability in using a model checker to generate the attack paths, and the level of attack and vulnerability abstraction may be at a lower level than optimal for a quick estimate of risk reduction.

Byres et al. [7] describe how the attack tree methodology may be applied to the common SCADA protocol MODBUS/TCP with the goal of identifying security vulnerabilities inherent in the specification and in typical deployments. Attack trees are a promising technology but no method is provided for weighting the attack paths.

While a number of the above methods and techniques seem promising and merit future research, none could provide a quantitative measure of time-to-compromise that was necessary for our risk reduction estimation case study.

3. Estimate time-to-compromise

The time-to-compromise (T_{pi}) is defined as the time needed for an attacker to gain some level of privilege p on some system component i. T_{pi} depends on the nature of the vulnerabilities and the attacker skill level. T_{pi} is modeled as a random process composed of the following three attacker subprocesses:

- **Process 1** is for the case where at least one vulnerability is known on component i that would achieve privilege level p, and the attacker has at least one exploit readily available that can be successfully used against one of the known vulnerabilities.

- **Process 2** is for the case where at least one vulnerability is known on component i that would achieve privilege level p, but the attacker does not have an exploit readily available that can be successfully used against any of the known vulnerabilities.

- **Process 3** is the identification of new vulnerabilities and exploits. Process 3 is a parallel process to processes 1 and 2, and is constantly running in the background. The attacker of a particular system may use the results of process 3 or may be an active participant in process 3. That is, the attacker may wait for new vulnerabilities/exploits to be identified and announced, or probe for new ones.

Each of the above processes has a different failure probability distribution. Process 1 and 2 are mutually exclusive and Process 3 is ongoing and in parallel with the other two processes.

3.1. Process 1 model

The Process 1 activities are shown in flow chart form in Figure 1. Notice that Process 1 always has a successful completion. The Process 1 model has two parts: 1) the probability estimate that the attacker has an exploit readily available to use against one of the component's vulnerabilities, that is, the probability the attacker is in Process 1, and 2) the time estimation for Process 1.

3.1.1. Probability the attacker is in process 1

The probability that the attacker is in Process 1 is calculated by using search theory in a similar fashion as has been applied to physical security systems by Major [12]. The following equation makes use of the simplifying assumption that the available exploits are uniformly distributed over all vulnerabilities:

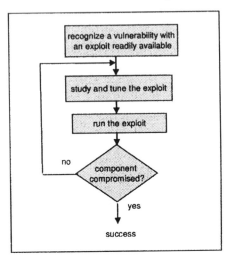

Fig. 1. Process 1

$$P_1 = 1 - e^{-vm/k}. \tag{1}$$

where P_1 is probability that the attacker has an exploit readily available that will compromise the component, v is number of vulnerabilities on the component of interest, m is the number of exploits readily available to the attacker, and k is the total number of vulnerabilities. The value of k is 9447 and is defined to be the total number of nonduplicate-known vulnerabilities found in the ICAT database.

Table 1. Model parameters—number of readily available exploits by skill level.

Skill Level	m (number of readily available exploits)
novice	50
beginner	150
intermediate	250
expert	450

The value of m is a function of the attacker skill level. The novice skill level is defined as m = 50 because there is a Web site (metasploit) that has 50 exploits that are trivial to use. The higher skill levels are defined by increasing the value of m for each increase in skill level as shown in Table 1. The specific choices in Table 1 are based on a postulated exponential growth in readily available exploits as a function of skill level.

3.1.2. Time estimation for process 1

The probability density function (PDF) for Process 1 is expected to be zero at time zero, rise rapidly then decrease to zero for times greater than some maximum time value. The shape of the PDF for this process is anticipated to look something like the beta distribution [3] shown in Figure 2.

The mean time for Process 1 was estimated as follows. Process 1 assumes that the attacker is familiar with at least one of the available vulnerabilities and has experience with at least one exploit to take advantage of the known vulnerabilities. Currently, the time it takes for an expert or novice to compromise a component under these conditions is considered to be roughly similar. Thus, the mean time-to-compromise for Process 1 is not modified based on skill or any other external factors. Cohen [2] states: "It takes a few days to program a few new attacks into systems, test them out, and prepare for a serious attack if you are already in the business of attacking other people." This suggests that the mean should be a few days. However, experiments conducted by Jonsson [4] suggest that a team of two nonprofessional attackers can execute a compromise in approximately 4 hours, on average. Based on the specification of time used by Jonsson, the 4 hours could represent the total time used for the attack or the time devoted by each team member, for a possible total of 8 hours. Somewhat arbitrarily, we decided to use 8 hours (one working day) as the mean time for a successful attack in Process 1, since it is at least marginally more in line with Cohen's comment.

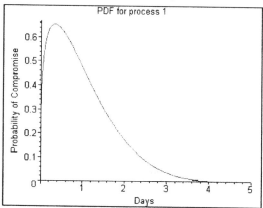

Fig. 2. PDF for Process 1. Time-to-compromise a component for the case where the attacker has an exploit readily available. This PDF is a 'beta' distribution with shape parameters == 1.3, 5.2; range == 0..5; mean = 1:

3.2. Process 2 Model

The Process 2 activities are shown in flow chart form in Figure 3. Notice Process 2 can have multiple tries and may end in failure or success. The Process 2 model has two parts: 1) the probability estimate that the attacker is in Process 2, and 2) the time estimation for Process 2.

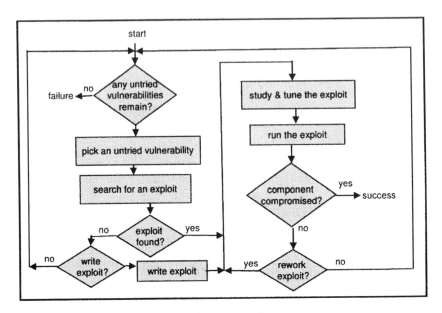

Fig. 3.. Process 2

3.2.1. Probability the attacker is in process 2
Since Process 1 and Process 2 are mutually exclusive, when $v > 0$ the probability that the attacker is in Process 2 is the complement of the probability that Process 1 applies. That is

$$P_2 = e^{-vm/k} = 1 - P_1. \tag{2}$$

where P_2 is the probability that the attacker does not have an exploit readily available that will compromise the component and P_1 is from Equation 1.

3.2.2. Time estimation for process 2
The PDF of Process 2 is expected to look similar to the gamma distribution [3] shown in Figure 4. A gamma distribution was chosen because the PDF is zero at time zero, and as time increases it peaks and then trends towards but never reaches zero. We chose a PDF that is non-zero at infinity because Process 2 has no guarantee of successful completion within any given time. The PDF in Figure 4 is a baseline PDF for process 2 and represents the case where the attacker is expected to find or write a usable exploit for the first vulnerability they try to exploit. As the expected number of vulnerabilities that an attacker must try to exploit before being successful increases, the PDF will be modified according to the number of "tries" needed as explained below. The average value of the baseline PDF for Process 2 was chosen as the average time from vulnerability announcement to exploit code availability, which according to [6] is 5.8 days.

The mean time estimation for Process 2 should be dependent on the number of known vulnerabilities and the probability the attacker will be able to find or write

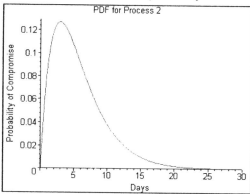

their own exploit code to take advantage of the weakness. This was modeled as a serial process in which the attacker randomly selects one of the known vulnerabilities and then tries to find or create an exploit for it. The average time it takes for each of these tries is considered constant and is the baseline mean of the hypothesized gamma PDF (5.8 days). The mean time of Process 2 is modeled as the expected value of the number of tries times 5.8 days; that is:

Fig. 4. Baseline PDF for Process 2. Time-to-compromise for the case of at least one vulnerability but the attacker has no exploit readily available. The PDF is a gamma distribution. Shape parameters == 2, 2.9; Mean == 5.8.

$$t_2 = 5.8 \; ET. \tag{3}$$

where t_2 is expected value of Process 2 and ET is the expected number of tries.

The expected number of tries may be written as:

$$ET = \frac{AM}{V} * \left(1 + \sum_{tries=2}^{V-AM+1} \left[tries * \prod_{i=2}^{tries} \left(\frac{NM - i + 2}{V - i + 1} \right) \right] \right) \tag{4}$$

where AM is the average number of the vulnerabilities for which an exploit can be found or created by the attacker given their skill level, NM is the number of vulnerabilities that this skill level of attacker won't be able to use (V-AM), and V is the number of vulnerabilities on the component of interest. See appendix for derivation of equation 4.

Equation 4 was obtained by assuming each try is an independent sample from the list of vulnerabilities where the unusable vulnerabilities are randomly distributed among the list.

Table 2. Fraction of vulnerabilities exploitable by attacker as a function of skill level.

Skill Level	Fraction of Vulnerabilities that are Exploitable (AM/V)	20 vulnerabilities from ICAT database judged by expert to be exploitable by this and lower levels.
novice	.15	CAN-2003-0004 CAN-2001-1039 CAN-2002-1048
beginner	.30	CAN-2004-1306 CAN-1999-1457 CVE-2000-0359
intermediate	.55	CAN-2004-0893 CAN-2005-0416 CAN-2002-0053 CAN-2003-0345 CAN-2004-0206
expert	1.00	CAN-2003-0897 CAN-2004-0117 CAN-2004-0208 CAN-2004-0575 CAN-2003-0724 CAN-2004-0118 CAN-2004-0119 CAN-2004-0123 CAN-2004-0897

To determine the values of AM/V as a function of skill level, we sampled 20 vulnerabilities to assess the availability of corresponding exploits. See table 2 for list of vulnerabilities. If our team expert assessed the vulnerability as requiring no code, or the code was available and trivial, it was then assumed a novice attacker could make use of the vulnerability/exploit pair. This criteria was met by three (15%) of the 20 vulnerabilities that were assessed. If our team expert assessed the vulnerability as being available to the novice or that it required exploit code that was readily accessible (and appeared easy to understand), it was assumed a beginner attacker could execute the code and take advantage of the vulnerability. Three additional

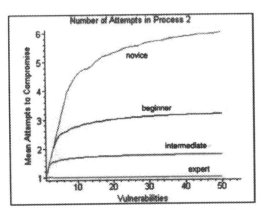

Fig. 5. Average number of attempts to compromise a component for Process 2 as a function of number of known component vulnerabilities and the attacker skill level. (Equation 4)

vulnerability/exploit pairs also met this criteria, bringing the total to six pairs (30%) available to the beginner attacker. If, in addition to the above six vulnerability/exploit pairs, our team expert found the exploit code to be difficult to understand, found only example code conveying the essence of the exploit, or assessed from experience that it was not easy to get the type of required exploit to work properly, it was assumed it would require an intermediate level attacker to take advantage of the vulnerability/exploit pair. Five additional pairs met this criteria so that 11 pairs (55%) were available to the intermediate attacker. If, in addition to the 11 exploits above, no exploit code was readily available or what code there was required significant modification to adapt, we assumed that it would require an expert attacker. All of the remaining vulnerabilities fit into this category for a total of 20 vulnerability/exploit pairs (100%) available to the expert. The results of this exercise are summarized in Table 2 and were used as part of the time-to-compromise model.

The average number of tries as described by Equation 4 is plotted in Figure 5. For an expert, the average number of tries is one, because an expert is expected to have access to an exploit for every vulnerability. As the skill level decreases, the average number of tries increases as expected.

3.3. Time estimation for process 3

The Process 3 activities are shown in flow chart form in Figure 6. Notice Process 3 continues until "success". The time to the discovery of a new usable vulnerability is modeled as a constant rate of new vulnerabilities/exploits occurring on a component. This model is the same form as the classic exponential distribution for constant failure rates as shown in Figure 7.

This exponential distribution was chosen for its simplicity and because research by Rescorla [5] indicates that the hypothesis stating that the vulnerability discovery rate is constant over time could not be rejected for the operating systems he studied. Using data from the same source, it also appears that a reasonable estimate for the mean time between vulnerabilities (MTBV) is 30.42 days. In addition to a vulnerability, an exploit would be needed. The time between the announcement of a vulnerability and the release of a corresponding exploit is now approximately 5.8 days [6]. The vulnerability rate estimate will be scaled by V/AM according to the portion of vulnerability/exploit pairs each attacker level can use (see Table 2). For example, the beginner attacker will on average require 1/(0.3) vulnerability/exploit pair occurrences before one becomes usable. To determine the expected time-to-

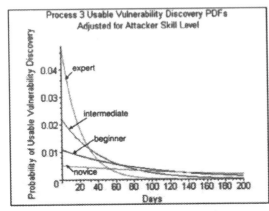

compromise for Process 3, the MTBV was multiplied by the scaling factor then half the MTBV was subtracted because, on the average, the midpoint of the fault cycle is the start point, and the mean time to create an exploit (5.8 days) is added. Thus:

Fig. 7. PDF for probability of discovery of a new usable vulnerability. (Process 3).

$$t_3 = ((V/AM) - 0.5) \, 30.42 + 5.8 \tag{5}$$

where t_3 is the expected time-to-compromise of Process 3, and V/AM is the appropriate value from Table 2.

One might assume that development and release of patches might be effective in mitigating the window of opportunity for an attacker, but as indicated by [1] the hypothesis of 'poor system administration' seems to be confirmed. In other words, it takes quite a long time for administrators to actually apply patches, and although there are some indications that the time between release of a patch and its application may be decreasing in the IT domain, control systems may be slower.

3.4 Overall compromise time estimation

Given the three attacker processes for compromising a component, their probabilities, and their time-to-compromise probability distributions we can now generate an overall time-to-compromise probability distribution for the component. For now, the analysis only uses the expected value of the time-to-compromise. The expected value of the overall distribution is approximated as a weighted sum of the expected values of each of the three attacker processes, where each weight is the probability that the respective process is operative.

Although Process 3 is a parallel process continually running in the background, we simplify the estimation of time-to-compromise and obtain a good first order approximation by assuming that Process 3 only applies if Processes 1 and 2 do not apply or are unsuccessful. This approximation is valid because the PDF for Process 3 is much more dispersed than the other processes, therefore its contribution to the composite PDF is small when Processes 1 or 2 are active. The following formula is valid under the assumption that all three processes are approximately mutually exclusive.

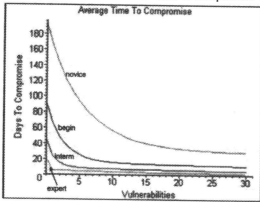

Fig. 8. Expected time-to-compromise a component for various numbers of vulnerabilities and attacker skill levels. (Equation 6 plotted)

$$T = t_1 P_1 + t_2 (1-P_1)(1-u) + t_3 u(1-P_1).$$ **(6)**

where

T is the expected value of time-to-compromise
t_1 is the expected value of Process 1 (1 day)
t_2 is the expected value of Process 2 (from Equation 3)
t_3 is the expected value of process 3 (from Equation 5)
$u = (1 - (AM/V))^V \equiv$ probability that Process 2 is unsuccessful (u=1 if V=0)
V is number of vulnerabilities, P_1 from Equation 1, AM/V from Table 2.

Equation 6 is plotted in Figure 8 where the number of known vulnerabilities for a component range from zero to 30 and attacker skill levels range from novice to expert. The time-to-compromise the component increases as the skill level decreases. Time-to-compromise decreases as the number of vulnerabilities increases, but for skilled attackers the time-to-compromise is not a strong function of the number of vulnerabilities. The shape of the curves shown in Figure 8 is consistent with intuition, although the numerical values are only approximations.

4. Case study

Our risk reduction methodology was applied to a small SCADA system (CS60) consisting of 8 generic component types connected to a local Ethernet LAN. The only potential attack target component identified was the RTU because it controls the physical state of equipment in the field. The system was tested as delivered from the manufacturer and did not include a firewall. The only perimeter component for the

CS60 system is the Ethernet switch that connects the system to the internet. For the purposes of testing, this perimeter component was assumed to be a simple switch that prevents locally addressed packets from external observation and prevents flooding of the local network from external sources.

Both the baseline and enhanced, more secure, versions of the CS60 system were tested with a variety of commercial and freeware scanning tools (including Nessus), password crackers and local tools. Tests of the baseline system revealed potential vulnerabilities in every component. The network scans found a total of 298 open ports, and 79 unknown services. Nessus vulnerability scans found 174 warnings and 154 holes. A 'hole' is a vulnerability that has the potential to allow an attacker to gain a foothold on the component. We were only concerned with holes that were noted by Nessus as high severity to increase confidence that they were significant vulnerabilities. High severity implies that the hole might allow one to run

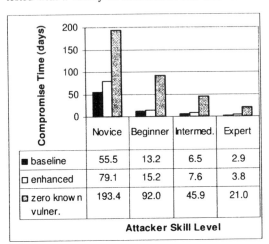

Fig. 9. Estimated compromise time of the most vulnerable component of the CS60 baseline system, enhanced system, and for hypothetical case of no known vulnerabilities.

	Novice	Beginner	Intermed.	Expert
■ baseline	55.5	13.2	6.5	2.9
▢ enhanced	79.1	15.2	7.6	3.8
▨ zero known vulner.	193.4	92.0	45.9	21.0

Attacker Skill Level

'arbitrary code' on the component to gain user or root access. The password testing found weak passwords on virtually all of the componentss. Network scans of the enhanced system found 95 open ports and nine unknown services. Nessus vulnerability scans of the enhanced system found a total of 101 warnings and 21 holes. Some of the vulnerabilities identified by the tools were validated for the enhanced system. INL expertise was used for the identification and validation of additional vulnerabilities. The passwords in the enhanced system were found to be much stronger than for the baseline system. We identified additional potential vulnerabilities by searching vulnerability identification libraries.

The time-to-compromise was calculated using Equation 6 and the number of vulnerabilities we identified that could be used to gain root access for each component in the CS60 system. Component APPS1 had the highest number of vulnerabilities in the baseline system (19) and in the enhanced system (11) for the type compromise that allows root access from a launch site, therefore the path through component APPS1 is considered to be the dominant attack path. The time to compromise APPS1 for various attacker skill levels is shown in Figure 9 for the baseline system, the enhanced system and for the hypothetical case of no known vulnerabilities. The total number of CS60 system vulnerabilities was reduced by 86% but the number of vulnerabilities for the component APPS1 was reduced by only 42% and the time-to-compromise APPS1 was increased by only 13% to 30% depending on attacker skill level. For the hypothetical case of 100% reduction in known vulnerabilities, the time-to-compromise is estimated to increase by 240% to 624% depending on attacker skill level.

These estimates of time-to-compromise have not been validated but simply show how the model may be applied to a real system. The numbers can be interpreted as a measure of risk and therefore may be used to trade off the value of cyber security mitigation actions versus the cost.

5. Alternative simplistic time-to-compromise models/metrics

Consider some simplistic alternative time-to-compromise models/metrics. One such model is the binary open/closed door model in which any known vulnerability is considered an open door that a determined attacker will enter as easily as if there were many other open doors. The application of this model to the case study yields a time-to-compromise reduction of zero on the APPS1 component because there are known vulnerabilities (open doors) remaining that lead to a successful attack, even though many doors have been closed. This model has some merit, particularly if the attacker is highly skilled and is determined to attack that particular site, but is considered too pessimistic and too simplistic because it does not take into account the various types of potential attackers, and the difficulty associated with the attacker in exploiting different sets of vulnerabilities is not considered.

Another alternative time-to-compromise metric for components may be obtained by counting the reduction in number of vulnerabilities. This can be done in several ways. For example: the total number of vulnerabilities for each component (before and after system enhancements) may be counted. An alternative view of vulnerabilities is the number of open TCP services rather than CVE entries. For this case study, the total holes found by Nessus (http://www.nessus.org) was reduced from 154 to 21 (86%), the number of vulnerabilities on the most vulnerable component was reduced from 19 to 11 (42%), and the total number of open TCP services was reduced from 298 to 95 (68%). This model is also believed to be too simplistic and too optimistic because it implies a linear relationship between number of vulnerabilities and the time-to-compromise a component, and ignores other important considerations such as skill of attacker.

6. Conclusions

We proposed a model for estimating the time-to-compromise a system component that is visible to an attacker. The model can be used as part of a risk reduction estimation methodology for control systems. Time-to-compromise was modeled as a function of known vulnerabilities and attacker skill level and was applied to a specific SCADA system and for a specific set of control system security remedial measures.

The nature of the numerical results obtained show that time-to-compromise is related to system attributes in ways consistent with intuition, and reinforces the types of remedial actions that truly reduce risk. For example, the model emphasizes the dynamic nature of cyber security such that the time-to-compromise a component decreases over time, unless there is constant effort to install patches or disable services as soon as new vulnerabilities are discovered.

The model also suggests some new strategies for reducing the risk of cyber threats: the publication of false exploits or government restrictions on the publication of valid exploits could theoretically increase the time necessary for an attacker to compromise components. Software that spoofs vulnerability scanning tools could trick potential attackers into trying exploits that would not be successful, but would raise alarms.

The time-to-compromise model has the following drawbacks. The model does not currently take into account dependencies between vulnerabilities on different components. For example, if two components are not identical but have some of the same vulnerabilities, compromising them are not independent events. Whether the number of available exploits is representative of the skill level of an attacker and estimates of the number of exploits available to various skill levels were not validated. The assumption that exploits are uniformly distributed over vulnerabilities is incorrect. It is our hypothesis that certain exploits are far more likely to be in the hands of an attacker, since the vulnerability is found on many more systems. The PDFs were not validated for Processes 1 and 2.

The proposed model for estimating time-to-compromise provides a quantitative assessment mechanism that fits within an overall methodology of risk assessment. The level of abstraction is high enough to avoid detailed analysis of each known vulnerability but detailed enough to provide useful security and defensive information for guiding risk assessments and mitigation strategies.

7. Future Work

The time-to-compromise model needs to be validated through experiments and measurement where possible. We plan to run realistic tests to collect information about attacker processes. We would like to perform a sensitivity analysis to determine how sensitive the model is to changes in our underlying assumptions.

The kind of data needed to effectively estimate control system cyber security risk is currently lacking. For example: the industry needs a vulnerability library specific to control systems similar to the existing IT CVE vulnerability library. The existing CVE libraries do not always clearly identify where vulnerabilities apply, nor do they indicate how difficult it is to exploit a given vulnerability. Existing vulnerability scanning tools do not clearly identify which vulnerabilities are tested and which are not. We would like to run experiments that measure the statistics associated with Processes 1 and 2. Validated statistical models may allow for a measure of the error bounds associated with future time-to-compromise estimates.

When dealing with a system many components will have common vulnerabilities. A method should be developed to account for such dependencies. Also, many components may be of equal use to an attacker. In such a case it may be more appropriate to aggregate the appropriate components into a higher level meta-component with the union of all its components vulnerabilities. This needs to be assessed.

References

1. Browne, H. K., McHugh, J., Arbaugh, W.A. and Fithen, W.L., "A trend Analysis of Exploitations," technical report CS-TR-4200, University of Maryland and Software Engineering Institute, November 2002.
2. Cohen, F., "Managing Network Security The Millisecond Fantasy," http://all.net/journal/netsec/1999–2003.html, 2003.
3. Evans, M., Hastings, N. and Peacock, B., "Statistical Distributions," Second Edition, 1993.
4. Jonsson, E., "A Quantitative Model of the Security Intrusion Process Based on Attacker Behavior," IEEE Transactions on Software Engineering, Vol 23 No 4, April 1997.
5. Rescorla, E., "Is Finding Security Holes a Good Idea," IEEE Security & Privacy, January-February 2005.
6. Turner, D., ed., "Symantec Internet Security Threat Report," Volume VI, September, 2004, http://enterprisesecurity.symantec.com/content.cfm?articleid=1539, 2004.
7. Byres, E. J., Franz, M. and Miller, D., "The Use of Attack Trees in Assessing Vulnerabilities in SCADA Systems", International Infrastructure Survivability Workshop (IISW '04), IEEE, Lisbon, Portugal, December 4, 2004
8. Carlson, R. E., Turnquist, M. A. and Nozick, L. K., Expected Losses, Insurability, and Benefits from Reducing Vulnerability to Attacks, SAND2004-0742, Sandia National Laboratories, Albuquerque, New Mexico, 2004.
9. Dacier, M., Deswarte, Y. and Kaaniche, M., "Quantitative Assessment of Operational Security: Models and Tools" Information Systems Security, ed. by S. K. Katsikas and D. Gritzalis, London, Chapman & Hall, p.179-86, 1996.
10. Haimes, Yacov Y., "Accident Precursors, Terrorist Attacks, and Systems Engineering," Presented at the NAE Workshop, 2003.
11. Madan, B. B., Goševa-Popstojavova, K., Vaidyanathan, K. and Trivedi, K. S., "Modeling and Quantification of Security Attributes of Software Systems," International Conference on Dependable Systems and Networks, Washington, DC,, 2002.
12. Major, J. A., "Advanced Techniques for Modeling Terrorism Risk," Journal of Risk Finance, Fall 2002.
13. McQueen, M. A., Boyer, W. F., Flynn, M. A. and Beitel, G. A., "Quantitative Cyber Risk Reduction Estimation for a SCADA Control System", INL/EXT-05-00319, Idaho National Laboratory, CSSC Report, prepared for U.S. Department of Homeland Security, May 17, 2005.
14. Sheyner, O., Haines, J., Jha, S., Lippmann, R. and Wing, J. M., "Automated Generation and Analysis of Attack Graphs," Proceedings of the IEEE Computer Society Symposium on Research in Security and Privacy, Berkeley, California, May 2002, 273–284.
15. Taylor C., Krings, A. and Alves-Foss, J., "Risk Analysis and Probabilistic Survivability Assessment (RAPSA): An Assessment Approach for Power Substation Hardening," Proc. ACM Workshop on Scientific Aspects of Cyber Terrorism, (SACT), Washington DC, November 21, 2002.

Appendix A

Derivation of Equation 4.
E(X) is expected value of **X** where **X** is a discrete random variable:

$$E(X) = \sum_{k=1}^{V} x_k * p_k$$

where x_k are the possible values of **X** (outcomes) and p_k is the probability of outcome k.

$$1 = \sum_{k=1}^{V} p_k$$

p_1 = Probability of matching an available exploit to the first vulnerability chosen.
p_1 = AM/V, because of uniform distribution of exploits over vulnerabilities. AM is number of usable exploits available, V is number of vulnerabilities.
p_2 = Probability of matching an available exploit to the 2nd vulnerability chosen.
p_2 = (probability of matching an available exploit to a vulnerability chosen from those remaining after first try)*(probability exploit not matched on the first try)
p_2 = (AM/(V-1))*((V-AM)/V)
p_2 = (AM/V) * (V-AM)/(V-1)
p_3 = (AM/(V-2))*(probability exploit not matched on the first two tries)
p_k = (AM/(V-k+1))*(probability exploit not matched on the first k-1 tries)

$$p_k = (AM/V) * \left(\prod_{i=2}^{k} \left[\frac{NM - i + 2}{V - i + 1} \right] \right) ; 2 \le k \le V\text{-AM}+1$$

p_k = 0; k > V-AM+1 (because there are AM usable exploits available, therefore there are no **untried** vulnerabilities with exploits available to the attacker for these cases. Attacker is successful for some previous value of k.)

$$ET = E(X) = \sum_{k=1}^{V-AM+1} k * p_k$$

$$ET = \frac{AM}{V} * \left(1 + \sum_{tries=2}^{V-AM+1} \left[tries * \prod_{i=2}^{tries} \left(\frac{NM - i + 2}{V - i + 1} \right) \right] \right)$$

Assessing the risk of using vulnerable components

Davide Balzarotti[1], Mattia Monga[2], and Sabrina Sicari[3]

[1] Politecnico di Milano
Dip. di Elettronica e Informazione - Piazza Leonardo da Vinci, 32
I 20133 Milan, Italy
[2] Università degli Studi di Milano
Dip. di Informatica e Comunicazione - Via Comelico, 39
I 20135 Milan, Italy
[3] Università di Catania
Dip. di Ing. Informatica e delle Telecomunicazioni
Viale Andrea Doria 6, I-95125 Catania, Italy

Abstract. This paper discusses how information about the architecture and the vulnerabilities affecting a distributed system can be used to quantitatively assess the risk to which the system is exposed. Our approach to risk evaluation can be used to assess how much one should believe in system trustworthiness and to compare different solutions, providing a tool for deciding if the additional cost of a more secure component is worth to be afforded.

1 Introduction

The issue of software security is increasingly more relevant in a world where most of our life depends directly on several complex computer-based systems. Today Internet connects and enables a growing list of critical activities from which people expect services and revenues. In other words, they *trust* these systems to be able to provide data and elaborations with a degree of confidentiality, integrity, and availability compatible with their needs. Unfortunately, this trust is often not based on a rational assessment of the risk to which the system could be exposed. Users tipically know only the interface of the system and, for example, they have too little information for evaluating the confidentiality of their credit card number: it could be even transmitted on an SSL armored link, but this does not help if on the other side it will be stored on a publicly available database! Surprisingly, the designers of the system are often in a similar situation. In fact, software systems are increasingly assembled from components that are developed by and purchased from third-parties and used as black boxes. Web services, for example, give to software engineers the ability of building complex applications by assembling third-parties components that expose a web interface[7], an extreme case of *components off the shelf* (COTS) software.

Thus, black box components make clear that nobody has enough information for evaluating how secure is every single computation. However, several public services exist (for example, BugTraq[1]) that publish known vulnerabilities of commercial components. The problem this paper wants to discuss is whatever this information can be used to assess how secure is a system built by assembling vulnerable components. In the following we propose a quantitative approach to measuring risk based on the knowledge of:

- the vulnerabilities of components and links and a measure of their "exploitability".
- the logical dependencies that the architecture of the system induces among vulnerabilities, since it is often the case that a vulnerability can be exploited more easily by leveraging on another one.
- the envisioned attacks against the system.

Risk evaluation can be used to assess how much one should believe in system trustworthiness, but also– more interestingly– to compare different solutions. In fact, designers have often the option of using different components and different architectural choices. A quantitative risk assessment is key in providing a tool for deciding if the additional cost of a more secure component is worth to be afforded.

The paper is organized as follows: in Section 2 we describe our approach to evaluate the risk associated with a given architecture, in Section 3 we present an example of application, in Section 4 we discuss related work, and finally in Section 5 we draw some conclusions and sketch future work.

2   Our approach to risk assessment

The goal of risk assessment is to determine the likelihood that identifiable threats will harm, weighting their occurrence with the damage they may cause. An ideal risk assessment requires enumeration of all possible failure modes, their probability of happening and their consequences. Unfortunately, this information is rarely available in its gory detail and, when it is, it is very difficult to analyze it in order to draw sensible considerations.

We aim at both (1) reducing the complexity of risk analysis and (2) using information that can be managed, discussed, and agreed by high-level designers of a distributed system. For this reason we consider a distributed system as a composition of black-box elements communicating through directed links. We call *architecture* of the system the directed graph $< C, L >$ in which C is the set of all black-box components and L the set of all directed links. A link (c_1, c_2) means that c_1 may send input to c_2.

Moreover, we consider each element $\in (C \cup L)$ as *vulnerable*. A vulnerability is a flaw or weakness in a system's design, implementation, or operation and management that could be exploited to violate the system's security policy [10]. The RFC definition adds also that

"Most systems have vulnerabilities of some sort, but this does not mean that the systems are too flawed to use. Not every threat results in an attack, and not every attack succeeds. Success depends on the degree of vulnerability, the strength of attacks, and the effectiveness of any countermeasures in use. If the attacks needed to exploit a vulnerability are very difficult to carry out, then the vulnerability may be tolerable. If the perceived benefit to an attacker is small, then even an easily exploited vulnerability may be tolerable. However, if the attacks are well understood and easily made, and if the vulnerable system is employed by a wide range of users, then it is likely that there will be enough benefit for someone to make an attack."

As stated by Howard and Le Blanc[11]: "You cannot build a secure system until you understand your threats". Therefore, in order to assess the trustworthiness of a system (or, dually, its risks), one has to identify possible threats and how attacks could be performed. Obviously enough, the risk of an unforeseen threat cannot be positively assessed and unknown attacks fall outside a systematic analysis of risks. Similarly, in the following we consider only *known vulnerabilities*, however it is possible to apply our approach even to *unknown vulnerabilities* (or a mix of known and unknown ones) if their nature is predicted.

Safety engineering has a long tradition of using *fault trees* or *event trees* to analyze hazards in complex systems[15]. A similar approach it is commonly used also in information technology. Attack trees[17, 6] provide a formal, methodical way of describing how an attack can possibly be performed against a system. Basically, one represents attacks in a tree structure, with the goal as the root node and different ways of achieving that goal as leaf nodes. There are and nodes and or nodes. or nodes are alternatives; and nodes represent different steps toward achieving the same goal. The ultimate objective in building an attack tree is identifying how vulnerabilities can be exploited to harm a system, therefore the basic leaves represent system vulnerabilities. However, these are often dependent one on another, but this information is partially lost in attack tree representation. In fact, only structural dependencies are made explicit (i.e., the attack has a given structure and implies the exploitations of some vulnerabilities), while indirect dependencies (i.e., a vulnerability might ease an attack, even if the attack is possible without its presence) are neglected. Therefore, we propose to take into account all vulnerabilities dependencies and we devise an analytical approach for computing the risk associated to a specific threat (described by an attack tree) starting from the assessment of the exploitability of vulnerabilities. Moreover, our analysis starts from the architecture of the system, since we found that most (but not all) of the dependencies among vulnerabilities stem from the basic topology of the system.

2.1   Measuring risk

Risk is measured by means of a function of two variables: one is the damage potential of the hazard (H) and another one is the level of exploitability (E) by which we consider the difficulty to make an attack. Damage potential can be defined as the average loss of money an attack may cause, but any sensible numerical measure can be used in our approach.

The meaning that we give to the term exploitability, E, is a general value that includes both the exploitability and reproducibility of an attack, defined in the STRIDE/-DREAD theory[11]. At the same time we also attribute to damage potential (H) the meaning of total damage taking into account also the number of affected users.

$$Risk = f(H, E) \qquad (1)$$

We want to evaluate the total risk of a threat described by an attack tree.
Our approach consists of four steps:

- **At step 1**: A threat to the system under examination is modelled by using an attack tree. The attack objective is the root node and children nodes represent different ways of achieving it. Children can be alternative (or subtrees) or needed jointly (and subtree). The final leaves of the tree are *potential* vulnerabilities of the system that should be matched with the *actual* known vulnerabilities. To each vulnerability v is associated a numerical index E, called *exploitability*, which measures how probable is that v will be exploited to perform a successful attack. Evaluation of E can be quite approximate: in order to apply our computation it is sufficient that the partial order of indexes among dependent vulnerabilities (see below) reflects the relative difficulty of exploitation. In fact, further calculation are based only on maximum and minimum operations and no complex arithmetics will be applied. However, to compare two different risk evaluations (possibly with respect to two different systems), the same scale should be used and a total order among exploitability indices is needed. A meaningful assessment of E is a matter of both experience and ingenuity, but as far as a single analysis is concerned only *relative* ease of exploitability has to be estimated, a judgement on which people often agree.
- **At step 2**: We introduce dependencies among identified vulnerabilities. A vulnerability A depends on a vulnerability B if and only if when B was already exploited, then A is easier to be exploited. Dependencies should be analyzed by taking into account context, architectural and topological information.
- **At step 3**: The index E of each vulnerability is updated taking into account mutual dependencies, according to the algorithm described in Section 2.2. since each vulnerability could be exploited *thanks to the previous exploitation of one of the vulnerabilities on which it depends*.
- **At step 4**: The risk associated to the threat under examination is finally computed by recursively aggregating exploitabilities along the attack tree. The exploitability of an or subtree is the easiest exploitability of children, and the exploitability of an and subtree is the most difficult exploitability of children. The aggregated exploitability measures the level of feasibility of the attack and can be combined with the damage potential (H) to assess the risk of the threat.

2.2   Exploitability of dependent vulnerabilities

Consider the system depicted in Figure 1. We will use this simple example to show our approach to risk assessment. The system can be described as a graph $S = < C, L >$ where $C = \{P, Q, R\}$ is the set of *components* and $L = \{(P, Q), (Q, R), (R, Q),$ $(R, P)\}$ is the set of *links* between components. A number of flaws affecting the software composing the system is known: let's them form the set $F = \{p_1, q_1, q_2, r_1, x_1, y_1,$ $z_1, z_2\}$. Components are exposed to the set of vulnerabilities $V_C = \{(P, p_1), (Q, q_1),$ $(Q, q_2)(R, r_1)\}$, where an element (v, ν) means that the component v is susceptible to be subverted thanks to the flaw ν. Links are exposed to the set of vulnerabilities $V_L = \{((P, Q), x_1), ((Q, R), z_1), ((Q, R), z_2), ((R, P), y_1)\}$, where an element (v, ν) means that the link v is susceptible to be subverted thanks to the flaw ν. Since link z is bidirectional, z_1 and z_2 affect also (R, Q), however it is not useful to take into account them twice. The set of all vulnerabilities is $V = V_C \cup V_L$. To ease notation, we denote $element(\nu) \in C \cup L$ the element of S to which the vulnerability ν applies.

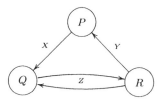

Fig. 1. System architecture

Initially, one has to assess how easy and repeatable is to exploit every single vulnerability to gain control of a component or a link in the given architecture. We call this the *exploitability* $E_0(\nu)$ of the vulnerability ν in the system S.

$$\forall \nu | (v, \nu) \in V \quad \text{assess} \quad E_0(\nu)$$

$$E : V \mapsto \mathbf{N}$$

where $\mathbf{N}$ is a total ordered set of degrees of exploitability; we will use $\mathbf{N} = \{x | 0 \leq x \leq 10\}$ where 0 means "not exploitable at all". This evaluation will be driven by the knowledge we have about the vulnerability itself and the constraints the architecture imposes on its exploitability. In fact, when a component or a link is part of a complex system, its vulnerabilities are typically more difficult to be exploited compared to the case when one has the total control of it.

However, the architecture of the system imposes dependencies among vulnerabilities. For example, we need to understand if it is easier to exploit a vulnerability of a component given that an input link attached to it was already compromised or a component attached to any of its input links was already compromised. Dependencies among vulnerabilities can be represented as a new graph $G = <V, D>$. We denote with $E(\alpha | \beta)$ the exploitability of α given that β was already exploited. The edge $(\beta, \alpha) \in D$ if $E(\alpha | \beta) \geq E_0(\alpha)$, i.e., if it is easier to compromise $element(\alpha)$ when one has compromised $element(\beta)$

$$\forall \nu, \alpha \in V \land \nu \neq \alpha \; : \; \text{assess } E(\nu | \alpha)$$

1 (Complexity)
The number of the exploitabilities to assess is $\leq |V|^2$ In fact, every vulnerability needs an exploitability evaluation ($|V|$ figures needed). Moreover, the graph G has at most $|V| \cdot (|V| - 1)$ edges.

Thus, in general one has to assess $|V|^2$ exploitabilities. However, most of the vulnerabilities are usually independent, and the numbers one has to *guess* is typically closer to $|V|$ than $|V|^2$. Moreover, in the following it will be clear that *only ordering is important*, i.e. absolute values of exploitabilities have no meaning: it is only a convenient

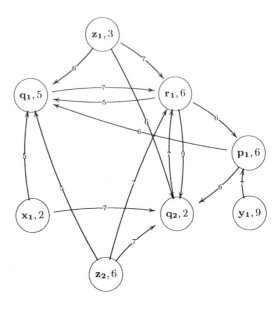

Fig. 2. Dependencies graph among vulnerabilities

way to express the relative easiness of acquiring control of an element thanks to one of them. Figure 2 shows an exploitability assessment for the example system: the dependencies among $|V| = 8$ vulnerabilities impose the assessment of 24 exploitabilities. The number associated to each node is E_0, that is the initial measure of how difficult is to exploit the vulnerability. The conditional exploitabilities are represented by the numbers on the edges. The assessment depicted in Figure 2 does not take into account that each vulnerability could be exploited *thanks to the previous exploitation of one of the vulnerabilities on which it depends*. Therefore, E_0 should be iteratively updated by considering the easiest (i.e., the maximum) way of exploiting an incoming vulnerability in the dependencies graph. In turn each incoming vulnerability could be exploited by controlling the affected element or leveraging on the dependency itself: the most difficult (i.e., the minimum) constraints the value.

$$\forall \nu \in V, (\nu, \gamma) \in D : E(\nu) = max(E_0(\nu), min(E(\nu|\gamma), E(\gamma))) \qquad (2)$$

Our methodology consists in iteratively applying the previous formula for each vulnerability, until the system converges to an equilibrium. Table 1 shows a possible sequence of iteration and the corresponding equilibrium.

2 (Convergence) *At each iteration the exploitability can only be updated with a greater value. Moreover, it is upper bounded by the maximum value of the incoming dependencies edges. Therefore no "oscillations" are possible and the algorithm always converges.*

3 (Order) *Only the relative order of exploitability values is important: in fact, only max and min operators are used in our formula, and no arithmetical functions are ever applied.*

	E_0	E_1	E_2
p_1	6	7	7
q_1	5	6	6
q_2	2	6	6
r_1	6	6	6
x_1	2	2	2
y_1	9	9	9
z_1	3	3	3
z_2	6	6	6

Table 1. Exploitability update

Risk assessment could be effectively used to evaluate design choices. For example, making links not exploitable at all (by protecting them with logical and physical defenses) would virtually change nothing.

Our approach can also be used to evaluate the impact of adding a new vulnerable component to a preexisting system. In fact, due to the presence of new dependencies between vulnerabilities, the new component can affect the security of the whole system, increasing the exploitability of some of the old vulnerabilities.

3   An example

In this section we introduce a numerical example based on an hypothetical Insecure Airlines web site. For the sake of simplicity we maintain the same simple architecture represented in fig.1.

According with the new airline scenario, Node P represents the company web server, node Q represents the database containing the flights information, and node R is a web service that manages the frequent flier accounts. Links X and Z connect the web server to the database and the frequent flier services respectively. Link Y allows some automatic script on the database to update the mileage of a customer account.

We associate the following vulnerabilities to the system components:

V_1 **(node P)** SQL injection. An authenticated user can submit a malicious query that allows him to read or modify any row in the database.

V_2 **(node Q)** Buffer Overflow. The CGI page that loads and displays the flight information copies the flight number into a small static buffer without checking for possible buffer overflow.

V_3 **(node Q)** A race condition in a local command allows an attacker to read any file in the web server machine.

V_4 **(node R)** Weak authentication. The access to each frequent flyer account is protected by a numeric PIN of 4 digits.

The threat that a malicious user could sniff[1] the traffic between two components is represented introducing three more vulnerabilities: V_5 (for X link), V_6 (for Y link) and V_7 (for Z link).

The airline company is interested in evaluating the risk that an external user (not a company employee) can add a fake flight reservation. The security analyst starts enumerating all the possible attacks and combining them to form a large attack tree. Fig 3 reports a piece of the tree in outline form.

```
Goal: Fake Reservation
1. Convince an employee to add a reservation
 1.1 Blackmail an employee
 1.2 Threaten an employee
2. Access and Modify the flight database
 2.1 SQL Injection from the web page (V1)
 2.2 Log into the database
  2.2.1 Guess the password
  2.2.2 Sniff the password (V7)
  2.2.3 Steal the password from the Web-Server machine (AND)
  2.2.3.1 Get an account on the Web-Server
  2.2.3.1.1 Exploit a buffer overflow (V2)
  2.2.3.1.2 Get access to an employee account
  2.2.3.2 Exploit a race condition to access a protected
          file (V3)
```

Fig. 3. Attack Tree

The next step consists in assigning the exploitability values of each vulnerability. The following table summarizes the values and the dependencies between each vulnerability:

Vuln.	E_0	V_1	V_2	V_3	V_4	V_5	V_6	V_7
V_1	2		-	10	-	10	-	-
V_2	0	5		-	-	-	-	-
V_3	0	-	3		-	-	-	-
V_4	4	8	-	10		-	7	10
V_5	7	-	-	-	-		-	-
V_6	7	-	-	-	-	-		-
V_7	7	-	-	-	-	-	-	

We do not have enough space to justify the choice of every values in the table, but in order to provide an idea of what is behind the numbers, we can consider the case of V_2. The second column represents $E_0(V_2)$, that is the exploitability of V_2 given that none

---

[1] We do not consider spoofing and man-in-the-middle attacks in order to do not complicate the example.

of the other vulnerabilities have been previously exploited by the attacker. In our case the value is zero. In fact, it is not possible for a malicious user to directly exploit the buffer overflow since the input the attacker should manipulate comes directly from the flight repository. For this reason, if the attacker would be able to insert a malicious row into the database, he could then force the web server to display that information taking control of the machine. This dependence is shown in the third column: $E(V_2|V_1) = 5$.

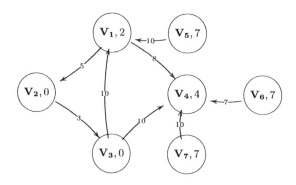

Fig. 4. Vulnerabilities Dependence Graph

Figure 4 shows the *Vulnerability Dependence Graph* representation of our system. Applying our algorithm to the graph, after a couple of iterations, the system converges to the following fixed point:

$E(V_1) = 7$
$E(V_2) = 5$
$E(V_3) = 3$
$E(V_4) = 7$

This result can seem obvious due to the simplicity of the example but in a real scenario that can involve dozen of components, also for a skilled user can be very difficult to figure out all the possibles chain of attacks just looking at the graph. Moreover, it is possible to see how the presence of a vulnerability in a branch of the attack tree can affect the exploitability values associated to leaves belonging to a different branch of the tree.

Anyway, the evaluation of the risk in a distributed environment is just the first step in a more complicate and interesting process. In fact, one of the main purpose of our approach is to allow user to locate, analyze, and compare the impact of security solutions on the whole system under analysis.

In the case of Insecure Airlines, a security manager can propose different solutions in order to mitigate the total risk of the system. Since security solutions are usually expensive, it is very important to reduce any possible waste of money. For this reason the possibility to quickly simulate and explore the impact of multiple actions allows the user to choose the right solution in order to guarantee a good security level according to business requirements.

In our example, the only way to log into the database is by knowing the password (that is stored into the web server host). The file containing the password can be read thanks to the race condition vulnerability present in one of the programs installed on the host. Suppose the security manager proposes the following possible solutions:

- *Solution A*: Update the vulnerable program with a more secure one.
- *Solution B*: Fix the buffer overflow vulnerability. So, no one can have the chance to perform the race condition attack.
- *Solution C*: Encrypt the communication between the web-server and the database to make a sniffing attack much more difficult.

Translating these three solutions in numbers, the first is equivalent to setting V_3 and its dependencies to zero, the second to setting V_2 and its dependencies to zero, and the last one to setting V_5 to one.

Running again our algorithm in the three different scenarios, we obtain the following results:

Scenario	V_1	V_2	V_3	V_4
Base	7	5	3	7
Solution A	7	5	0	7
Solution B	7	0	0	7
Solution C	2	2	2	7

The previous table shows that the first solution does not affect the rest of the system. The second solution makes the system more secure since it removes the possibility to exploit V_3. Nevertheless, an attacker can still exploit V_1 modifying the database at his will. The third solution seems the better one, since it makes very hard to exploit three of the four initial vulnerabilities.

Of course, in order to decide if a solution is worthwhile or not, it is necessary to propagate the exploitability values from the leaves to the root of the attack tree. In such a way a security analyst can evaluate what is the real danger and which solution is more appropriate to mitigate it.

4   Related work

Risk, trust, security requirements mapping, and component interdependence are concepts that are linked together and have been widely discussed in literature.

Baskerville [3] describes the evolution of different methods to measure risk that sometimes could be used together to improve the result accuracy. Even though software security risk is extensively discussed in risk management methodologies [20, 5, 2], among information security experts there appears to be no agreement regarding the best or the most appropriate method to assess the probability of computer incidents [18].

We started our investigation analyzing the STRIDE/DREAD theory [11] and proposing a simplified way to combine together the assessment values. We then took into account the problem of risk aggregation that represents a key point to enable modular reasoning in distributed environments that involve multiple and heterogenous components.

O.Sami Saydjari et al.[9]present a system security engineering methodology for discovering system vulnerabilities, and determining what countermeasures can best close those vulnerabilities.Their approach improves the process "*analyzing IS through an adversary's eyes*".

Evaluation and analysis of vulnerabilities in isolation is insufficient because it is important to consider the effects of the interactions among vulnerabilities. There are many approaches for taking into account vulnerability dependencies [9, 13].Using a graph representation to model security-related concepts is not a new approach. For instance, attack graphs [19, 14] use state-transition diagrams to describe complex attacks that can involve multiple steps. Different techniques, such as model checking [19], can then be applied to attack graphs in order to evaluate security properties. The goal of our vulnerability dependence graph is different since we only need to describe the relationships among vulnerabilities in order to improve information obtained by the attack tree model [6, 17].

Software components have received a great deal of interest from both industries and academia as the component based software development paradigm promises maximum benefits of component reusability and distributed programming. A software component is independently developed and delivered as an autonomous unit that can be composed to become part of a lager application. The component interdependence is often ignored or overlooked [4] leading to incorrect or imprecise models. In order to avoid this problem, one must specify more complete models taking into account interconnections among system components. In agreement with this point of view [8, 18, 4, 9, 16] present models for assessing security risks taking into account interdependence between components.

Even though there is no easy way to assess risks and choose the damage values, there are various approaches that provide methodologies by which the risk evaluation can be made more systematic. In particular, Sharp et al.[18] develop a scheme for probabilistic evaluation of the impact of the security threats and proposes a system for risk management with the goal of assessing the expected damages due to attacks also in terms of the cost. Z. Dwaikat et al.[8] define security requirements for transactions and provide mechanisms to measure likelihood of violation of these requirements. Unlike us, the authors base the evaluation of risk on transaction traces combining security requirements, context information and risks presented by various components. K.Khan et al [12] propose a framework to characterize compositional security contracts of software components.

At the same time, there is a need to automate the modeling phase in the risk assessment and analysis process. G. Biswas, et al. [4] proposed the use of qualitative modeling techniques based on deriving behavior from structural descriptions and causal reasoning to aid automating and enhancing the risk analysis. Hierarchical schemes are used for describing component structure and system functionality is derived from a set of primitive functions and parameters defined for the domain. The authors want to (1) incorporate uncertainty analysis using probabilistic schemes or belief functions for estimating risk probabilities, and (2) use causal reasoning and qualitative modeling for consequence analysis. We introduced an automatic evaluation of the total exploitability of each vulnerability that will then influence the value of total risk. In agreement to [4, 9, 16] the information computed by the model to calculate the risk could be used as effect analysis and decisional support.

5 Conclusions

Risk analysis of large distributed systems is still a hard problem for security managers since it requires a perfect balance of skills, experience, and "black magic" to be solved.

This paper presents a quantitative approach to evaluate risk in a distributed environments based on the knowledge of the system architecture and the list of vulnerabilities of links and components.

The choice of dividing the analysis into four steps simplifies the study of the problem allowing the security designer to acquire and manipulate risk information step by step in an incremental way.

Starting from an attack tree we build a Vulnerability Dependencies Graph that emphasizes the possible dependencies among vulnerabilities/leaves. In this way we point out the dependencies among system vulnerabilities that can be lost in an attack tree representation and that can make the system more vulnerable. We then propose an equilibrium condition that can be iteratively applied to propagate exploitability values from one node of the graph to the others.

Even though the number of values that must be initially assigned to each vulnerability can be fairly high, we strongly belief that our system simplify the risk analysis process. In fact, since we never use any arithmetic operation to combine exploitabilities, we only requires (and preserve) that the initial values respect some kind of ordering criterion.

Finally, our algorithm can be used to automatically evaluate different security solutions, enabling a security manager to perform a "what if" analysis in order to analyze the impact of a local modification on the security of the whole system.

We are currently experimenting by applying our approach on real world examples, in particular focusing on systems based on web services. In principle, our approach is independent from the level of abstraction one uses to analyze a system, thus we are planning to extend our analysis to the relationship between hierarchical assessments.

References

1. http://msgs.securepoint.com/bugtraq/.
2. Christopher Alberts, Audree Dorofee, James Stevens, and Carol Woody. Introduction to the Octave approach. http://www.cert.org/octave/, 2003.
3. Richard Baskerville. Information system security design methods: Implications for information systems development. *ACM Computing Survey*, 25(4):375–412, 1993.

4. Gautam Biswas, Kenneth A. Debelak, and Kazuhiko Kawamura. Application of qualitative modelling to knoweledge-based risk assessment studies. *IEA/AIE '89: Second International Conference on Industrial & Engineering Applications of Artificial Intelligence & Expert Systems-ACM*, pages 92–101, 1989.
5. B.Jenkins. Risk analysis helps establish a good security posture; risk management keeps it that way. *whitepaper*, pages 1–16, 1998.
6. CERT. Technical report 2001-tn-001.
7. Harvey M. Deitel, Paul J. Deitel, B. DuWaldt, and L. K. Trees. *Web Services: A Technical Introduction*. Prentice Hall, 2002.
8. Zaid Dwaikat and Francesco Parisi-Presicce. Risky trust: Risk-based analysis of software system. *Proceedings of the first workshop on Software Engineering for Secure Systems (SESS05)*.
9. S. Evans, D. Heinbuch, E.Kyle, J. Piorkowski, and J.Wallener. Risk-based system security engineering: Stopping attacks with intention. *IEEE Security & Privacy*, pages 59–62, 2004.
10. Network Working Group. Internet security glossary. http://rfc.net/rfc2828.html, May 2000. Request for Comments: 2828.
11. Michael Howard and David Leblanc. *Writing secure Code*. Microsoft Press, 2003.
12. Khaled Khan, Jun Han, and Yuliang Zheng. A framework for an active interface to characterize compositional security contracts of software components. *2001 Australian Software Engineering Conference (ASWEC01)-IEEE Computer Society Press*, pages 117–126.
13. I.S. Moskowitz and M.H. Kang. An insecurity flow model. *Proceedings of New Security Paradigms workshop*, 1997.
14. S. Noel, S.Jajoidia, B.O'Berry, and M. Jacobs. Efficient minimum-cost network hardening via exploit dependency graphs. *Proceedings of ACSAC'03*.
15. M. Elisabeth Pate-Cornell. Fault tree vs. event trees in reliability analysis. *Risk Analysis*, 4(3):177–186, 1984.
16. Mehmet Sahinoglu. Security meter:a pratical decision-tree model to quantify risk. *IEEE Security & Privacy*, 3(3):18–24, May/June 2005.
17. Bruce Schneier. Modelling security threats. *Dr. Dobb's Journal*, dec 1999.
18. Gunter P. Sharp, Philip H. Enslow, Shamkant B. Navathe, and Fariborz Farhmand. Managing vulnerabilities of information system to security incindets. *ACM International Conference:5th international conference on Electronic commerce*, pages 348–354, 2003.
19. O. Sheyner, J. Haines, S.Jha, R. Lippmann, and J.M. Wing. Automated generation and analysis of attack graphs. *Proceedings of the 2002 IEEE Symposium on Security and Privacy (S&P'02)*.
20. Thomas Siu. Risk-eye for IT security guy. *Gsec*, pages 1–20, 2004.

Collection and analysis of attack data based on honeypots deployed on the Internet

E. Alata[1], M. Dacier[2], Y. Deswarte[1], M. Kaâniche[1], K. Kortchinsky[3], V. Nicomette[1], V.H. Pham[2], and F. Pouget[2]

[1] LAAS-CNRS,
7 Avenue du Colonel Roche, 31077 Toulouse Cedex 4, France,
{ealata, deswarte, kaaniche, nicomett}@laas.fr
http://www.laas.fr
[2] Eurécom,
2229 Route des Crêtes, BP 193, 06904 Sophia Antipolis Cedex, France,
{dacier, pham, pouget}@eurecom.fr
http://www.eurecom.fr
[3] CERT-RENATER, c/o ENSAM, 151 Boulevard de lHôpital, 75013, Paris, France,
kostya.kortchinsky@renater.fr
http://www.renater.fr/Securite/CERT_Renater.htm

Abstract. The CADHo project (Collection and Analysis of Data from Honeypots) is an ongoing research action funded by the French ACI "Securité & Informatique" [1]. It aims at building an environment to better understand threats on the Internet and also at providing models to analyze the observed phenomena. Our approach consists in deploying and sharing with the scientific community a distributed platform based on honeypots that gathers data suitable to analyze the attack processes targeting machines connected to the Internet. This distributed platform, called *Leurré.com* and administrated by Institut Eurécom, offers each partner collaborating to this initiative access to all collected data in order to carry out statistical analyzes and modeling activities. So far, about thirty honeypots have been operational for several months in twenty countries of the five continents. This paper presents a brief overview of this distributed platform and examples of results derived from the data. It also outlines the approach investigated to model observed attack processes and to describe the intruders behaviors once they manage to get access to a target machine.

1 Introduction

Since the very first large distributed denial of service attacks launched in February 2000, an apparently increasing number of major security problems have been reported. In particular, a large number of worms have been observed during the last years. Surprisingly, the number of observed attacks does not seem to be influenced by the ever increasing deployment of efficient security protection tools, such as personal desktop firewalls. Is this apparent raise in the number of attacks backed up by some undisputable data? If yes, what are the attack processes that lead to such phenomena?

As of today, we are unfortunately unable to answer these questions because of the lack of precise and unbiased data to assess the seriousness of the situation. A few qualitative indicators exist, such as, for instance, the yearly survey conducted by the Computer Security Institute (CSI) and the Federal Bureau of Investigations (FBI). However, these reports provide only high-level trends, based on statistical data obtained in various heterogeneous environments, without having a precise knowledge of the configuration of these environments. Also, the collected data is not rich enough to enable scientists to carry out rigorous analyses of the malicious behaviors at stake, and to model attack processes and their impact on the target systems security. Some companies, such as IBM, have access to a very large amount of security incident-related information collected from their customers, which, in theory, could be used to model and analyze the attack processes. In practice, however, all previous experience with such data has revealed that they are not suitable for that purpose. The main reasons lie in the complexity, diversity and dynamicity of the systems that are under scrutiny. Recently, various initiatives have been taken to monitor real world data related to malware and attacks propagation on the Internet. The Internet Telescopes, so-called blackholes/darknets and the DShield projects are among them. These projects provide valuable information for the identification and analysis of malicious activities on the Internet [2–4]. Nevertheless, such information is not sufficient to model attack processes and analyze their impact on the security of the targeted machines.

The CADHo project described in this paper is complementary to the above initiatives. It intends to address these issues by means of the following actions:

1. The project aims at deploying and sharing with the scientific community a distributed platform of honeypots [5] that gathers data suitable to analyze the attack processes targeting a large number of machines connected to the Internet.
2. The project aims at validating the usefulness of this platform by carrying out various analyses, based on the collected data, to characterize the observed attacks and model their impact on security. In particular, we will investigate how to use the modeling results to improve the design and validation of secure systems. Our objective consist in providing solid rationales for those who need to validate the fault assumptions they make when designing, for instance, intrusion tolerant systems.
3. Finally, the project aims at going beyond the study of the most frequent and automated attacks. Our objective consists here in investigating and modeling the behavior of malicious attackers once they have managed to compromise and get access to a new host. Indeed, we are not interested in monitoring all kinds of attackers. Instead, we want to monitor only those that are representative of large classes of attackers so that the knowledge derived from their observation is symptomatic of a large amount of real attacks. To fulfill this objective, we need to develop and deploy a sophisticated environment that gives the attackers the "apparent" possibility of compromising a target system, under strict control and monitoring. This is a real challenge given the current the state of the art.

The CADHo project started in September 2004. The honeypot platform we have built has been deployed in thirty sites, from academia and industry, in twenty countries over the five continents. In the following sections, we describe our honeypot based data collection platform (called *Leurré.com*), and we present some examples of results obtained from the analysis of the data collected so far. In addition, the paper includes a preliminary discussion of the problems and the directions investigated for the modeling activities.

Section 2 presents the data collection environment *Leurré.com*. Section 3 provides a summary of the various analyses carried out on the collected data. Section 4 focuses on the modeling of attacks observed on the various honeypots deployed so far. Finally, Section 5 discusses the future evolution of the current platform toward the development of high-interaction honeypots that will enable us to model the behavior of attackers once they manage to control a target system and try to progress to defeat some security objectives.

2   The data collection environment *Leurré.com*

As mentioned in Section 1, one of the goals of the CADHo project is to share with the scientific community an open distributed platform to collect data from a large number of honeypots. This platform is deemed to evolve over the years, well beyond the end of the CADHo project. New partners are allowed to get access to the complete collected data set if and only if they agree to set up a honeypot on their premises, thus enriching the overall setup by their presence. Names of the partners are protected by a Non Disclosure Agreement that each participating entity must sign. We have developed all the required software to automate the various regular maintenance tasks (new installation, reconfiguration, log collection, backups, etc.) to ensure the long term existence of this set up.

A honeypot is a machine connected to a network but that no one is supposed to use. In theory, no connection to or from that machine should be observed. If a connection occurs, it must be, at best an accidental error or, more likely, an attempt to attack the machine. Recently, several approaches have been proposed to build environments where several honeypots are deployed. The generic term *honeynet* is used to represent them. The most visible honeynet project is the one carried out by the so called Honeynet Research Alliance [5, 6]. The Alliance is made of national entities. Some CADHo members are active members of the French one, the French Honeynet Project [7].

So far, most of the attention has been paid to implementation issues. Institut Eurécom has been working for more than a year on the definition of a low-interaction honeypot dedicated to the tasks explained here above. A first environment has been deployed, based on the VMware [8] technology. Based on the acquired expertise during a one-year use of this environment and on the analyses carried out on the collected data, we are now convinced that, for the specific objectives of our project, the freely available software called *honeyd* [9] can be used instead of VMware. Indeed, it is known that the major drawback of *honeyd* is that an environment using that software can be remotely identified by a skilled attacker. This is less easy with VMware. Fortunately, data collected so far indicate that the risk of seeing attackers fingerprinting the environment under attack is negligible. This justifies the choice of a *honeyd* based solution.

Honeyd is a free software and it runs on various flavors of Linux and Windows. It does not consume a lot of resources and, therefore, old PCs can be used without any trouble. These are very interesting features since we are interested in building a large environment where many honeynets would run. The fact that we can add honeynets for almost no cost makes this solution very attractive. It is indeed unlikely that we could identify interested partners to join this platform on a voluntary basis otherwise.

The distributed platform Leurré.com itself is made of a potentially large number of identical honeynets deployed at the sites of our partners. All the honeynets are centrally managed to ensure that they have exactly the same configuration. This is very important if we want to keep the experiment under control. The data gathered by each honeynet are securely uploaded to a centralized database administrated by Institut Eurécom. This database contains, in a highly structured and efficient way, the complete content, including payload, of all packets sent to or from these honeynets. Furthermore, the collected data are enriched by additional information to facilitate their analysis, such as the IP geographical localization of packets source addresses, the OS of the attacking machine, the local time of the source, etc. In our context, each IP address interacting with the honeynets identifies an attacking machine. It is noteworthy that for attack processes that go through a chain of systems to attack a target, the IP address recorded in our database corresponds to the previous hop in the chain before reaching our honeynets, which does not necessarily correspond to the machine initiating the attack process.

Concretely, the distributed platform *Leurré.com* is constituted of three main components:

1. A set of computers connected to the Internet deployed at the partners sites, running *honeyd* with the same configuration. Each computer emulates three virtual machines running various operating systems (Linux RedHat, Windows 98, Windows NT) and services (ftp, web, etc.). All traffic received by or sent from each computer is saved in tcpdump files. A firewall ensures that connections cannot be initiated from the computer, only answers to external solicitations are allowed. Every day, a secured communication is established from a trusted machine during a short period of time to copy the tcpdump files archived on each computer. Integrity checks are also performed to ensure that the platform has not been compromised.
2. A centralized relational database where all the collected data are archived. All partners have the possibility to send queries to that database through a secure web interface.
3. A set of software programs that are used to collect, process and enrich the data collected from each platform. For instance, three different software are used for passive fingerprinting the OS of the attacking machines: *p0f* [10], *ettercap* [11], and *disco* [12]. *Maxmind* [13] is used to identify the geographic location of the attacks.

3 Data analysis: Summary of the main results

Several analyses have been carried out on the data collected from VMware and the *honeyd* based platforms. The results obtained from these analyses have been published in international conferences in the course of 2004-2005. An up to date list of publications on this topic can be found in [14]. In the following, we provide a short summary of the main conclusions and lessons learned from the data.

- The analyses reported in [15, 16] were based on the data collected from the initial VMware platform during a 10 month observation period. In particular, we have observed that the data exhibit a stable behavior from various perspectives, for instance with respect to the geographic location of the attacking machine, the target of the attack (virtual machine, port), etc. Such regularity suggests that there are some real values in using the data collected from honeypots to model attack processes and threats. Also, the data revealed the existence of two distinct sets of machines that targeted our honeypot platform. The first set of machines were only seeking to gather information on our environment, without really trying to perform an attack. Their activity mainly consisted in scanning our network in a systematic way considering a limited number of ports. The second set of machines (about 25%) were attacking only specific open ports of our honeypot. This suggests that they have already acquired such information from other machines belonging to first set (the scanning machines). It is noteworthy that such observation has been also confirmed by the more recent data collected from the *honeyd* distributed platform. However, we observe a higher proportion of *attacking* machines than *scanning* machines.

- A deep and thorough analysis of honeypots data is generally required to have a good understanding of malicious activity. In [17, 18], a new clustering algorithm is used to identify similar attack traces associated to attacking machines that are likely to use the same attack tool. The application of this algorithm to our honeypots data confirmed that it is very useful to highlight interesting phenomena that remain hidden if we analyze the data at a higher macroscopic level only (e.g., considering the number of attacks observed at the different ports without analyzing the root causes of the attacks).

- In the study reported in [19], we present a methodology to analyze the potential bias introduced by the use a low interaction *honeyd* platform compared to the VMware based platform. We show that high interaction honeypots are useful to control the relevance of low interaction honeypot configurations, and that both interaction levels are required to build an efficient network of distributed honeypots.

- Finally, in [20], we present a comparative analysis of the attack processes observed on various platforms deployed at different geographic locations. In particular, we can highlight the three following observations:
  1. Some attack processes have been observed on all the platforms
  2. Some attack processes have been observed only on a subset of platforms
  3. Some attack processes have been observed only on a single platform

The results obtained suggest that the data observed from a single platform is not sufficient to characterize the malicious activity observed on the Internet. Based on the data collected so far, it seems that this is only possible for a minority of observed attacks. This result highlights the necessity to have a largely deployed distributed platform to observe the malicious activity carried out on the Internet in order to be able to derive meaningful and representative conclusions.

The results summarized above are based on the qualitative analysis of the collected data. Additional useful insights can be obtained by using mathematical modeling techniques, in particular with respect to the definition of appropriate models that can be used for prediction purposes. In the next sections, we discuss the objectives and the main problems related to this topic and we outline some examples of preliminary results to promote discussion.

4   Modeling based on the collected data

Honeypots are generally attacked by different attackers from several geographic locations all over the world. In other words, the time when the attacks are launched, their source and consequences are not known in advance. Also, the vulnerabilities exploited by the attackers and the attack scenarios might differ significantly. On the other hand, the attack results might depend on the state of the target system when the attack is initiated. All these factors are uncertainty sources that have to be taken into account in the analysis and modeling tasks carried out on the data collected from the honeypots. Statistical and probabilistic analysis techniques are well suited to take into account such uncertainties in order to: i) characterize the attackers behavior and the attack scenarios, and ii) build stochastic models and evaluate quantitative measures reflecting targeted system capacity to resist to attacks.

The data collected from the honeypots can be processed in various ways to characterize the attack processes and perform predictive analyses. For example, we can build stochastic models characterizing the frequency and the distribution of attacks taking into account the geographic location of the attackers, the IP addresses of the attacking machines, the vulnerabilities exploited, the severity of the consequences of the attacks on the target system and data, etc. In particular, modeling activities can be used to fulfill the following objectives:

1. Identify the probability distributions that best characterize the attack occurrence and attack propagation processes.
2. Analyze whether the data collected from different platforms exhibit similar or different malicious attack activities.
3. Model the time relationships that may exist between attacks coming from different sources (or to different destinations).
4. Predict the occurrence of new waves of attacks on a given platform based on the history of attacks observed on this platform as well as on the other platforms.

The approach adopted in the CADHo project to fulfill these objectives consists in exploring the application of statistical analysis and probabilistic modeling techniques that are traditionally used to model and evaluate the dependability of software and hardware based systems using data collected in operation, and extending their use to the data collected from the honeypots.

For the sake of illustration, we present in the following simple preliminary models based on the data collected from our honeypots. The examples address: i) the time-evolution modeling of the number of attacks observed on different honeypot platforms deployed so far, and ii) the analysis of potential correlations for the attack processes observed on the different platforms taking into account the geographic location of the attacking machines and the relative contribution of each platform to the global attack activity. We remind that in our context, an attacking machine is identified by an IP address interacting with our honeypots, which does not necessarily correspond to the machine initiating the attack process (see Section 2).

The data collection period considered for the examples corresponds to 46 weeks. We take into account the attacks observed on 14 honeypot platforms among those deployed so far. The honeypots selected correspond to those that have been active for almost the whole considered period. The total number of attacks observed on these honeypots is 816476. These attacks are not uniformly distributed among the platforms. In particular, the data collected from three platforms represent more than fifty percent of the total attack activity.

Let us denote by:

- $Y(t)$ the function describing the evolution of the number of attacks per unit of time observed on all the honeypots during the observation period,
- $X_j(t)$ the function describing the evolution of the number of attacks per unit of time observed on all the honeypots during the observation period for which the IP address is located in country j.

In a first stage, we have plotted, for various time periods, $Y(t)$ and the curves $X_j(t)$ corresponding to different countries j. Visual inspection showed surprising similarities between $Y(t)$ and some $X_j(t)$. To confirm such empirical observations, we have then decided to rigorously analyze the phenomena using mathematical linear regression models.

Considering a linear regression model, we have investigated if $Y(t)$ can be estimated from the combination of the attacks described by $X_j(t)$, taking into account a limited number of countries j. Let us denote by $Y^*(t)$ the estimated model.

Formally, $Y^*(t)$ is defined as follows:

$$Y^*(t) = \sum \alpha_j X_j(t) + \beta \qquad j = 1, 2, ..k \qquad (1)$$

Constants α_j and β correspond to the parameters of the linear model that provide the best fit with the observed data, and k is the number of countries considered in the regression.

The quality of fit of the model is measured by the statistics R^2 defined by:

$$R^2 = \frac{\sum (Y^*(i) - Y_{av})^2}{\sum (Y(i) - Y_{av})^2} \qquad (2)$$

$Y(i)$ and $Y^*(i)$ correspond to the observed and estimated number of attacks for unit of time i, respectively. Y_{av} is the average number of attacks per unit of time, taking into account the whole observation period.

R^2 represents the proportion of total variation about the average explained by the regression. Indeed, R is the correlation factor between the estimated model and the observed values. The closer the R^2 value is to 1, the better the estimated model fits the collected data.

We have applied this model considering linear regressions involving one, two or more countries. Surprisingly, the results reveal that a good fit can be obtained by considering the attacks from one country only. For example, the models providing the best fit taking into account the total number of attacks from all the platforms are obtained by considering the attacks issued from UK, USA, Russia or Germany only. The corresponding R^2 values are of the same order of magnitude (0.944 for UK, 0.939 for USA, 0.930 for Russia and 0.920 for Germany), denoting a very good fit of the estimated models to the collected data. This result is confirmed by several statistical tests that provided significant *p-values* indicating that the data appear to be consistent with the linear regression model. For example, the estimated model obtained when considering the attacks from Russia only is defined by equation (3):

$$Y^*(t) = 44.568X_1(t) + 1555.67 \tag{3}$$

$X_1(t)$ represents the evolution of the number of attacks from Russia. Figure 1 plots the evolution of the observed and estimated number of attacks per unit during the data collection period considered in this example. The unit of time corresponds to 4 days. It is noteworthy that, similar conclusions are obtained if we consider another granularity for the unit of time, for example one day, or one week.

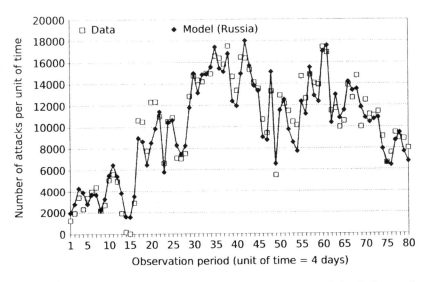

Fig. 1. Evolution of the number of attacks per unit of time observed on all the platforms and estimated model considering attacks from Russia only

These results are even more surprising that the attacks from Russia and UK represent only a small proportion of the total number of attacks (1.9% and 3.7% respectively). Concerning the USA, although the proportion is higher (about 18%), it is not significant enough to explain the linear model.

The fact that the linear regression models considering attacks originating only either from UK or USA, or Russia provide a good fit to the collected data, is related to the fact that the corresponding curves present similar trends. This is illustrated on Figure 4 which represents the evolution of the Laplace factor considering the data collected from the honeypot platforms with all source countries included (Figure 2a), and the data corresponding to attacks from UK, USA or Russia only (Figures 2b, 2c and 2d). It clearly shows that there exists a striking similarity between all the curves.

As detailed in [21], the Laplace factor $u(i)$ computed at unit of time i is based on all the data observed before i. This explains the smooth evolution of the Laplace curve compared for example to Figure 1. The global and the local trends exhibited by the data are identified respectively by analyzing the sign and the variation (increase or decrease) of the Laplace factor curve. From a practical point of view, the curves presented on Figure 4 can be analyzed as follows:

- values oscillating between -2 and 2 indicate a stable behavior (i.e., there is no significant trend toward an increase or a decrease of the number of attacks per unit of time)
- positive values > 2 (respectively, negative values < -2) suggest a global trend towards an increase (respectively a decrease) of the intensity of attacks.
- decreasing or increasing values of the Laplace factor over a subinterval indicate a local decrease or increase of the intensity of attacks, respectively, for that subinterval.

It can be noticed that all the curves in Figure 4 present similar trends. In particular, significant trend changes occur almost around the same units of time (e.g., 15, 45, 54).

We have applied similar analyses by respectively considering each honeypot platform in order to investigate if similar conclusions can be derived by comparing their attack activities per source country to their global attack activities. The results are summarized in Table 3. The second column identifies the source country that provides the best fit. The corresponding R^2 value is given in the third column. Finally, the last three columns give the R^2 values obtained when considering UK, USA, or Russia in the regression mode.

It can be noticed that the quality of the regressions measured when considering attacks from Russia only is generally low for all platforms (R^2 less than 0.80). This indicates that the property observed at the global level is not visible when looking at the local activities observed on each platform. However, for the majority of the platforms, the best regression models often involve one of the three following countries: USA, Germany or UK, which also provide the best regressions when analyzing the global attack activity considering all the platforms together. Two exceptions are found with P6 and P8 for which the observed attack activities exhibit different characteristics with respect to the origin of the attacks (Taiwan, China), compared to the other platforms.

The trends discussed above have been also observed when considering a different granularity for the unit of time (e.g., 1 day or 1 week) as well as different data observation period.

To summarize, two main observations can be derived from the results presented above:

1. Some trends exhibited at the global level considering the attack processes on all the platforms together are not observed when analyzing each platform individually (this is the case for example of attacks from Russia). On the other hand, we have observed the other situation where the trends observed globally are also visible locally on the majority of the platforms (this is the case for example of attacks from USA, UK and Germany)

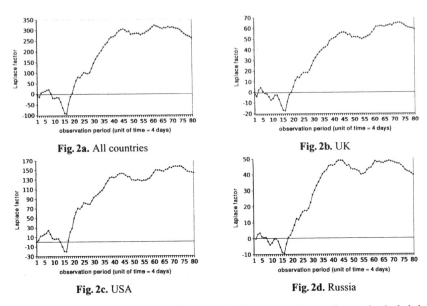

Fig. 2a. All countries

Fig. 2b. UK

Fig. 2c. USA

Fig. 2d. Russia

Fig. 2. Laplace Factor evolution considering attacks from all platforms, all countries included (2a), or only attacks from UK (2b), USA (2c) or Russia (2d)

Platform	Country providing the best model	R^2 Best model	R^2 UK	R^2 USA	R^2 Russia
P1	Germany	0.895	0.873	0.858	0.687
P2	USA	0.733	0.464	0.733	0.260
P3	Germany	0.722	0.197	0.373	0.161
P4	Germany	0.874	0.869	0.872	0.608
P5	UK	0.861	0.861	0.699	0.656
P6	Taiwan	0.796	0.249	0.425	0.212
P7	Germany	0.754	0.630	0.624	0.631
P8	China	0.746	0.303	0.664	0.097
P9	Germany	0.738	0.574	0.412	0.389
P10	Germany	0.708	0.510	0.546	0.087
P11	USA	0.912	0.787	0.912	0.774
P12	SPAIN	0.791	0.620	0.727	0.720
P13	USA	0.870	0.176	0.870	0.111
P14	USA	0.874	0.659	0.874	0.517

Fig. 3. Estimated models for each platform: correlation factors obtained for the countries providing the best fit and for UK, USA and Russia

2. The attack processes observed locally on each platform are very often highly correlated with the attack processes originating from a particular country. The country providing the best regressions locally, does not necessarily yield good regressions when considering other platforms or at the global level. These trends seem to result from specific factors that govern the attack processes observed from each platform.

A thorough analysis of the collected data is currently carried out in order to find a sound justification of the observed trends, taking into account the different attributes characterizing the attacks. Moreover, a particular emphasis is put on the elaboration of stochastic models that can be used from a predictive point of view to forecast the attack activities to be observed on a given platform based on past observations on the same platform and on the other platforms.

5   High-interaction honeypots

The honeypots that we have already deployed in the context of this project belong to the family of so-called "low interaction honeypots". This means that their design is such that attackers have not the possibility, at any point in time, to actually get access to the machine they are attacking. This property is enforced by the fact that there is no real machine. Instead, targets are implemented by means of virtual machines without any real operating system or server to compromise. Thus, hackers can only scan ports and send requests to fake servers without ever succeeding in taking control over them.

In the CADHo project, we are also interested in running experiments with "high interaction" honeypots where attackers can really compromise the targets. Collecting data from such honeypots would enable us to study the behaviors of attackers once they have managed to get access to a target. Obviously enough, we do not want to let them use these machines for launching attacks against third party machines. Instead, we will devise a simulated environment within which they could evolve. An important feature of the environment we are planning to build is that it will "select" the attackers that we will, or will not, let compromise our machines. Indeed, we are not interested in monitoring all kinds of attackers. On the contrary, we want to monitor only those that are representative of large classes of attackers so that the knowledge derived from their observation is symptomatic of a large amount of real attacks. Such high interaction honeypots will be deployed within a limited number of highly controlled environments.

The experiments and the data that will be collected based on the high-interaction honeypots will enable us to address two distinct objectives. First, we are interested in better understanding the attack scenarios, in particular those carried out by skilled intruders. This acquired knowledge will be useful to build concrete responses and to develop tools to counter this form of attack, which is known to be very costly, but which has received little attention up to now. Second, we want to propose concrete and efficient techniques to assess the impact of such ongoing attacks on the security of the targeted system. Along this line, we propose to use observations from this setup to validate a theoretical model initially developed in our previous work on quantitative analysis of operational security in the 90s [22, 23]. The original method is a probabilistic one that differs from classical qualitative approaches (red book, ITSEC, common criteria, etc.).

The core of the method lies in a so called privilege graph which highlights the various possibilities offered to an intruder to increase his privileges thanks to identified vulnerabilities or features of the system he has access to. We have shown how to use this model to derive probabilistic estimations of the ability of a system to resist attacks. These estimations are expressed as a *mean effort to security failure* (METF, similar to the MTTF measure for reliability), assessing the effort necessary for an attacker to realize a violation of a given security policy. The effort is considered as a multi-dimensional variable, taking into account the attacker competence and knowledge, the time needed to prepare and perform the attack, the efficiency of the protection mechanisms (e.g., the difficulty to guess a given password), etc. An automatic tool has been developed to compute these measures, and has been used for a campaign of more than one year on a relatively complex system (a network of several hundred workstations in an academic environment). The results have been analyzed in detail [23], giving convincing arguments on the interest of the method, and the significance of the quantitative measures. The limitations of that approach reside in the absence of real world validation of the assumptions made about the behaviors of the intruders. Common sense has dictated our design but a more rigorous approach requires running some experiments to validate our claims. Thanks to high-interaction honeypots, this is something that now becomes feasible and something that we aim to do within the CADHo project.

6   Conclusion

The distributed data collection platform *Leurré.com* based on honeypots has been operational for many months. The data collected so far and our preliminary analyses have revealed that very interesting observations and conclusions can be derived from this data with respect to the attack activities observed on the Internet. Our objective is to deploy a large number of honeypots all around the world, in various places, in order to get comprehensive data that will allow to derive meaningful results reflecting the main phenomena that characterize the malicious activities on the Internet. It is our wish to share with the scientific community the data contained in our database. We invite all teams interested in using our data for analytical purposes to join us. All partners who accept to deploy one honeypot in their premises are allowed to have access to the database.

As summarized in the paper, the data collected can be analyzed from several perspectives, using qualitative as well as quantitative analysis and modeling techniques. Regarding modeling activities, there are several open issues that need to be addressed in future research in order to be able to build stochastic models that can be used to quantify security or to analyze from a predictive point of view the level of threat and the types of attack processes carried out on the Internet. We believe that the data collected from our honeypots, in particular, high interaction honeypots, will be very useful to identify realistic assumptions and build models that reflect the observed activities. The preliminary models discussed in this paper and the experiments that we are planning to carry out with high interaction honeypots constitute a starting point toward this objective.

References

1. ACI "Sécurité et Informatique", http://acisi.loria.fr/
2. M. Bailey, E. Cooke, F. Jahanian, J. Nazario, and D. Watson, "The Internet Motion Sensor: A Distributed Blackhole Monitoring System", Proc. 12th Annual Network and Distributed System Security Symposium (NDSS), San Diego, CA, Feb. 2005.
3. Home Page of the CAIDA Project, http://www.caida.org/, last visited 06/2005
4. DShield Distributed Detection System homepage, http://www.honeynet.org/, last visited 06/2005
5. L. Spitzner, Honeypots: Tracking Hackers, Addison-Wesley, ISBN from-321-10895-7, 2002
6. Home Page of the Honeynet Project, http://www.honeynet.org/, last visited 06/2005
7. Home page of the French Honeynet Project, http://honeynet.rstack.org/
8. VMWARE, Home page, http://www.vmware.com/
9. Honeyd Home page, http://www.citi.umich.edu/u/provos/honeyd/
10. p0f passive fingerprinting tool homepage, http://lcamtuf.coredump.cx/p0f-beta.tgz
11. The ettercap tool home page, http://ettercap.sourceforge.net/
12. The Disco tool home page, http://www.altmode.com/disco/
13. MaxMind   GeoIP   Country   Database   Commercial   Product: http://www.maxmind.com/app/products/
14. F. Pouget, Publications web page, http://www.eurecom.fr/ pouget/papers.htm
15. M. Dacier, F. Pouget, H. Debar, "Honeypots: Practical Means to Validate Malicious Fault Assumptions on the Internet", Proc. 10th IEEE International Symposium Pacific Rim Dependable Computing (PRDC10), Tahiti, March 2004, pages 383-388.
16. M. Dacier, F. Pouget, H. Debar, "Attack Processes found on the Internet", Proc. OTAN Symposium on Adaptive Defense in Unclassified Networks, Toulouse, France, April 2004.
17. F. Pouget, M. Dacier, "Honeypot-based Forensics", Proc. AusCERT Asia Pacific Information Technology Security Conference (AusCERT2004), Brisbane (Australia), May 2004.
18. F. Pouget, M. Dacier, V. H. Pham, "Towards a Better Understanding of Internet Threats to Enhance Survivability", Proc. International Infrastructure Survivability Workshop (IISW04), Lisbon (Portugal), December 2004.
19. F. Pouget, T. Holz, "A Pointillist Approach for Comparing Honeypots", Proc. Conference on Detection of Intrusions and Malware & Vulnerability Assessment (DIMVA 2005), Vienna (Austria), July 2005.
20. F. Pouget, M. Dacier, V. H. Pham, "Leurré.com: On the Advantages of Deploying a Large Scale Distributed Honeypot Platform", Proc. E-Crime and Computer Evidence Conference (ECCE 2005), Monaco, Mars 2005.
21. K. Kanoun, M. Kaâniche, J-C. Laprie, "Qualitative and Quantitative Reliability Assessment", IEEE Software, Vol. 14, n2, pages 74-86, 1997.
22. M. Dacier, Y. Deswarte, M. Kaâniche, "Models and tools for quantitative assessment of operational security", Proc. 12th International Information Security Conference (IFIP SEC'96), Samos (Greece), May 1996, pages 177-186
23. R. Ortalo, Y. Deswarte, M. Kaâniche, "Experimenting with Quantitative Evaluation Tools for Monitoring Operational Security", IEEE Transactions on Software Engineering, Vol.25, N5, pages 633-650, September/October 1999.

Multilevel Security and Quality of Protection

Simon N. Foley[1], Stefano Bistarelli[3,4], Barry O'Sullivan[1,2], John Herbert[1], and Garret Swart[5]

[1] Department of Computer Science, University College, Cork, Ireland.
[2] Cork Constraint Computation Centre, University College Cork, Ireland
[3] Dipartimento di Scienze, Università "G. D'Annunzio" di Chieti-Pescara, Italy
[4] Istituto di Informatica e Telematica, CNR, Pisa, Italy
[5] IBM Almaden Research Center, San Jose, CA, USA

Abstract. Constraining how information may flow within a system is at the heart of many protection mechanisms and many security policies have direct interpretations in terms of information flow and multilevel security style controls. However, while conceptually simple, multilevel security controls have been difficult to achieve in practice. In this paper we explore how the traditional assurance measures that are used in the network multilevel security model can be re-interpreted and generalised to provide the basis of a framework for reasoning about the quality of protection provided by a secure system configuration.

1 Introduction

Multilevel security is concerned with controlling the flow of information in systems. The traditional view of multilevel security is one of ensuring that information at a high security classification cannot flow down to a lower security classification [1–3]. However, constraining how information may flow within a system is at the heart of many protection mechanisms and many security policies have direct interpretations in terms of multilevel security style controls. These include: Chinese Walls [4, 5]; separation of duties and well formed transactions [4, 6, 7]; Role-Based Access Control [8] and a variety of policies where a degree of data separation is required, for instance, Digital Rights Management [9] and Multi-applicative Smart Cards [10].

Multilevel security, while conceptually simple, has been notoriously difficult to achieve in practice [11]. From the earliest efforts, there have been problems in reconciling multilevel security models with actual multilevel secure systems, leading to problems such as covert channels [12] and how to properly interpret the model [13]. This led to more abstract formal definitions such as [14–16] and more recently [17–20] that effectively attempted to capture the meaning of information flow in some possibilistic information-theoretic sense. These properties of non-interference, information flow and a great many variations have been extensively studied. Designing and verifying security mechanisms that uphold these classes of property is accepted to be difficult [21, 22].

Using formal methods to analyse and verify information flow properties of secure systems requires considerable specification effort. The cost of such in-depth specification and subsequent analysis may be justified for small critical security mechanisms such as authentication protocols and security kernels. However, such in-depth security analysis would not scale to the configuration of a large and/or complex application system.

We are interested in developing shallow and pragmatic security analysis methods for systems. This is achieved through the analysis of how a system is *configured*, rather than an analysis of its underlying mechanisms and protocols. Instead of concentrating on detailed semantics and complete formal verification of components, we are concerned more with the ability to trace, at a practical level of abstraction, how component security requirements relate to each other and any overall security requirements. We believe that a complete security verification of a system is not achievable in practice; we seek some degree of useful feedback from an analysis that a particular system configuration is reasonable.

We adopt this view when re-visiting the problem of multilevel security. Rather than seeking 'beyond A1' multilevel security [3, 11, 21], we seek to measure the degree and/or quality of the multilevel protection that is provided by a system configuration. Weaker, but reasoned, assurances of security are a pragmatic way of providing practical multilevel systems, such as [23], that can be built from Commercial Off-The-Shelf (COTS) components. Systems may be configured from components in which we have varying degrees of confidence in their security. In [24], confidence-rated information flow policies are used to model interoperation between PDAs and Workstations: we have a higher degree of confidence in the flows that are constrained by the workstation security mechanism than we have in flows constrained by the PDA application. In [25] we considered how best to configure Storage Area Networks from components having varying security guarantees, while ensuring that mandatory security rules are enforced. These approaches do not consider covert-channels or in-depth formal analysis of protection mechanisms. Rather, they seek useful feedback that a particular configuration is reasonable.

In this paper we describe a general framework for measuring quality of protection for information flow and/or multilevel security. The model builds on earlier work on information flow security [4, 7, 24, 26] by considering the relative risks of configuring various components into multilevel systems. Risk measurement is used to characterise the quality of protection that is provided by a multilevel system configuration. This gives rise to a novel approach to describing multilevel security policies that combine both risk and information flow. The model that is developed in this paper is a consistent interpretation of multilevel security, allowing us to draw on a wide range of existing results from the area.

The model that is proposed in this paper forms a part of our ongoing research in using constraint solving techniques as a practical approach for reasoning about security [25, 27–30]. Building on the results in [28] we demonstrate in this paper that determining whether a particular system configuration meets a quality of protection measure can be described as a constraint satisfaction problem. Constraint solving is an emerging software technology for modelling and solving large-scale optimisation problems [27, 31] and there are many results on solving this problem for large systems of constraints in a fully mechanised manner.

Section 2 describes the underlying model of multilevel security. As with past security criteria, this model is extended in Section 3 to support assurance levels. However, our interpretation of assurance is more general: every system component has an assurance level that reflects the degree of confidence that it cannot be compromised. In Section 4 we illustrate how configurations within our model can exhibit cascade vulnerabilities [3, 32] and outline in Section 5 a soft constraint-based framework [28] that can be used in their detection and elimination. The advantage of taking a soft constraint approach is that assurance can be described in terms of a c-semiring [27] and Section 6 explores how aggregate risk measurements can be made across configurations. Section 7 provides further discussion on how this framework provides a basis for quality of protection.

2   Interpreting Multilevel Security

An information flow policy is defined in terms of a lattice ordering $(\_ \leq \_)$ over a set of security labels $\mathcal{L}$. Given $x, y : \mathcal{L}$ then $x \leq y$ means that information may flow from level x to level y. The simplest interpretation of an information flow policy is multilevel security [1] whereby the labels correspond to sensitivity levels, for example, unclass $\leq$ secret $\leq$ topsecret. A more general interpretation [7] is that a label represents an abstract data type that is used to encode security relevant characteristics of entities that are subject to flow constraints. With this interpretation a wide variety of access control policies can be represented within the multilevel security model. Techniques for specifying more general (non-lattice) information flow constraints and translating them into lattice-based policies are considered in [4, 7, 26].

Let the set of entities $\mathcal{E}$ represent the set of all components that can source and/or sink information. In addition to the conventional 'subject' and 'object' interpretation, entities are regarded as anything that can store, process and/or manage information [24, 26]. Examples include devices, workstations, controllers, sessions, datasets and applications (examples can be found in [7, 24, 25]). An entity is anything that can have an associated security state (and to which the flow constraints must apply).

Every entity, e, is bound to an interval of the policy lattice, where $int(e) = [x, y] \in \mathcal{L} \times \mathcal{L}$, and $x \leq y$, is interpreted to mean that entity e may sink information at class y or lower and may source information at class x or higher [26]. We also write $int(e) = [int_\perp(e), int_\top(e)]$. If entity e is a 'subject' then $int(e) = [x, y]$ corresponds to a partially trusted subject (in the sense of [33]) that may view/read information at class y and lower and may write/alter information at class x and higher; these are defined as $vmax$ and $amin$, respectively, in [33]. Conventional objects may be interpreted within this model as entities that are bound to a point interval $[x, x]$ with a single level. Intuitively, we interpret [26], $int(e) = [x, y]$ to mean that the entity can be trusted to properly manage multilevel information within the security interval $[x, y]$.

Let $A \leadsto B$ represent information flow in our system from entity A to entity B. We do not consider a semantics for $\leadsto$; it could be simply based on read-write access controls (effectively [1, 33]), based on a non-interference interpretation, or even based on some informal characterisation of what flows are considered to be possible [24] in a system. Under this interpretation, a system is secure if for all entities, A, B, such that $A \leadsto B$ then $int_\perp(A) \leq int_\top(B)$ holds [26]. In this paper we use a variant of this definition to reflect the *specific* information that can flow. Let $A_x \leadsto B_y$ represent a flow of x information in entity A to y information in entity B. A system is secure, if for all entities A and B then,

$$A_x \leadsto B_y \Rightarrow x \leq y \wedge int_\perp(A) \leq x \leq int_\top(A) \wedge int_\perp(B) \leq y \leq int_\top(B)$$

Example 1 A multilevel secure network is composed of systems A and B. System A is a multilevel secure and configured to manage unclass and secret information and is thus partially trusted with $int(A) = [\mathsf{u}, \mathsf{s}]$. Similarly, system B is trusted to manage secret and topsec information, and $int(B) = [\mathsf{s}, \mathsf{t}]$. The systems communicate/share secret information. The flows are defined as $A_\mathsf{s} \leadsto B_\mathsf{s}$ and $B_\mathsf{s} \leadsto A_\mathsf{s}$, and by definition, the configuration is secure. Note that we may use the initial character(s) of a security level to represent it, if no ambiguity can arise. In general, a flow between entities need not necessarily be sourced and sunk at the same level. For example, the flow $F_\mathsf{s} \leadsto P_\mathsf{t}$ might represent a secret file F that is read by a single level process P with $int(P) = [\mathsf{t}, \mathsf{t}]$. $\triangle$

3   Interpreting Assurance

Define a lattice, $\mathcal{A}$, of assurance levels with ordering $\leq$. Given $x, y : \mathcal{A}$, then $x \leq y$ means that a system evaluated at y is no less secure than a system evaluated at x, or alternatively, that an attacker that can compromise a system evaluated at y can compromise a system evaluated at x. For example, the 'Orange' and 'Red' Book security criteria [3, 34] define assurance levels A1 > B3 > B2 > B1 > .... This conventional notion of assurance can be generalised to assurance for entities [24] if we regard assurance as reflecting our degree of confidence that an entity can be relied upon to properly manage the information that is entrusted to it. For example, we might have high confidence in a firewall-based email proxy (entity) managing multilevel information, but have low confidence in a `sendmail` process (entity) managing the same information.

We define $rating : \mathcal{E} \to \mathcal{A}$ where $rating(e)$ gives the assurance rating of entity e, and is also taken to represent the minimum effort that is required by an attacker to compromise entity e.

Security evaluation criteria [3] also define a minimum required assurance function $req : \mathcal{L} \times \mathcal{L} \to \mathcal{A}$, such that $req(l, l')$ defines the minimum required assurance for a system managing information at classes $l, l' : \mathcal{L}$. For example, $req(\mathsf{unclass}, \mathsf{topsec}) = \mathsf{B3}$ means that in order for an entity to manage information with labels between unclass and topsec, a B3 assurance rating is needed. In general a system must meet the minimum required assurance.

$$\forall e \in \mathcal{E} : req(int_\perp(e), int_\top(e)) \leq rating(e)$$

This has a similar interpretation for the more general notion of an entity used in this paper. Entities represent anything that can source and/or sink information. For example, the rating of an entity may incorporate the methodology that was used to develop the entity, as in the conventional Orange/Red Book rating, the level of testing the entity has received, or the level of complexity of the function the entity is implementing. A general purpose workstation, W, may be just fine for managing single level of information, like [secret, secret] but be unacceptable for managing multilevel data such as [secret, topsec]. In the model this is represented by setting $rating(W)$ to FAIR, and setting req(secret, secret) to FAIR. But req(secret, topsec) must be set to a higher assurance rating, say GOOD, to ensure that W, and other workstations like it, are not used for such information. Another example, $rating(A)$ could represent how much we can rely on the user A (given their associated security interval); for example, one would presume that a CEO has a higher assurance rating than a clerk in the same organisation.

A further example, $rating(S)$ could represent the rating of application software S: a COTS product may have a low rating, while an in-house developed application may have a high rating, when handling multilevel information. While it may be acceptable to trust the high assurance email proxy process with multilevel information (for example, int(proxy) $= [\mathsf{u}, \mathsf{t}]$), it may only be acceptable to trust sendmail with single-level information (for example, int(sendmail) $= [\mathsf{s}, \mathsf{s}]$). This could be reflected by requirement $req(\mathsf{u}, \mathsf{t}) = hi$ and $req(\mathsf{s}, \mathsf{s}) = lo$, where $lo < li$, and so forth.

Example 2 In the Chinese Wall policy a stock market analyst may not advise an organisation if he has insider knowledge of another competing organisation. Encoding this policy in terms of a multilevel security policy has been demonstrated elsewhere [4, 5, 7]. In this example we describe a new multilevel encoding of the Chinese Wall policy in terms of an assurance requirement.

Let $\mathcal{L} = 2^{\{\mathsf{ibm,hp,sun,elf,shell,...}\}}$ be the powerset of organisations. Define the assurance lattice as: audit $<$ cons $<$ over, where audit represents the degree of trust in an auditor, cons represents the degree of trust in a consultant, and over represents the degree of trust in a stock exchange partner who is trusted to access everything for the purposes of oversight. Consultants are trusted to consult for multiple organisations so long as there is no conflict of interest. We define some minimum required assurance levels for intervals of trust as follows.

$$req(\{\}, \{\mathsf{hp}\}) = \mathsf{aud} \quad req(\{\}, \{\mathsf{ibm, elf}\}) = \mathsf{cons} \quad req(\{\}, \{\mathsf{ibm, hp}\}) = \mathsf{over}$$
$$req(\{\}, \{\mathsf{elf}\}) = \mathsf{aud} \quad req(\{\}, \{\mathsf{hp, shell}\}) = \mathsf{cons} \quad req(\{\}, \{\mathsf{ibm, hp, elf}\}) = \mathsf{over}$$
$$req(\{\}, \{\mathsf{ibm}\}) = \mathsf{aud} \quad req(\{\}, \{\mathsf{hp, elf}\}) = \mathsf{cons} \quad req(\{\}, \{\mathsf{ibm, hp}\}) = \mathsf{over}$$

Assume that any entity that is controlled by a consultant will never have an assurance rating higher than cons. While a consultant may be trusted to simultaneously manage ibm and elf information (bound to interval $[\{\}, \{\mathsf{ibm, elf}\}]$), the minimum assurance rule dictates that a consultant cannot be trusted to access conflicting ibm and hp data (bound to interval $[\{\}, \{\mathsf{ibm, hp}\}]$). $\triangle$

Note that we assume that the execution system will properly classify entities. For example, a session entity corresponding to a consultant executing low assurance software would have an assurance level equal to the greatest lower bound of the consultant assurance and the software assurance level. Similar calculations are necessary to determine the interval for the session (the greatest lower bound of the intervals of the entities involved). For reasons of space we do not consider the execution model in this paper, however models such as [7] are applicable in this case.

4   The Cascade Problem

The *cascade vulnerability problem* [3, 32] is concerned with secure interoperation, and considers the *assurance risk* of composing multilevel secure systems that are evaluated to different levels of assurance according to the criteria specified in [3]. The transitivity of the multilevel security policy upheld across all secure systems ensures that their multilevel composition is secure; however, interoperability and data sharing between systems may increase the risk of compromise beyond that accepted by the assurance level. For example, it may be an acceptable risk to store only secret and top-secret data on a medium assurance system, and only classified and secret data on another medium assurance system; classified and top-secret data may be stored simultaneously only on 'high' assurance systems. However, if these medium assurance systems interoperate at classification secret, then the acceptable risk of compromise is no longer adequate as there is an unacceptable cascading risk from top-secret across the network to classified.

Example 3 Continuing the Chinese Wall example, consider two consultant sessions (entities) A and B, that are trusted to the following extent.

$$rating(A) = \mathsf{cons} \quad int(A) = [\{\}, \{\mathsf{ibm}, \mathsf{elf}\}]$$
$$rating(B) = \mathsf{cons} \quad int(B) = [\{\}, \{\mathsf{hp}, \mathsf{elf}\}]$$

Suppose that the system permits these sessions to share information classified at $\{\mathsf{elf}\}$, that is, we have $A_{\{\mathsf{elf}\}} \rightsquigarrow B_{\{\mathsf{elf}\}}$ and $B_{\{\mathsf{elf}\}} \rightsquigarrow A_{\{\mathsf{elf}\}}$. While the individual entities are secure based on the req assurance rule defined above, their interoperation is not. There is a cascading path from $\{\mathsf{ibm}\}$ on entity A to $\{\mathsf{hp}\}$ on entity B via shared channel $\{\mathsf{elf}\}$. The assurance rules require an assurance level of at least over in order to be able to simultaneously access both $\{\mathsf{hp}\}$ and $\{\mathsf{ibm}\}$ information. However, with a configuration that allows A and B share elf information, entities with an assurance rating of just cons can obtain this access.

This can be interpreted in two ways. The assurance level reflects how much we can rely on an entity to properly manage the different information. The configuration implies that we have cons level confidence that hp and ibm information is properly managed, which is contrary to the requirement. The second interpretation is when one regards assurance as representing the degree of confidence that one can have that an entity cannot be compromised. In this case the effort required by an attacker corresponds to the effort to compromise cons rated systems to effectively copy hp into ibm data. However, the requirement is that it must require at least the effort to compromise a level over rated entity.   △

The above example illustrates that avoiding conflict of interest when entities share information corresponds to detecting and eliminating the cascade vulnerability problem. Existing research has considered schemes for detecting these cascading security vulnerabilities and for eliminating them by reconfiguring system interoperation. While the detection of cascade vulnerabilities can be easily achieved [3, 32], their *optimal* elimination is NP-complete [35].

5   Soft Constraints and Semirings

In [28], a soft constraint-based framework is described for modelling, detecting and eliminating the cascade vulnerability problem. A soft constraint may be seen as a constraint where each instantiation of its variables has an associated value from a partially ordered set that can be interpreted as a set of preference values. Combining constraints will then have to take into account such additional values, and thus the formalism has also to provide suitable operations for combination ($\times$) and comparison ($+$) of tuples of values and constraints. This is why this formalisation is based on the concept of c-semiring, which is just a set plus two operations.

The framework described in [28] is directly applicable to the information flow model described in this paper. A network (a system of entities) is modelled in terms of constraints, reflecting all possible flows as a result of the network configuration (the $\leadsto$ relation). This constraint network also considers the effective assurance along all possible communication paths in the network. The network is cascade free if these constraints uphold the overall assurance criteria (the req relation).

The security label ordering $(\mathcal{L}, \leq)$ is modelled as a lattice and the assurance ordering $(\mathcal{A}, \leq)$ in [28] is modelled as a more general c-semiring structure [27, 36]. While [28] only considered the cascade problem for conventional lattice-based assurance ordering, the framework is applicable for any c-semiring. A semiring is a tuple $\langle \mathcal{S}, +, \times, 0, 1 \rangle$ such that: $\mathcal{S}$ is a set and $0, 1 \in \mathcal{S}$; $+$ is commutative, associative and 0 is its unit element; $\times$ is associative, distributes over $+$, 1 is its unit element and 0 is its absorbing element. A c-semiring is a semiring $\langle \mathcal{S}, +, \times, 0, 1 \rangle$ such that: $+$ is idempotent, 1 is its absorbing element and $\times$ is commutative.

Let us consider the relation $\leq_S$ over $\mathcal{S}$ such that $a \leq_S b$ iff $a + b = b$. Then it is possible to prove that (see [36]): $\leq_S$ is a partial order; $+$ and $\times$ are monotone on $\leq_S$; 0 is its minimum and 1 its maximum. Informally, the relation $\leq_S$ gives us a way to compare semiring values and constraints. In fact, when we have $a \leq_S b$, we will say that b *is better than* a. In the following, when the semiring will be clear from the context, $a \leq_S b$ will be often indicated by $a \leq b$.

The classical Constraint Satisfaction Problem (CSP) is a Soft CSP (SCSP) where the chosen c-semiring is: $S_{CSP} = \langle \{false, true\}, \vee, \wedge, false, true \rangle$. Fuzzy CSPs (FCSP) can instead be modelled in the SCSP framework by choosing the c-semiring $S_{FCSP} = \langle [0, 1], max, min, 0, 1 \rangle$. Many other soft CSPs (probabilistic, weighted, ...) can be modelled by using a suitable semiring structure ($S_{prob} = \langle [0, 1], max, \times, 0, 1 \rangle$, $S_{weight} = \langle \mathcal{R}, min, +, +\infty, 0 \rangle$, ...). Therefore, a wide range of 'soft' ways to consider degree of assurance can be considered and can be effectively reasoned about within our model.

6   Interpreting Risk

While conventional assurance ratings are defined in terms of a lattice, the model proposed in this paper can use any *measure* that can be defined as a c-semiring. The assurance rating, $rating(A)$, of an entity A provides a measure of how much the entity can be relied upon not to be compromised. Whether we use numbers, enumerations

(A1, B3, . . .), and so forth, in the c-semiring is not important; rather it is the ability to compare different rating which give a measure of how much we can rely on an entity.

We can interpret an assurance rating as providing an indication of the minimum amount of effort that is required by an attacker to compromise an entity. By 'compromise' we mean that the attacker can force the entity to violate its interval of trust, that is, to violate the information flow ordering. For example, compromising the system B in Example 1 corresponds to the attacker breaking the protection mechanism, and outputting topsec labelled as secret (copying topsec information to secret). This corresponds to the usual threat model used in [3]. In this paper we generalise this to any entity. An attacker could compromise another user by tricking them into revealing incorrectly labelled information; an attacker could compromise an application by a stack smashing attack, causing it to copy information from one file to another, violating the flow policy.

The c-semiring provides a convenient way to measure aggregate threats across the collections of entities that make up a system. The minimum effort required to break a series of entities along a path is given by the combination (under the c-semiring) of the ratings of the individual broken entities. In this case, the weighted c-semiring $S_{weight} = \langle \mathcal{R}, min, +, +\infty, 0 \rangle$ provides the appropriate measure. A path that can cause a flow of level x information to level y can start at any system that is trusted to manage x information and can end at any system trusted to manager y information. Given a series of possible compromising paths that facilitate a flow from level x to level y, where $x \not\leq y$, then the least effort required to create a compromise from x to y is the shortest path (using S_{weight}) from x to y. There is a cascade vulnerability if the value calculated for this shortest path is more than $req(x, y)$.

This is effectively a characterisation of a cascading path from [3], but defined in terms of a c-semiring using the model [28]. It is the definition in terms of a c-semiring that allows the determination of effort along a cascading path as the combination of the efforts required to break individual systems along the path. Practical techniques for calculating shortest paths across weighted constraint networks are considered in [27].

Definition 1 Quality of Protection. Let constraint specification $\mathcal{CONFIG}$ represent the flows (and cascades) that are a consequence of entity interoperation constructed using the model [28]. The assurance requirements function $req(x, y)$ provides an acceptable lower bound on the quality of protection for this system configuration. Let constraint specification $\mathcal{QOP}$ represent these ratings for all permitted flows. A configuration $\mathcal{CONFIG}$ meets the quality of protection requirement $\mathcal{QOP}$ if no path in $\mathcal{CONFIG}$ violates $\mathcal{QOP}$.   △

The assurance requirements function $req(x, y)$ provides an acceptable lower bound on the quality of protection for an overall system configuration. The soft constraint model described in [28] can be used to encode the quality of protection problem as a constraint satisfaction problem. For reasons of space we do not provide the details of the constraint model.

Example 4 Figure 1 depicts a configuration of the consultant sessions A and B from Example 3. We introduce a third session entity C, that connects entity A and entity B, permitting controlled sharing of $\{elf\}$ information. This is represented by the flows

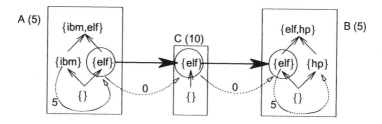

Fig. 1. Entity Information Flows with Weighted Cascading Path.

$A_{\{elf\}} \rightsquigarrow C_{\{elf\}}$ and $C_{\{elf\}} \rightsquigarrow B_{\{elf\}}$. Using the weighted c-semiring to define assurance ratings, the sessions are trusted to the following extent.

$$rating(A) = 5 \quad int(A) = [\{\}, \{ibm, elf\}]$$
$$rating(B) = 5 \quad int(B) = [\{\}, \{hp, elf\}]$$
$$rating(C) = 10 \quad int(C) = [\{\}, \{elf\}]$$

and some defined minimum required ratings are as follows.

$$
\begin{array}{l|l|l}
req(\{\}, \{hp\}) = 3 & req(\{\}, \{ibm, elf\}) = 5 & req(\{\}, \{ibm, hp\}) = 15 \\
req(\{\}, \{elf\}) = 3 & req(\{\}, \{hp, shell\}) = 5 & req(\{\}, \{ibm, hp, elf\}) = 18 \\
req(\{\}, \{ibm\}) = 3 & req(\{\}, \{hp, elf\}) = 5 & req(\{\}, \{ibm, hp\}) = 15
\end{array}
$$

This configuration has a cascading path vulnerability. The effort required to break entity A and copy $\{ibm\}$ information to $\{elf\}$, copy this to entity C, and copy it again to a broken entity B which allows it to be copied to $\{hp\}$ is 5+5=10, which is less than the minimum effort required, that is, $req(\{\}, \{ibm, hp\}) = 15$. Note that it is not necessary to break entity C as the attacker inputs and outputs $\{elf\}$ information, and thus, the effort to carry out this copy is 0. This is dealt with within the cascade framework [28] by defining permitted flows as having minimum rating, the lowest level in the lattice. In the case of $\mathcal{S}_{weight}$ this is the value 0, that is, $req(\{elf, elf\}) = 0$. The dashed arcs in Figure 1 represents the weighted cascading path calculated from $\{ibm\}$ to $\{hp\}$. $\triangle$

In suggesting the use of the weighted c-semiring $\mathcal{S}_{weight} = \langle \mathcal{R}, min, +, +\infty, 0 \rangle$ as one example of a risk measure, we are assuming that the effort required by an attacker to compromise one entity is independent of the effort to compromise any other entity. This means that having expended 'effort' $rating(A)$ to compromise system A, an attacker must, in addition, expend 'effort' $rating(B)$ to subsequently compromise system B, regardless of whether lessons learnt in compromising A can be subsequently used to attack B. This is quite a restrictive assumption; however, there are examples where this kind of measure is useful. For example, in practice, the more firewalls/subnets that have to be traversed to directly access a system, then the more 'secure' the system is considered to be. The notion of *security distance* is defined in [30] as the minumum number of servers and/or firewalls that an attacker on the Internet must compromise to obtain direct access to some protected service. We conjecture that security distance in this case is equivalent to using a weighted c-semiring with each system having an equal rating of '1'. This can be generalized within our model to the *weighted security distance*, whereby, a weight is associated with each server and/or firewall to indicate the amount of effort that is required to compromise that component.

An alternative measure to using the weighted c-semiring is to interpret the probabilistic c-semiring $\mathcal{S}_{prob} = \langle \{x| \in [0,1]\}, max, \times, 0, 1 \rangle$ [27] in terms of aggregation of risk along a path, which is calculated as combination (multiplication) of probabilities. As an attacker compromises systems along a cascading path, then overall, less and less 'effort' is required to attack subsequent systems.

These measures are unlike the lattice-based assurance measure used by the Orange/Red Book. This reflects an assumption that once one system rated at degree x (for example, B2) is compromised then all systems rated at this degree or lower (for example, B2, B1,...) are considered compromised. In practice, we believe that a practical risk measure will use a variety of such measures; exploring suitable c-semirings is a topic for future research.

7   Discussion and Conclusion

In this paper we describe how the network multilevel security model can be generalised to provide an approach to measuring the degree of confidence that one can have in the security of a system configuration. A system configuration is modelled as a collection of entities. These entities can represent system components, users, COTS components, and so forth, whose potential accesses and interoperation are articulated abstractly in terms of information flows. It is not necessary for these components to have an *explicit* access control mechanism; the flow relations represents the access limitations that we believe the entities effectively uphold. Thus, in the sense of [37], every entity in the system can be regarded as contributing to the overall Trusted Computing Base. In our framework we can distinguish the merit of each entity's contribution.

While the results in this paper are presented in terms of a multilevel security model, we argue that they have wider application. Constraining how information may flow within a system is at the heart of many protection mechanisms. Many security policies have direct interpretations in terms of multilevel security style controls. Furthermore, modelling a configuration in terms of information flows provides a form of traceability on interoperation that can provide useful feedback on the quality of protection achieved.

A multilevel security model for Storage Area Networks (SANs) is proposed in [25]. This SAN model also takes a measurement approach to achieving security. Hard (crisp) constraints are used to measure the risk associated with SAN configurations. However, the SAN model uses an ad-hoc adaptation of multilevel security, and does not have the same strict interpretation within the network security model as does the model proposed in this paper. As a consequence, the SAN model does not address the cascading channel problem. We are currently investigating how the risk framework in [25] can be re-coded in terms of the c-semiring-based framework proposed in this paper. The advantage of this is a simplification of the SAN model that solves the channel cascade problem, and provides access to a greater range of measures (c-semirings) for risk. A soft constraint encoding of the revised SAN model will also provide access to techniques for exploring and manipulating SAN configurations. This will be especially useful when making tradeoffs of quality of protection against other attributes such as cost and performance [25, 30]. Exploring how our soft constraint framework can facilitate making such tradeoffs is a topic for future research.

Determining whether a system configuration provides quality of protection as required by $req(x, y)$ is easily achieved as it corresponds to the channel cascade *detection* problem. Any solution to the constraint model represents a cascading path, which provides significantly more information regarding the vulnerabilities in the network than existing approaches for detecting cascading paths [32, 35]. The set of solutions to the constraint model provides a basis for removing the cascade vulnerability problem.

Reconfiguring such a system by attempting to eliminate an optimal minimum number of links (flows) between entities is NP-complete as it corresponds to the cascade *elimination* problem [35]. Previous approaches [32, 35, 38] detect a single cascading path in polynomial time, but eliminating the cascade in an optimal way is NP-complete. Detecting all paths in the constraint model is NP-hard, however elimination of a minimal number of links is polynomial. While constraint solving is NP-complete in general, this has not detracted from its uptake as a practical approach to solving many real-world problems [31]. Using a constraint model, we can rely on a significant body of successful techniques for finding the set of cascading paths, which once found, can be eliminated in polynomial time.

Acknowledgements

The authors would like to thank the anonymous referees for their useful comments and feedback on the paper. This work has received partial support from from Enterprise Ireland under their Basic Research Grant Scheme (SC/02/289 and SC/2003/007) and their International Collaboration Programme (IC/2003/88) and from the Italian MIUR project "Constraint-Based Verification of Reactive Systems" (COVER).

References

1. Bell, D.E., Padula, L.J.L.: Secure computer system: unified exposition and MULTICS interpretation. Report ESD-TR-75-306, The MITRE Corporation (1976)
2. Denning, D.: A lattice model of secure information flow. Communications of the ACM **19**(5) (1976) 236–243
3. TNI: Trusted computer system evaluation criteria: trusted network interpretation. Technical report, National Computer Security Center (1987) Red Book.
4. Foley, S.: Aggregation and separation as noninterference properties. Journal of Computer Security **1**(2) (1992) 159–188
5. Sandhu, R.: Lattice based access control models. IEEE Computer **26**(11) (1993) 9–19
6. Lee, T.: Using mandatory integrity to enforce 'commerical' security. In: Proceedings of the Symposium on Security and Privacy. (1988) 140–146
7. Foley, S.: The specification and implementation of commercial security requirements including dynamic segregation of duties. In: ACM Conference on Computer and Communications Security. (1997) 125–134
8. Sandhu, R.: Role hierarchies and constraints for lattice-based access controls. In: ESORICS. (1996)

9. Popescu, B., Crispo, B., Tanenbaum, A.: Support for multi-level security policies in drm architectures. In: 13th New Security Paradigms Workshop. (2004)

10. Schellhorn, G., Reif, W., Schairer, A., Karger, P., Austel, V., Toll, D.: Verification of a formal security model for multiapplicative smart cards. In: ESORICS. (2000) 17–36

11. Schaefer, M.: If A1 is the answer, what was the question? an edgy naif's retrospective on promulgating the trusted computer systems evaluation criteria. In: Annual Computer Security Applications Conference, IEEE Press (2004) 204–228

12. Millen, J.: 20 years of covert channel modeling and analysis. In: IEEE Symposium on Security and Privacy. (1999) 113–114

13. McLean, J.: Reasoning about security models. In: Proceedings 1987 IEEE Symposium on Security and Privacy. (1987) 123–131

14. Goguen, J.A., Meseguer, J.: Unwinding and inference control. In: Proceedings 1984 IEEE Symposium on Security and Privacy. (1984) 75–86

15. Foley, S.: A universal theory of information flow. In: Proceedings 1987 IEEE Symposium on Security and Privacy. (1987) 116–121

16. Sutherland, D.: A model of information. In: Proceedings 9th National Computer Security Conference. (1986)

17. Focardi, R., Gorrieri, R.: A classification of security properties for process algebras. Journal of Computer Security 3(1) (1995) 5–33

18. Roscoe, A., Woodcock, J., Wulf, L.: Non-interference through determinism. Journal of Computer Security 4(1) (1995)

19. Ryan, P., Schneider, S.: Process algebra and non-interference. In: IEEE Computer Security Foundations Workshop. (1999) 214–227

20. Sabelfeld, A., Myers, A.C.: Language-based information-flow security. IEEE Journal on Selected Areas in Communications, special issue on Formal Methods for Security 21(1) (2003)

21. McLean, J.: 20 years of formal methods. In: IEEE Symposium on Security and Privacy. (1999) 113–114

22. Schneider, F.: Enforcable security policies. ACM Transactions on Information and Systems Security 3(1) (2000) 30–50

23. Lewis, S., Wiseman, S.: Securing an object relational database. In: ACSAC, IEEE Computer Society (1997) 59–68

24. Foley, S.: Conduit cascades and secure synchronization. In: ACM New Security Paradigms Workshop. (2000)

25. Aziz, B., Foley, S., Herbert, J., Swart, G.: Configuring storage area networks for mandatory security. In: Proceedings of the 18th IFIP Annual Conference on Data and Applications Security, Kluwer (2004)

26. Foley, S.: A model for secure information flow. In: Proceedings of the Symposium on Security and Privacy, Oakland, CA, IEEE Computer Society Press (1989)

27. Bistarelli, S.: Semirings for Soft Constraint Solving and Programming. Volume LNCS 2962. Springer (2004)

28. Bistarelli, S., Foley, S., O'Sullivan, B.: Detecting and eliminating the cascade vulnerability problem from multi-level security networks using soft constraints. In: Proceedings of AAAI/IAAI-2004 (16th Innovative Applications of AI Conference), AAAI Press San Jose (2004) 808–813

29. Bistarelli, S., Foley, S., O'Sullivan, B.: Reasoning about secure interoperation using soft constraints. In: Proceedings of FAST-2004 Workshop on Formal Aspects of Security and Trust. (2004)

30. Swart, G., Aziz, B., Foley, S., Herbert, J.: Trading off security in a service oriented architecture. In: 19th Annual IFIP WG 11.3 Working Conference on Data and Applications Security. (2005)

31. Wallace, M.: Practical applications of constraint programming. Constraints 1(1–2) (1996) 139–168

32. Millen, J., Schwartz, M.: The cascading problem for interconnected networks. In: 4th Aerospace Computer Security Applications Conference, IEEE CS Press (1988) 269–273

33. Branstad, M., et al.: Trusted Mach design issues. In: Proceedings Third Aerospace Computer Security Conference. (1987)

34. U. S. Department of Defense: Trusted computer system criteria. Technical Report CSC-STD-001-83, U. S. National Computer Security Center (1983)

35. Horton, R., et al.: The cascade vulnerability problem. Journal of Computer Security 2(4) (1993) 279–290

36. Bistarelli, S., Montanari, U., Rossi, F.: Semiring-based Constraint Solving and Optimization. JACM 44(2) (1997) 201–236

37. Blakley, G., Kienzle, D.: Some weaknesses of the TCB model. In: IEEE Symposium on Security and Privacy, IEEE CS Press (1997)

38. Fitch, J., Hoffman, L.: A shortest path network security model. Computers and Security 12 (1993) 169–189

A Conceptual Model for Service Availability*

Judith E. Y. Rossebø[1,2], Mass Soldal Lund[3,4], Knut Eilif Husa[5], and Atle Refsdal[3]

[1] The Norwegian University of Science and Technology
[2] Telenor R&D, Norway, judith.rossebo@telenor.com
[3] University of Oslo, Norway, atler@ifi.uio.no
[4] SINTEF ICT, Norway, mass.s.lund@sintef.no
[5] Ericsson Applied Research Center, Norway, knut.eilif.husa@ericsson.com

Abstract Traditionally, availability has been seen as an atomic property assert-
ing the average time a system is "up" or "down". In order to model and analyse
the availability of computerized systems in a world where the dependency on and
complexity of such systems are increasing, this notion of availability is no longer
sufficient. This paper presents a conceptual model for availability designed to
handle these challenges. The core of this model is a characterization of availability by means of accessibility properties and exclusivity properties, which is
further specialized into measurable aspects of availability. We outline how this
conceptual model may be refined to a framework for specifying and analysing
availability requirements.

1 Introduction

Availability is an important aspect of today's society. Vital functions as e.g. air traffic
control and telecom systems, especially emergency telecommunications services, are
totally dependent on available computer systems. The consequences are serious if even
parts of such systems are unavailable when their services are needed.

Traditionally, the notion of availability has been defined as the probability that a
system is working at time t, and the availability metric has been given by the "uptime"
ratio, representing the percentage of time that a system is "up" during its lifetime [1].
This system metric has been applied successfully worldwide for years in the PSTN/-
ISDN telephony networks along with failure reporting methodologies [2].

With this traditional understanding, a web-based application such as a concert ticket
sales service may have $99,999\%$ availability, however if it is down for the 5 minutes
when concert tickets to a popular artist are put out for online sale while at the same tickets can be purchase via competing distributors, this means a considerable loss of profit
for the adversely affected ticket sales website even though the service is considered to
be highly available along traditional lines. Service availability needs a more enhanced
metric in order to measure availability in a way that meets the demands of today's services which have been shown to have much more bursty patterns of use than traditional

* The research on which this paper reports has been funded by the Research Council of Norway
project SARDAS (152952/431). Thanks to Manfred Broy, Rolv Bræk, Øystein Haugen, Terje
Jensen, Fabio Massacci, Birger Møller-Pedersen, Ina Schieferdecker, Ketil Stølen and Thomas
Weigert for commenting on earlier versions of this paper

PSTN/ISDN services [3]. Such burstiness in usage patterns also affects the ability of the service to provide to all users requiring the use of a service at a given moment.

Indeed, as the environment where services are deployed becomes more and more complex [4] a more "fine-grained" view on "what is availability" is needed. Several global virus attacks have recently showed that availability is indeed affected by security breaches, e.g., when e-mail servers are flooded by infected e-mails, the availability for "real" e-mails decreases. Another example is the so called denial of service attack, for which a service is overloaded with requests with the only purpose of making the service unavailable for other users.

In this paper we motivate and introduce an augmented notion of availability. In the heart of the resulting conceptual model lies a characterization of availability as aspects of accessibility and exclusivity. Further, we seek to preserve well-established definitions from our main sources of inspiration: security, dependability, real-time systems, and quality of service (QoS). The paper shows how the conceptual model may be used as a basis for specifying service availability requirements in a practical setting.

In Sect. 2 we provide the basis for our analysis of availability including our analysis of different viewpoints and approaches on availability and other aspects in the fields of security and dependability. Motivated by this discussion on related work in the fields of dependability and security research, we identify the requirements a conceptual model of availability should satisfy. In Sect. 3 the properties of availability are discussed, in Sect. 4 the means to achieve availability are classified, and in Sect. 5 we present some of the threats to availability. In Sect. 6 the overall conceptual model including an availability measure is presented. Summary and conclusions are provided in Sect. 7.

2   Requirements to a Refined Notion of Availability

The setting for our availability analysis is derived from the fields of dependability and security, and we therefore strive to conform to the well-established concepts and definitions from these fields where there is a consensus. We also look to different approaches and viewpoints in dependability and security research to motivate and derive a set of requirements for an availability concept model which enables an augmented treatment of availability that is more suited to securing availability in today's and future services.

2.1   Classifying Availability

Availability has been treated by the field of dependability and the field of security. The definitions of availability commonly used in these fields are:

1. Readiness for correct service [5].
2. Ensuring that authorised users have access to information and associated assets when required [6].
3. The property of being accessible and usable on demand by an authorized entity [7,8].

We find the first of these definitions to be insufficiently constraining for practical application to design of systems and services with high availability requirements. An integral part of securing availability is ensuring that that the service is provided to authorised users only; this is not addressed by the first definition. This aspect is addressed by the second, but neither of these two definitions captures the aspect of a service being *usable*. The third definition, however, does capture all of these aspects, and therefore is the basis for our analysis of availability in more detail.

We claim that there is a need to provide an enhanced classification of availability in order to thoroughly analyse and enable the rigorous treatment of availability throughout the design process depending on the requirements of the individual services. *Our availability model should therefore characterise the properties/attributes of availability.*

2.2   Classification of Threats and Means

The IFIP WG 10.4 view on dependability is elaborated by J. C. Laprie in [5]. This conceptual model of dependability consists of three parts: the *attributes* of, the *threats* to and the *means* by which dependability is attained [9]. This is a nice approach which motivates us to use a similar approach in our classification of availability. *Clearly, threats to availability such as denial of service, and means to availability such as applying redundancy dimensioning techniques, have an important place in our availability model.*

However, in order to classify threats to availability and means to achieve availability in a security setting, we are also motivated by the approach used in the security field of risk analysis and risk management as in [10,11].

This is because, incidents resulting in loss of availability do not necessarily transpire due to faults and therefore classification of means in terms of faults as in [5,9] is, in our view, insufficient for availability analysis. An example is the hijacking of user sessions by an attacker or group of attackers, preventing the authorised user or group of users from accessing the service. This incident results in loss of service availability for a set of users, without incurring a fault in the system. An *unwanted incident* is defined in [12] as an incident such as loss of confidentiality, integrity and/or availability. A fault is an example of an unwanted incident. *The availability model should therefore classify the means to achieve availability in terms of countering unwanted incidents.*

In [5,9], the *threats* to dependability are defined as faults, errors and failures, and these are seen as a causal chain of threats to dependability:

fault $\longrightarrow$ error $\longrightarrow$ failure

This understanding of threats serves nicely in the dependability model, however, we use the definition of threat, as defined in [8]: a *threat* is a potential cause of an unwanted event, which may result in harm to a system or organisation and its assets. Unlike [9], we do not consider such a causal chain alone as the sole threats to availability, as service availability may be reduced by e.g. a denial of service (DoS) attack which reduces the service availability without causing a fault, error, or failure to the actual service itself. *The conceptual model of availability should classify known threats to availability while conforming to existing literature on the classification of security threats.*

2.3 Viewpoints for Analysing Availability

For our availability analysis, it is appropriate to evaluate whether we should consider a system from a black box or white box perspective. In [13,14], Erland Jonsson provides a conceptual model for security/dependability with a black box view.

In this system model view, Jonsson considers availability to be a purely behavioural aspect related to the outputs of the system, solely with respect to the users. Availability is defined as the ability of a system to deliver its service to the authorised user [13]. This viewpoint is valid and useful for some aspects of availability analysis; however, we see the need for evaluating availability from other viewpoints as well. Availability aspects of the internal components of the system must also be analysed.

We claim that aspects of availability must indeed be observed from both the input and output sides as well as the internal components of the system. For example, denial of service attacks can be observed as malicious input to a system to either flood the system and render it unavailable, or in order to alter the integrity of the system, e.g., by deleting a group of users from the database of authorised users. In the latter case, the input messages of the intruder can be observed, and the changes to the internal database, resulting in a loss of availability for those users that were deleted, will also be registered.

With a black box view only, as in [13], only the externally observable behavioural aspects of availability can be studied. However, it is also important to observe and analyze the internal behaviour in the system in order to analyze the availability aspects of components, in particular service components which collaborate to deliver the service. Motivated by a service-oriented system view, it is important to consider a whitebox view also, so that the internal means to achieve availability can be specified and internal causes that affect availability can be examined. *The conceptual model should therefore address internal and external concerns of availability.*

2.4 Requirements of Different Services

In the current and future telecommunications market, there are many different types of services each of which may have different requirements with respect to availability. Telephony services, and in particular, emergency services, are examples of services with stringent availability requirements. Internet-based services, however, have somewhat different requirements. Requirements for what may be tolerated of delays or timing out of services are rather lax currently for e.g., online newspaper services. Yet, a citizen who leaves the tax return to the last minute before the deadline for filing requires urgently that the online tax return submission service is available at that particular moment [15].

For traditional telecommunications services, the traditional availability requirement of $99,999\%$ availability is still valid, however, it does not sufficiently address all of the differentiated requirements with respect to service availability. More precisely, as advocated by the Service Availability Forum (SAF) [16], there is also a need for a customer centric approach to defining availability requirements. The availability concern of the Service Availability Forum is readiness for correct service and in particular continuity of service, with a focus on the demands of the customers.

We intend to incorporate the ideas of the SAF in our model, to enable customer oriented availability requirements, however, extending these to include the aspects of ensuring that unauthorised users cannot interrupt, hijack, or prevent the authorised users from accessing a service. *The model must address the availability requirements in a flexible manner, in order to address the different aspects of availability.*

2.5 Measuring Availability

As discussed in the introduction, we need a more fine grained measure of availability than pure "up" or "down". Services can exist in numerous degraded but operational/-usable/functional states between "up" and "down" or "correct" and "incorrect". For example, an online newspaper may behave erratically with slow response times for displaying articles browsed without going down or becoming completely unavailable. It should be possible to describe various states of availability in order to specify just how much a reduction of service quality may be tolerated.

While both the Common Criteria [17] and Johnson [14] define security measures and provide techniques for measuring security in general, there is a need for a more fine grained metric for measuring availability that takes into account, for example, measurement of how well user requirements are fulfilled, as well as a need for measuring the ability to adequately provision a service to all of the authorised users requiring the service at a given moment. Such a metric needs to take into account the appropriate set of parameters, not just the usual average based on the mean time to failure (MTTF) and the mean time to repair (MTTR). *Our aim is to incorporate techniques from the existing initiatives in the fields of security and dependability in order to arrive at a more complete composite measure of availability.*

3 Properties of Availability

Availability encompasses both exclusivity, the property of being able to ensure access to authorised users only, and accessibility, the property of being at hand and useable when needed. As such, contrary to, e.g., the IFIP WG10.4 [18], which treats availability as an atomic property, we see availability as a composite notion consisting of the following aspects:

– Exclusivity
– Accessibility

We elaborate on these two properties in Sect. 3.1 and Sect. 3.2.

3.1 Exclusivity

By *exclusivity* we mean the ability to ensure access for authorised users only. More specifically, this involves ensuring that unauthorised users cannot interrupt, hijack, or prevent the authorised users from accessing a service. This aspect is essential to prevent the denial of legitimate access to systems and services. That is, to focus on prohibiting unauthorised users from interrupting, or preventing authorised users from accessing services. Our definition of exclusivity involves both users and non-users, i.e., ensuring access to users while keeping unauthorised users out. This is in order to properly address means to achieve exclusivity. Some of these will address ensuring access for authorised users and others will address techniques for preventing unauthorised users from accessing or interrupting services.

The goal with respect to exclusivity is to secure access to services for authorised users in the best possible way. Essentially this means:

- Secure access to services for the authorised users.
- Provide denial of service defence mechanisms. Here we focus on prohibiting unauthorised users from interrupting, or preventing users from accessing services.
- Ensure that unauthorised users do not gain access to services.

Note that attacks via covert channels or by eavesdropping can lead to loss of confidentiality without loss of exclusivity as the attacker is not accessing the service, but passively listening in on service activity. Confidentiality, however, consists of exclusivity and absence of unauthorised disclosure of information.

3.2 Accessibility

We define *accessibility* as the quality of being at hand and usable when needed. The notion of "service" is rather general, and what defines the correctness of a service may differ widely between different kinds of services. Accessibility is related to quality of service (QoS) [19,20,21], but what is considered relevant qualities vary from one domain to another. Furthermore, QoS parameters tend to be technology dependent. An example of this is properties like video resolution and frame rates [20], which are clearly relevant for IP-based multimedia services and clearly not relevant in other service domains, such as SMS or instant messaging services.

What all services do seem to have in common is the requirement of being timely; for a service to be accessible it must give the required response within reasonable time. In addition to being timely, a service will be required to perform with some quality to be usable. Hence, we divide accessibility properties into two major classes of properties: *timeliness* properties and *quality* properties. Timeliness is the ability of a service to perform its required functions and provide its required responses within specified time limits. A service's quality is a measure of its correctness and/or how usable it is.

Consider an online booking service. From the viewpoint of a user at a given point in time, we could say that the quality of the service is either 1 or 0 depending on whether the user gets a useful reply (e.g. confirmation) or unuseful reply (e.g. timeout). (Over time this can be aggregated to percentages expressing how often one of the two kinds of responses will be given.)

In a multimedia service like video streaming, the frame rate may be seen as a timeliness property (each frame should be timely) while the resolution of each frame and the colour depth are quality properties.

In both these examples we may see a dependency between timeliness and quality. In the first example (Fig. 1) we may assume a deadline t_2 for the response to the user for the service to be accessible. However, we must also assume some processing time t_1

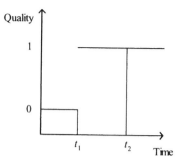

Figure 1. Quality vs. timeliness

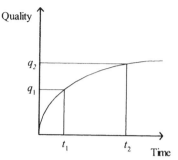

Figure 2. Quality vs. timeliness

for the service to be able to produce an answer. This means that the quality requirement enforces a lower bound on the timeliness; if the deadline is too short the user will always receive the timeout message. In other words we must have that $t_1 < t_2$ for the service to be accessible.

In the other example (Fig. 2) we may assume that higher quality requires more processing time per frame. This means that a required quality q_1 provides a lower limit t_1 on the processing time of each frame. Further, to get the required frame rate there must be a deadline t_2 for each frame, which provide an upper bound q_2 on the quality. This means the service must stay between this lower and upper bound to be accessible. This approach may be seen as an elaboration of Meyer's concept of *performability evaluation* [22].

These considerations motivates a notion of *service degradation*. We define service degradation to be reduction of service accessibility. Analogous to accessibility we decompose service degradation into timeliness degradation and quality degradation, and see that these are quantities mutually dependent on each other. For example, graceful degradation in timeliness may be a way of avoiding quality degradation if resources are limited, or the other way around. A combination of graceful degradation in timeliness and graceful degradation in quality may also be applied. Related to QoS, accessibility may actually be considered a QoS tolerance cut-off, i.e., the point at which the QoS deteriorates to a level where the service is deemed no longer usable, so that the service is considered unavailable.

4   Means to Ensure Availability

Traditionally, the approach to meeting availability requirements has primarily focused on ensuring accessibility aspects of availability such as by introducing redundancy, and by service replication. This is a valid approach to availability, but it does not ensure, e.g., that the service is accessible to authorised users only. There are costs involved in introducing redundancy and replication, which need to be justified. The goal should be to obtain more comprehensive, more cost-effective means to achieve availability, and to specify, design, and implement a set of measures that enable delivery of services and/or systems according to availability requirements.

By means to ensure availability we address *protection* of the service from incidents leading to a loss of availability. Therefore, in our model, we categorise the means into the following three groups: *incident prevention*: how to prevent incidents causing loss of availability; *incident detection*: how to detect incidents leading to loss of availability; and *recovery from incident*: the means to recover after an incident has lead to a loss of availability. We do not attempt to create an exhaustive list of all such measures, but do provide examples that illustrate the different aspects of securing availability.

4.1 Incident Prevention

Preventative means are defined as the internal aspects of a system that are designed to prevent, stop or mitigate intrusions, faults, errors, or other incidents which have a negative effect on the availability of a system.

Access control is an important preventative means for achieving the exclusivity aspect of availability. Access control is the prevention of unauthorised use of a resource, including the prevention of use of a resource in an unauthorised manner [7].

Providing *integrity protection* mechanisms is important for example, in order to protect against manipulation and redirection of messages resulting in denial of service for the authorised user.

It is also important to ensure that the required resources e.g. in the network that an authorised user has permission to use during a session are indeed allocated to the user to ensure that the service is delivered according to the user availability requirements.

Another example of a means for avoiding loss of availabilty is *graceful degradation* [23], that is degradation of a system in such a manner that it continues to operate, but provides a reduced level of service rather than failing completely. By applying graceful degradation schemes a complete loss of availability can be prevented.

4.2 Incident Detection

Incident detection consists of means to discover incidents such as denial of service attacks, faults, errors or failures, which lead to a loss or reduction of availability.

Detective measures will commonly be coordinated with recovery aspects of the system in order to adapt and restore system availability. Fault detection, traffic flow monitoring, intrusion detection systems (IDS), and accounting audits are all examples of detective measures.

For an efficient approach to unwanted incident detection, it is wise to combine monitoring, fault detection and IDS techniques along with audit logs generated and process the information and data collected in real time or close to real time in order to detect and thwart attacks or incidents that have the potential to result in loss or reduction of availability.

4.3 Recovery from Incident

Recovery from incident consists of the means to recover from incidents leading to loss or reduction of availability. This includes techniques for adapting the service, e.g. in the case that anomalies are detected by the IDS so that major unwanted incidents of loss of availability are avoided. Recovery means may entail, e.g., making changes to the internal aspects of the system, such as correction of faults or removal of system vulnerabilities. Additionally, external filters may be implemented to filter away the discovered cause of the incident such as malicious traffic or traffic from unauthorised users. Recovery addresses the *adaptability*, *robustness*, *maintainability* and *redundancy* aspects of the system.

5   Threats to Availability

The most explicit threat to availability is *denial of service* (DoS) attacks. *Replay*, *masquerade*, *modification of messages*, *man-in-the-middle* and *misuse of service* are examples of other kind of active threats that may affect availability. Threats may originate on the inside (inside attackers) or the outside (outside attackers) of the system. The impact of threats varies with the nature of the threats; some threats may result in degradation of the service, others in complete loss of service. Going into detail on this issue is outside the scope of this paper, but below we give some examples on how some of these threats may affect availability.

Denial of service attacks may lead to loss of use due to unauthorised use of the service preventing authorised users from accessing the service. Unauthorised use may also create over-usage problems having an overload effect and in this way degrading the quality of the service for the authorised users.

In a masquerade, an attacker steals the identity of a real user and obtains fraudulent access by masquerading as the real user while preventing the valid user from accessing services. Or, the other way around, an attacker replaying or masquerading as a service may deceive the user, and the service the user intended to access is then not available.

6   Conceptual Model for Service Availability

Based on the requirements from Sect. 2 and our discussion above we propose the overall model presented in Fig. 3 (represented in UML 2.0) and further explained in the following text.

In the figure the relationships between availability, threats and means are shown. Availability is affected by means and threats. Means ensures availability and protects against threats. Threats may cause reduction of availability.

There are many different types of services, and they may have different requirements with respect to availability. Availability requirements should be flexible enough to address the different services consistently. We propose that availability is specified by the means of availability policies and predicates over measurable properties of services, and that these policies and predicates are decomposed in accordance with the decomposition of availability in the conceptual model. An availability policy consists of an accessibility policy (e.g., required resources) and an exclusivity policy (e.g., which entities have permissions to use the service or system).

The predicates place conditions on the allowed behaviour of the service. In order to express these predicates, there is a need to describe rules for allowed or prohibited

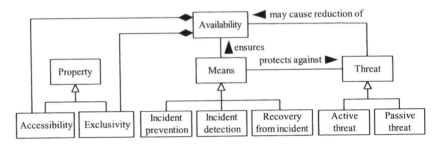

Figure 3. The overall picture

behaviour and to provide a means for measuring the availability properties of a service. Figure 4 illustrates how availability properties are related to services, i.e., as part of the relation between the service and the user entity using the service.

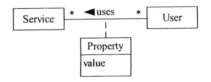

Figure 4. Service availability

Our conceptual model provides the foundation for an availability metric in that it provides decomposition of availability properties that may be mapped to measurable quantities. This metric includes behavioural measures, preventative measures, and correctness measures such as the measurement of degree of degradation.

The following is the mathematical representation of the availability metric for a service. Let A denote a service with an availability property for a user group U, and let X denote the availability metric for service A. We represent X as an n-tuple $X = (x_1, \ldots, x_n)$ where x_i is a measure of an aspect of availability. By this we mean that x_i describes requirements for a particular availability aspect. The minimum requirement for each x_i must be satisfied in order to fulfil the total availability requirement X.

Using our conceptual model this idea can be refined as follows: We represent X as a tuple $X = (X_1, X_2)$ where X_1 measures the exclusivity properties, and X_2 measures the accessibility properties.

Essentially, the requirement aims to describe the degree of accessibility and exclusivity that is sufficient for the user to be able to activate and use the service. Examples of measures of aspects of exclusivity may be illustrated by the following: For a measurement of exclusivity we need to be able to answer questions such as "how well does the system keep out unauthorised users while still granting access to authorised users?" This leads to the following examples of exclusivity requirements:

- The probability that an authorised user is denied access to the service at a given time t should be less than x.
- The probability that an unauthorised user obtains access to the service at a given time t should be less than y
- User u should be prohibited from accessing service s when user v is using the service.
- The number of intrusions at a given time t (e.g. during a critical moment) should be less than z.

Similar measures may be defined for accessibility. These may be defined with basis in measures for service degradation, timeliness, performance, and quality.

In order to apply the model, the availability requirements must be determined. Threats must then be analysed to understand what affects availability and means for ensuring availability need to be identified to meet requirements and counter threats. Measurements of the different aspects are then used to evaluate how well the availability requirements are met. A more in depth discussion of how to apply the model is the subject of further work. We are currently applying the model to our work on ensuring availability in service composition.

7   Conclusions

The contribution of this paper is a conceptual model for availability that takes into account a much broader spectrum of aspects that influence availability than previously addressed by work in this area. We have argued that exclusivity is an aspect of availability that has been generally neglected in the literature, and shown where it fits in an enhanced notion of availability. Further we have shown how QoS, real time and dependability considerations may be integrated in the model and treated as accessibility properties.

We have established that there is a need for a more fine grained metric for measuring availability and have provided a representation of the availability metric for a service that allows specification of the measurable requirements for exclusivity and accessibility properties.

Our conceptual model for availability embraces both a white box view as well as a black box view of availability and, hence, addresses both internal and external concerns of availability. The need for this is apparent in our current work on ensuring availability in service composition that encompasses a collaboration of roles, which are slices of behaviour across distributed systems. These must be composed correctly in order to achieve a service with the required availability.

The model also contains a classification of threats to availability and means to ensure availability, and establishes the relationship between threats, means and availability properties. Together these elements provide a framework in which all relevant views and considerations of availability may be integrated, and a complete picture of service availability may be drawn.

References

1. Ross, S.M.: Inroduction to probability models. 6th edn. Academic Press (1997)
2. Enriquez, P., Brown, A.B., Patterson, D.A.: Lessons from the PSTN for dependable computing. In: Workshop on Self-Healing, Adaptive and self-MANaged Systems (SHAMAN 2002). (2002)
3. Clark, D., Lehr, W., Liu, I.: Provisioning for bursty internet traffic: Implications for industry and internet structure. In: MIT ITC Workshop on Internet Quality of Service. (1999)
4. Arbaugh, W.A., Fithen, W.L., McHugh, J.: Windows of vulnerability: A case study analysis. IEEE Computer **33** (2000) 52–59
5. Laprie, J.C., ed.: Dependability: Basic Concepts and Terminology. Springer-Verlag (1992)
6. International Standards Organization: ISO/IEC 17799, Information technology – Code of practice for information security management. (2000)
7. International Standards Organization: ISO 7498-2, Information Processing Systems – Interconnection Rreference Model – Part 2: Security Architecture. (1989)
8. International Standards Organization: ISO/IEC 13335, Information technology – Security techniques – Guidelines for the management of IT security. (2001)
9. Avižienis, A., Laprie, J.C., Randell, B.: Fundamental concepts of dependability. In: Third Information Survivability Workshop (ISW-2000). (2000)
10. den Braber, F., Lund, M.S., Stølen, K., Vraalsen, F.: Integrating security in the development process with UML. In: Encyclopedia of Information Science and Technology. Idea Group, 2005 (2005) 1560–1566
11. Lund, M.S., den Braber, F., Stølen, K.: Maintaining results from security assessments. In: Proc. Seventh European Conference on Software Maintenance and Reengineering (CSMR 2003), IEEE Computer Society (2003) 341–350
12. Standards Australia: AS/NZS 4360:1999, Risk Management. (1999)
13. Jonsson, E.: An integrated framework for security and dependability. In: The New Security Paradigms Workshop (NSPW'98). (1998) 22–29
14. Jonsson, E., Strömberg, L., Lindskog, S.: On the functional relation between security and dependability impairments. In: The New Security Paradigms Workshop (NSPW'99). (1999) 104–111
15. Ryvarden, E.: Skatte-servere tålte ikke trykket. digi.no, April 30 (2005) (In Norwegian).
16. Service Availability Forum: Backgrounder. (http://www.saforum.org/home, accessed March, 2004)
17. International Standards Organization: ISO/IEC 15408, Information technology – Security techniques – Evaluation criteria for IT security. (1999)
18. IFIP WG10.4:   IFIP WG10.4 on dependable computing and fault tolerance. http://www.dependability.org/wg10.4/ (2005)
19. Barbacci, M., Klein, M.H., Longstaff, T.A., Weinstock, C.B.: Quality attributes. Technical report CMU/SEI-95TR-021, Software Engineering Institute, Carnegie Mellon University (1995)
20. Vogel, A., Kerherve, B., von Bochmann, G., Gecsei, J.: Distributed multimedia and QoS: A survey. IEEE Multimedia **2** (1995) 10–18
21. Group, O.M.: UML profile for modeling quality of service and fault tolerance characteristics and mechanisms. OMG Adopted Specification ptc/2005-05-02 (2005)
22. Meyer, J.F.: Performability evaluations: Where it is and what lies ahead. In: Proc. International Computer Performance and Dependability Symposium, IEEE (1995) 334–343
23. Shin, K.G., Meissner, C.L.: Adaption and graceful degradation of control system performance by task reallocation and period adjustment. In: Proc. 11th Euromicro Conference on Real-Time Systems, IEEE (1999) 29–36

A SLA evaluation methodology in Service Oriented Architectures

Valentina Casola[1], Antonino Mazzeo[1], Nicola Mazzocca[1]
and Massimiliano Rak[2]

[1] Universita' degli Studi di Napoli, Federico II
Dipartimento di Informatica e Sistemistica
Naples, Italy
{casolav,mazzeo,n.mazzocca}@unina.it
[2] Seconda Universita' di Napoli
Dipartimento di Ingegneria dell'Informazione
Aversa (CE), Italy
{massimiliano.rak}@unina2.it

Abstract. Cooperative services in Service Oriented Architectures (SOA) interact and delegate jobs to each other; when they have to respect a Service Level
Agreement (SLA) they need to explicitly manage it amongst each other. SLAs
and, above all, security-SLAs, are usually expressed in ambiguous ways and this
implies that they need to be manually evaluated both in a mutual agreement to
"qualify a service" and in the monitoring process. Due to this approach, usually,
service composition cannot be dynamically performed. In this paper we introduce
a methodology which helps in security SLA automatic evaluation and comparison. The methodology founds on the adoption of policies both for service behavior and SLA description and on the definition of a metric function for evaluation
and comparison of policies. We will illustrate the applicability of the proposed
methodology in different contexts of great interest for e-government projects.

1 Introduction

Large diffusion of Internet has lead to the explosion of complex infrastructures distributed all over the world. These infrastructures offer services for e-business, public administration, health care information (e.g. distributed medical case history), and other
different services. At the state of the art all these infrastructures found on a Service oriented Architecture model (SOA). SOA is an architectural style whose goal is to achieve
loose coupling among interacting software agents. A service is a unit of work done by
a service provider to achieve desired end results for a service consumer. Both provider
and consumer are roles played by software agents on behalf of their owners [19].

Cooperative services are capable of intelligent interaction and are able to discover
and negotiate with each other, mediate on behalf of their users and compose themselves
into more complex services. For example, Web Services technologies [1, 2] and the
emerging standards such as SOAP, UDDI, and WSDL allow a dynamic composition to
offer advanced services.

In Service oriented architecture the problem of guaranteeing a given "quality" of services to final users, in terms of functional and non-functional requisites like performance or security, is one of the hot topic. In general, a service provider is able to guarantee a predefined service level and a certain security level (supposing you are able to measure it); in this context, an open issue needs to be addressed when the service is an aggregated one, i.e. it is offered thanks to the cooperation of different service providers which belong to different domains, each one characterized by different Service Levels [21].

Usually, these and other interoperability problems are faced by an explicit and initial agreement among services which will be part of the same aggregated service, and these agreements will be periodically monitored to guarantee that all providers meet the promised levels. Cooperative services interact and delegate jobs to each other and they need to create and manage "'Service Level Agreements'" amongst each other.

A Service Level Agreement (SLA) is a contract between a network service provider and a customer that specifies, usually in measurable terms, what services the network service provider will furnish. Many Internet service providers provide their customers with a SLA. More recently, enterprises have adopted the idea of writing a service level agreement too, so that services for their customers can be measured, justified, and perhaps compared with those of outsourcing network providers.

Usually each service domain expresses the set of SLAs by means of free text documents and, often, in ambiguous ways. A common problem that arises, is how to help different domains to reach an agreement in order to cooperate and offer advanced and integrated services, assuring at the same time a quantifiable Service Level. At the state of the art, the main solution focuses on manual evaluation of the proposed SLAs, expressed is "some way" and on mutual agreement from experts of the two domains.

At the state of the art SLAs are strictly related to the quality of service and not to security. The main reason why security has never been expressed through SLA is the lack of an objective mean to measure a security service; to date only few experimental security metrics have been proposed to classify, evaluate and compare security practices [14, 13, 11, 12]. In this paper, instead, we are interested in facing the problem of security in this context.

In service oriented architectures we need to re-define the concept of trust between end-users and services and between services and services; in fact, providing and accessing an applicative service needs the adoption and cooperation of third parties that offers infrastructural services needed to aggregate the services. It is necessary to ensure that the consumer perceives that the provider is adhering to its promised service level agreements; but the provider will use other services to perform its task.

Some available approaches include the definition of a "network of trust" among services by previous agreements among actors [18, 10, 22, 20]; this is a static approach to face the problem as it requires that only a predefined set of services could cooperate; this unfortunately is a strong limitation. In a dynamic context, a service that needs some other service providers to complete its task, could locate them in the Internet (for example trough a public registry) and decide to adopt the offered services.

So, how can the end-user trust in a cooperative service that claims a predefined security SLA? How can the end-user evaluate the real SLA of that service? In this paper we propose an evaluation methodology to face this problem.

Our proposal founds on SLA dynamic management. SLA management involves the procedure of signing SLAs thus creating binding contracts, monitoring their compliance and taking control actions to enable compliance. SLA monitoring is difficult to automate as it would need precise and unambiguous specification and a customizable engine that collects the right measurement, models the data and evaluates the SLA at certain times or when certain events happen. In a cross-domains scenario like web services it will be important to obtain measurements at multiple sites and to guarantee SLAs on them.

Automating SLA evaluation for agreements and monitoring involves minimizing human involvement in the over-all monitoring process and it is a very interesting research field.

Within this context, the main research issue that we want to face in this paper is related to a quantitative evaluation of the system SLAs and, in particular, we will focus our attention on SLAs related to security aspects (security-SLA, for brevity) [14].

We will introduce a theoretical model to formalize SLAs by means of policies and we will illustrate a policy evaluation methodology that helps in both initial and run time agreement phases. The methodology we propose is based on security-SLA formalization through the use of standard *policy* languages and on the formalization of concepts like "security levels" against which we could measure the security of a system. In particular, we will introduce a Reference Evaluation Model to evaluate and compare different policies by quantifying their security levels.

The application of the methodology is very interesting especially if we think that, actually, there is a human Service Registration Authority that controls whether the entities respect SLAs and policies (service qualification). The applicability contexts we will refer, are *untrusted domains* where both parties that wish to inter-operate need to formally agree on SLAs and security policies; and *trusted domains* where an explicit security evaluation need to be continuously monitored.

The reminder of this paper is structured as follows: in Section 2 we will illustrate our approach to express security SLAs by means of a standard policy language. Section 3 introduces the Reference Evaluation Model, exploiting for each component of the model how to build correct and usable solutions. By examples we will show some solutions for policy formalization and evaluation techniques. Section 4 shows the methodology applicability in different phases of the agreement for different contexts. Finally Section 5 contains some conclusions.

2   Policies to express Service Level Agreements

We need a formal way to express Service Levels and automate the Agreement process; to do this we will adopt a policy language for the formalization and an evaluation methodology for the automatic agreement.

Policies can be expressed and formalized in many different ways, they could be informal (consider for example "some good practices to choose a password") or highly mathematical. We could identify a type of policy by the way in which it is expressed; for example we could classify the following types of policies:

Formal policies are usually expressed by mathematical or machine-parsable statements and languages.
Semi formal policies are partially expressed by machine-parsable languages.
Informal policies are usually expressed in a very informal language, with statements often ambiguous and or expressed in a free textual form.

Notice that formal policies are typically expressed by technical staff-members who need to express in an unambiguous way technical procedures, while organizational members who often need to express practical and behavioral aspects of the organization of a secure site typically prefer informal policies. Both technical and organizational aspects are very critical for security but often members of one part do not understand the criticality of the other ones. The more a policy is formalized, the more the evaluation process is easy when performed by an automatic machine; on the other side the evaluation process becomes very difficult for a non-technical member who needs to read the security statements.

The classification is not exhaustive, it intends to make the reader more sensitive to the policy formalization problem in terms of what to express in a security policy and in which formalism to express it [4, 15, 16].

Recently, some proposals and standards to formalize policies for WS [23] and the related security provisions have been provided [14]; we think that they could help in expressing security-SLAs and allow systems to *automate* the SLA evaluation process.

Really, available policy frameworks present some limits; they certainly represent a valid means to develop a textual policy, but they do not resolve ambiguity problems, they are not sufficiently structured to be used as a valid mean to evaluate and compare policies.

Policy ambiguity is often the primary reason for which a security expert is not able to completely trust a system declared secure and we are working on policy formalization at the aim of reducing such ambiguity to automatically evaluate the security level associated to the policy.

An Example of Formalization Talking about Web Services architectures, we think to adopt WS-policy framework to express policies for security-SLA. The framework is structured as a hierarchical tree to express all macro provisions. We have started the formalization by considering the set of items proposed by [14]; the first level of the tree structure includes:

- Security documentation,
- Security Auditing,
- Contingency Planning,
- User Security Training,
- Network Infrastructure Management,
- Physical Security,
- User Discretionary Access Control (DAC) Management,

- Password Management,
- Digital Certificate Management,
- Electronic Audit Trail Management,
- Security Perimeter or Boundary Services,
- Intrusion Detection and Monitoring,
- Web Server Security,
- Database Server Security,
- Encryption Services,
- Configuration Management.

All these items represent general categories (both technical and organizational) and they are actually expressed in natural language.

Second level provisions try to describe all the details about all macro-provisions and they express objects that are still complex but bring a more bounded security information; for example the Digital Certificate Management provision includes: Key Pair Generation, Key length, Private Key Protection, Activation Data, Key Controls and verification, Network Security Control, Cryptographic module engineering controls.

The provisions defined in the first two steps are very complex objects and this is the most important reason for ambiguity; to solve the ambiguities the proposed formalization supports a hierarchical structure which consists of several couples (element-type, value) representing topics and sub-topics, where the "value" itself is a complex object. A wide range of new data-structures has been defined to represent the values, and finally a grammar has been created based on such data-structures to formalize a policy for security-SLA. The used data-structures are new atomic or enumerative types and total order relations among their values may be defined, so as to solve the ambiguity problem; we will associate a Local Security Level to each provision instance. For most critical topics we were able to build such a structure that could be automatically processed by a numeric algorithm.

The proposed structure is a hierarchical tree represented by an XML document; tree nodes identify complex security provisions, leaves identify simple security provisions. Furthermore alternative representations can be easily derived; for example XML documents can be represented as trees and the set of leaves of the XML tree can be represented as a vector. In the following we will use both these syntactical representations for policy evaluation.

3   The Evaluation methodology

Having formalized and expressed SLAs by a policy language, we need an evaluation methodology to compare them and decide to extend trust to the new service or not.

The methodology we propose is based on a Reference Evaluation Model (REM, for short) to evaluate and compare different security policies, quantifying their security level. The model will define how to express in a rigorous way the security policy (formalization), how to evaluate a formalized policy, and what is its security level. In particular the REM is made of three different components:

1. The policy formalization,

2. The evaluation technique,
3. The reference levels.

The policy formalization

A formalized policy instance expresses in a rigorous way, who, how and where security SLAs will be applied. The way in which we formalize a policy is strongly dependent by the technique we intend to adopt [6, 7]; at this aim, the adopted formalization will be presented with the technique.

The evaluation technique

The REM we propose, includes the definition of a technique to compare and evaluate the policies; we have called this component the *REM Evaluation technique.*

Different evaluation techniques represent and characterize the security level associated to a policy in different ways, for example with a numerical value, a fuzzy number [8, 9] or a verbal judgment representing its security level.

In the following we introduce the adoption of an evaluation technique based on an innovative definition of a metric policy space. The policy space allows to represent policies as an homogeneous space on which we could define a distance criteria and a metric function.

For brevity sake we do not give details about how we have built the technique, but, in this paper we will give clear information on how it is able to represent and evaluate policies; further details are available in [5] .

The main characteristic of the metrical space technique could be summarized as follows:

- Given any tree-policy formalization, the evaluation process takes into account just the provisions of the policy which represent the leaves of the policy tree structure.
- With the formalization, each provision is represented by an enumerative data-type; the policy space "P" is defined as the vectorial product of all n provisions K_i i.e. P = K1 x K2 x . x Kn.
- The policy space "P" has been transformed into an homogeneous one, denoted "PS" thanks to a family of threshold functions (F-functions) which allow us to associate a Local Security Level (LSL for short) to each provision.
- "PS" is represented by a $n \times 4$ matrix whose n rows represent the single provisions K_i and 4 is the chosen number of LSLs admissible for each provision. For example, if the LSL associated to a provision is l_3, the vector corresponding to its row in the matrix is: (1,1,1,0).
- The distance criteria for the definition of the metric space is the Euclidean distance among matrices, defined as:
$$d(A, B) = \sqrt{(\sigma(A - B, A - B))}$$
where $\sigma(A - B, A - B) = Tr((A - B)(A - B)^T)$

In Figure 1 an example of provision representation is reported.

To show that the defined distance really represents the distance between policies, we will give two examples; the policy SLA-P is compared with two different policies

provision name				
Local Registration Authorities (LRAs)	1	1	1	1
Repositories	1	1	1	0
Policy applicability	1	1	0	0
Notification of certificate issuance and revocation	1	1	1	0
Time between certificate request and issuance	1	1	1	0

Fig. 1. An example of Policy provisions

SLA-X and SLA-Y; they both are globally stronger than SLA-P since they have a lot of provisions with a stronger Local Security Level. Each policy in the example has just 10 provisions, this is just a simplification which does not affect the validity of the method.

$$
\text{SLA-P} = \begin{pmatrix} 1\,1\,0\,0 \\ 1\,1\,0\,0 \\ 1\,0\,0\,0 \\ 1\,0\,0\,0 \\ 1\,0\,0\,0 \\ 1\,0\,0\,0 \\ 1\,0\,0\,0 \\ 1\,0\,0\,0 \\ 1\,1\,0\,0 \\ 1\,0\,0\,0 \end{pmatrix} \quad \text{SLA-X} = \begin{pmatrix} 1\,1\,1\,0 \\ 1\,1\,1\,0 \\ 1\,1\,0\,0 \\ 1\,0\,0\,0 \\ 1\,0\,0\,0 \\ 1\,1\,0\,0 \\ 1\,0\,0\,0 \\ 1\,1\,0\,0 \\ 1\,0\,0\,0 \\ 1\,0\,0\,0 \end{pmatrix} \quad \text{SLA-Y} = \begin{pmatrix} 1\,1\,1\,1 \\ 1\,1\,1\,1 \\ 1\,1\,1\,0 \\ 1\,1\,0\,0 \\ 1\,1\,1\,0 \\ 1\,1\,1\,1 \\ 1\,1\,1\,1 \\ 1\,1\,0\,0 \\ 1\,1\,0\,0 \\ 1\,1\,1\,1 \end{pmatrix}
$$

Example 1: SLA-X is a policy that appears stronger than SLA-P, just looking at the levels of the single provisions; we first calculate the trace:
$Tr((X-P)(X-P)^T) = 6$
The distance between SLA-X and SLA-P is: $d = 2,45$
That mirrors the fact that SLA-X is just a little stronger than SLA-P.

Example 2: SLA-Y is a policy that appear stronger than SLA-X and much stronger than policy SLA-P, while SLA-P is the same as that of the example 1; the trace is:
$Tr((Y-P)(Y-P)^T) = 19$
The distance between SLA-Y and SLA-P is: $d = 4,36$
This result mirrors the evident difference between the two cases.

These examples show how it is very simple to evaluate the distance between policies, once they have been represented as a matrix. The distance will be adopted to define the metric function.

The reference levels

The last component of the REM is the set of reference security SLAs levels that could be used as a reference scale for the numerical evaluation of security. When references are not available, the REM could be used for direct comparison among two or more policies.

To properly choose the references, we can proceed in two different ways:

- when possible, if n different policy instances are available and they certainly correspond to n different security levels, then we could use those ones as reference levels. This is the typical case of an existing Platform which publishes a set of predefined security SLAs corresponding, for example, to a Gold, Silver and Bronze class of services.
- when they are not available, we need to define an appropriate set of policy instances.

At this point, to define the **metric function**, we represent the reference levels according to the same technique of the REM and we evaluate the target policy against them.

So, we first evaluate the distances among the references (denoted as REFLi) and the origin of the metric space (denoted as $\emptyset$), then define the metric function which gives the resulting level as follows:

The references are:

$$d_{10} = d(REFL1, \emptyset)$$
$$d_{20} = d(REFL2, \emptyset)$$
$$d_{30} = d(REFL3, \emptyset)$$
$$d_{40} = d(REFL4, \emptyset)$$

Finally, the *security metric function* to evaluate the SLA associated to a target policy P_x is:

$$L_{Px} = \begin{cases} L_0 \ iff d_{x0} \leq d_{10} \\ L_1 \ iff d_{10} < d_{x0} < d_{20} \\ L_2 \ iff d_{20} < d_{x0} < d_{30} \\ L_3 \ iff d_{30} < d_{x0} < d_{40} \\ L_4 \ iff d_{40} \leq d_{x0} \end{cases}$$

where L_{Px} is the SLA Level associated to P_x

4 Methodology Applicability

The SLA evaluation technique could be easily applied in SOA. When an end-user choose a platform for services, he also express his desired SLAs and could evaluate them by himself whether they have been published. Each service which is part of the platform is able, in general, to offer the declared SLAs but, the same it is not so obvious if the service offered has been aggregated with open external services. To guarantee that aggregated services respect the requested SLAs, it is necessary to apply an explicit process of "service qualification among requestors and providers". We will denote this process as **"cross qualification"**.

Cross qualification is needed when a new service (external or just developed) wants to cooperate with existing ones and it consists of two steps, applied in different times:

1. initial evaluation of service SLAs to verify that they respond to the platform expectation which has already publish its own SLS toward end-users;
2. periodical monitoring of service SLA to verify if the service is still qualified (for example if the declared performance are still verified even if the number of requesters has considerably grown).

This context is actually predominant (for example it is applied in numerous Italian e-government projects [20]) but it is very expensive as it is manually performed, and limited, especially when we think that having open standards and free service available, we could aggregate them by using public registry and public services with a very low cost. The main constraints in the application of such mechanisms are, above all, the impossibility to evaluate the open service SLAs at run time to decide to extend trust to them or not and decide to use them for aggregation or not by guaranteeing, at the same time, the user requested SLAs.

Having SLA formalized and expressed by a policy language, we could apply the proposed methodology to evaluate them in both the following cases:

a) CASE A: predefined cross-qualification among services.
b) CASE B: run-time cross-qualification among open services.

Adoption of the REM helps in all these approaches, giving a tool which helps in automating the evaluation process. We explicitly note that there are different actors in such kind of architectures and they need to adopt the same REM for the evaluation; the main constraints is not on the evaluation technique but on the policy formalization. Indeed, each one could decide to adopt different policies and include different provisions and we need to face all these aspects.

In the following we will show the applicability of the evaluation techniques through the REM in these two cases of cross-qualification.

4.1 Predefined cross-qualification

When a new service (target service, TS for short) should be added to an existing platform, its security SLAs need to be evaluated against the SLA adopted by the platform itself. In other words, in this architecture there is a master which decides both the policy formalization (including the provisions) and the SLA reference levels. The evaluation of SLA-TS consists in assigning a security level evaluated against the platform SLA reference security levels.

In this case the formalization step of the REM building phase will take place using the master policy as the policy template. The choice of the REM technique can be carried on taking into account that the rules of the master *must* be respected and flexible judgments are not useful and the result of the evaluation technique should be a yes/no or the resulting level to which the service is associated.

Security reference levels are defined by the master, too.

Once the REM is built, the TS evaluation is made up of the following steps:

− the TS-SLAs are formalized according to the master policy template;
− the TS-SLAs are evaluated with the chosen REM technique and a SLA Level is assigned to it according to the defined metric function (see Section 4).

The result of the methodology is the numerical SLA Level of TS. And the new service will be included in the architecture for aggregation with services of the same SLA-level.

The same process is periodically (and automatically) repeated when the master needs to monitor all TSs.

4.2   Run-time cross-qualification

This model rests on peer-to-peer agreement between TSs couples. When a TS, retrieved in a public registry, asks to cooperate with an existing domain of services, it has to agree with one or more services of the group.

In this case there is no external master that can be used as reference for policy formalization; being a peer-to-peer agreement, the TSs have the same role. It is impossible to build the formalization on the basis of only one of the two parts so, in this case, each TS proceeds by building its own REM and evaluation phase. In this case each policy needs to be first formalized according to the other template and then the evaluation could begin. All this process is performed at run-time; the service that has found the TS retrieves its SLAs, formats them according to its template and evaluates the SLA level to decide to cooperate or not.

The application of our methodology to this last context is very promising and we are actually working on the integration of an automatic tool to adopt the REM in a Regional project and apply this theoretical model on a very complex infrastructure.

5   Conclusions and Future Works

In this paper we have introduced a theoretical methodology to evaluate Service Level Agreement in SOA. The methodology is based on two fundamental features; the first one is the security-SLA formalization through the use of standard *policy* languages while the second one is the formalization of "qualifiable service levels" against which we could measure the SLA. In particular, we have adopted a Reference Evaluation Model, developed for different infrastructures, to evaluate and compare different policies and quantifying their levels. The application of the methodology in different contexts seems very promising and we intend to adopt it in the integration of an automatic tool in complex infrastructure in which aggregated services dynamically vary and, at the same time, are able to guarantee the same perceived service level to the end-user.

6   Acknowledgments

This work was supported in part by the Italian National Research Council (CNR), by Ministero dell'Istruzione, dell'Universita' e della Ricerca (MIUR), by the Consorzio Interuniversitario Nazionale per l'Informatica (CINI), and by Regione Campania, within the framework of following projects: Centri Regionali di Competenza ICT, Serviceware and Telemedicina.

References

1. K. Beznosov, B. Hartman, D.J. Flinn, and S Kawamoto. Mastering Web Services Security. *Wiley.*
2. A. Bosworth. Developing Web Services. Proceedings 17th International Conference on Data Engineering. IEEE Comput. Soc, pp.477-81. Los Alamitos, CA, USA, 2001.
3. Bishop M., Computer Security, Art and Science, Addison-Wesley, 2003.
4. Brewer D., Nash M., The Chinese Wall Security Policy, Proceedings of the 1989 IEEE Symposium on Security and Privacy, pp.206-214 (May 1989).
5. Casola V., A Policy Based Methodology for the Analysis, Modelling and Implementation of Security Infrastructures, PhD Thesis, Second University of Naples, 2004.
6. Casola V., Mazzeo A., Mazzocca N., Vittorini V., Policy Formalization to combine separate systems into larger connected networks of trust -Proceedings of Net-Con'2002 Conference, Paris, France. 2002.
7. Casola V., Mazzeo A., Mazzocca N., Vittorini V., Policy based interoperability in distributed security infrastructures -Proceedings of 10th ISPE International conference on concurrent engineering: research and applications. Madeira, Spain. 2003.
8. Casola V., Preziosi R., Rak M. , Troiano L. 2004. Security Level Evaluation: Policy and Fuzzy Technique. In IEEE Proceedings of International Conference on Information Technology: Coding and Computing (ITCC 2004), vol. 2, pp. 752-756, Las Vegas, ISBN 0-7695-2108-8.
9. Casola V., Preziosi R., Rak M., Troiano L., A Reference Model for Security Level Evaluation: Policy and Fuzzy Techniques, in JUCS - Journal of Universal Computer Science - edited by Ajith Abraham, Oklahoma State University, USA and L.C. Jain, University of South Australia, January 2005
10. Curry I.,   Trusted Public-Key Infrastructures, Version 1.2,Entrust Technologies www.entrust.com. 2000.
11. DoD (Department of Defense) Trusted Computer System Evaluation Criteria, 26 December 1985 (Orange Book).
12. European Communities - Commission: ITSEC: Information Technology Security Evaluation Criteria; (Provisional Harmonised Criteria, Version 1.2, 28 June 1991) Office for Official Publications of the European Communities, Luxembourg 1991 (ISBN 92-826- 3004-8).
13. Harris Corporation,   Information Assurance Benchmark Analysis Study Final Report, 21 october 1999.
14. Ronda R. Henning Security Service Level Agreements: Quantifiable Security for the Enterprice? ACM Proceedings of New Security Paradigm Workshop 1999, Ontario, Canada.
15. Jajodia S., Samarati P., and Subrahmanian V. S., "A Logical Language for Expressing Authorizations," Published in the proceedings of IEEE Symposium on Security and Privacy, Oakland, USA, 1997.
16. Kagal L., Finin T., Joshi A.,2003. A Policy Language for a Pervasive Computing Environment, IEEE 4th International Workshop on Policies for Distributed Systems and Networks (Policy 2003)
17. Klobucar T., Jerman-Blazic B., A Formalization and evaluation of certificate policies, Computer Communication 22(1999), 1104-1110
18. Kokolakis S.A., Kiountouzis E.A., Achieving Interoperability in a multiple-security-policies environment , Computer & Security. Vol 19, no. 3 pp 267-281, Elsevier Science 2000.
19. Service Oriented Architectures http://webservices.xml.com/pub/a/ws/2003/09/30 /soa.html
20. SPCC. Sistema pubblico di cooperazione: ARCHITETTURA, versione 1.0 www.cnipa.org, 2004 (SPCoop-Architettura_v1[1].0_20041125_.pdf).

21. SPCC.   Sistema pubblico di cooperazione: ORGANIZZAZIONE, versione 1.0
    www.cnipa.org, 2004 (SPCoop-Organizzazione_v1[1].0_20041125_.pdf)
22. Turnbull J. "Cross-Certification and PKI Policy Networking" Version 1.1, Entrust Technolo-
    gies www.entrust.com. 2000.
23. WS-policy specification Web Services Policy Framework, september 2004.

Towards a Notion of Quantitative Security Analysis

Iliano Cervesato*

Department of Mathematics, Tulane University
New Orleans, LA 70118, USA
iliano@math.tulane.edu

Abstract. The traditional Dolev-Yao model of security limits attacks to "computationally feasible" operations. We depart from this model by assigning a cost to protocol actions, both of the Dolev-Yao kind as well as non traditional forms such as computationally-hard operations, guessing, principal subversion, and failure. This quantitative approach enables evaluating protocol resilience to various forms of denial of service, guessing attacks, and resource limitation. While the methodology is general, we demonstrate it through a low-level variant of the MSR specification language.

1 Introduction

Security protocols have classically been analyzed with respect to the Dolev-Yao intruder [8, 14], a model which gives the attacker complete access to the network, but limits its decryption capabilities to messages for which he possesses the appropriate keys. There is consensus among practitioners that the basic problems of protocol verification, namely secrecy and authentication, are by now solved for this model, as the most recent tools sweep through the standard Clark-Jacob benchmark [6] in mere milliseconds. Recent research has moved in two directions: apply the current tools to the much larger protocols used in the real world, and investigate intruder models that rely on capabilities beyond Dolev-Yao gentlemen correctness. We follow the latter path.

The three tenets of the Dolev-Yao model are (1) the symbolic representation of data, so that a key k is seen as an atomic object rather than a bit-string, (2) the unguessability of secret values such as nonces and keys, and (3) black-box cryptography, by which a message m encrypted with k can be recovered only by a principal in possession of $k^{(-1)}$. All three have been weakened in the last few years. Approaches have taken the bit length of messages and keys into account. Within the symbolic abstraction, effort has been undertaken to include guessing in the intruder's toolkit [11], and to let recurrent algebraic operations, in particular XOR and Diffie-Hellman exponentiation, out of the black box, allowing the intruder to use them to mount an attack (within the accepted computational bounds, *e.g.,* taking a discrete logarithm is not permitted) [4, 7].

The present work takes a symbolic view of data, but allows the intruder to guess values and perform computationally hard operations. That is, if he is willing and able to pay the price. Indeed, we are not so much interested in a *lucky* intruder breaking

---

* Partially supported by NRL under contract N00173-00-C-2086 and by ONR under contract number N000149910150.

the protocol, but in a *tenacious* one, who will spend Herculean effort in order to gain Alice's confidence or learn Bob's secret. The proposed methodology assigns a cost to both Dolev-Yao and non-standard intruder operations. Depending on the intended use, this cost can be a physical measurement, such as time, space or energy, a complexity class, or simply one of the two values 0 and ∞ in a purely Dolev-Yao model. This work directly extends Meadow's quantitative assessment of denial-of-service [13] and Lowe's analysis of verifiable guesses [11]. It is also related to [16].

Potential applications of this approach include:

- Provide a way for standard analysis methodologies to take intruder effort levels into account. For example, weak secrets are usually modeled as either unguessable or public values. Assigning them an appropriate cost and estimating the resources (or the persistence) of the intruder may help decide whether this secret is too weak for practical purposes. Intruder cost thresholds can be easily integrated into many model checking tools for example.
- Monitoring of network activity, by either an intruder or a law enforcement agency. This entity may then compute the cost of mounting an action against particular communicating agents, using the result to estimate the needed resources.
- Gauge the resilience of a system against denial-of-service scenarios. Cost functions have been used for this purpose [13, 15], but mostly limited to legal Dolev-Yao intruder operations.
- Assess the vulnerabilities of agents meant to operate in a potentially hostile environment with very limited resources in terms of computational power, bandwidth, battery life, etc [5], *e.g.,* , smart cards, PDAs and cellular phones.
- When building a system, compare protocols providing desired functionalities, with respect to their resilience to particular forms of attacks. During the development phase of a protocol, compare alternative designs or parameter choices for optimal resistance to certain attacks. In particular, proposals for denial-of-service protection, *e.g.,* , Juels and Brainard's client puzzles [10] or even the network level proposal of Gunter et al. [9], are good application candidates for this methodology.

As it allows asking "How secure is this protocol?", rather than "Is it secure or not?", the proposed methodology can also be seen as complementing performance and quality of service with an additional quantitative dimension on which to evaluate protocols.

We rely on a Fine-Grained variant of the MSR rule-based specification formalism [1, 2] as a vehicle to introduce this work. Fine-Grained MSR isolates individual verification operations and accounts for the possibility of failure. This is achieved by dividing rule application in a pre-screening phase that commits to a rule, and a more thorough check that fully assesses its applicability. Further details can be found in [3].

2 Background

In MSR, a protocol is specified as a number of *roles*. A role corresponds to the abstract sequence of actions executed by each participating principal. Roles are also used to describe the intruder capabilities. A role itself is given as a sequence of *multiset rewrite* *rules*, which describe each individual action. Each rule represents a local transformation of the execution state. It has a *left-hand side* that describes what should be taken out of the state, and a *right-hand side* denoting what it should be replaced with. State objects are modeled using first-order atomic predicates. They include messages in transit ($N(m)$), public information ($M_*(m)$), private data of a principal ($M_A(m)$), and a record of the status of every executing role ($L^v(m)$ — v acts as a program counter, and m is synchronization data). The right-hand side of a rule can additionally mention existentially bound variables to model the creation of nonces and other fresh data. See [3] for details. Example of rules will be shown later in this document.

Simplifying somewhat from [3], the execution semantics of MSR operates by transforming *configurations* of the form $\langle S \rangle_{\Sigma}^{R}$, where the *state* S is a multiset of ground predicates, the *signature* Σ keeps track of the symbols in use, and the *active role set* $R = (\rho_1^{a_1}, \ldots, \rho_n^{a_n})$ records the remaining actions of the currently executing roles (ρ_i), and who is executing them (a_i). In order to add costs to this framework, it is useful to take an even higher-level view of execution. This will also act as an abstract interface where other formalisms can experiment with the techniques in this paper.

An *abstract execution step* is a quadruple $C \xrightarrow{r,\iota} C'$, where C and C' are consecutive configurations, r identifies the rule from $\mathcal{P}$, and ι stands for the instantiating substitution. An abstract execution step is just a compact yet precise way to denote rule application. It is reasonable to think about it as a partial function from C, r and ι to C'. We say that r is *applicable* in C is there is are a substitution ι and a configuration C' such that $C \xrightarrow{r,\iota} C'$ is defined. A *trace* $\mathcal{T}$ is then a sequence of applications

$$C_0 \xrightarrow{r_1,\iota_1} C_1 \xrightarrow{r_2,\iota_2} \cdots \xrightarrow{r_n,\iota_n} C_{n+1}$$

While we rely on the notion of sequence here, this definition could be generalized to a lattice with minimum C_0 and maximum C_n to account for action independence. We will however stick to sequences for simplicity.

A *protocol requirement* for a safety property such as secrecy or authentication is simply given by a set $\mathcal{S}_\mathcal{I}$ of *initial configurations* and a set $\mathcal{S}_A$ of *attack configurations*, or some finite abstraction of them. A *verification procedure* decides, for a given protocol, whether there exists a valid trace from an initial to an attack configuration.

A *script* is a parametric sequence of actions $(r_1, \sigma_1), \ldots, (r_n, \sigma_n)$, where the codomain of the σ_i's may mention variables. A script is *realizable* if there are configurations $C_0, \ldots, C_{n+1}$, and grounding substitutions $\gamma_1, \ldots, \gamma_n$ such that $C_0 \xrightarrow{r_1,\iota_1} \cdots \xrightarrow{r_n,\iota_n} C_{n+1}$ is a trace. Scripts describe patterns of execution.

In general, there are two types of scripts of interest: the ones corresponding to the expected runs of the protocol (written $\mathcal{T}_{ER}$), and the scripts that an intruder devises to mount an attack. For our purposes, the latter are more interesting, and we shall extend their syntax for flexibility. An *attack script* is then given by the following grammar:

$$
\begin{aligned}
\mathcal{A} ::= \; & \cdot & \textit{(Empty script)} \\
& | \; \mathcal{A}\,(r, \sigma) & \textit{(Extension with an action)} \\
& | \; !_n\,\mathcal{A} & \textit{(Script iterated n times)} \\
& | \; \mathcal{A} + \mathcal{A} & \textit{(Alternative scripts)}
\end{aligned}
$$

We are particularly interested in attack scripts that are realizable in an initial configuration and end in an attack configuration. We further distinguish *any-time scripts*, which where honest principals are just responding to intruder solicitation, and *opportunistic scripts*, where the intruder takes advantage of moves initiated by honest principals.

3   Fine-Grained MSR

It is possible to use the definitions in Section 4 to endow MSR with a notion of cost. This would however not be a very precise model, in particular as far as rule application failure is concerned. Therefore, we dedicate this section to defining a finer-grained version of MSR. We isolate the verification operations implicit in an MSR left-hand side as separate rules. During execution, we split rule application into two steps: *pre-screening* commits to a rule, while *left-hand side verification* decides if it should succeed or fail (typically when messages have been tempered with). For space reasons, we describe the compilation of an MSR specification into fine-grained MSR only intuitively.

Fine-grained MSR inherits its language of messages from MSR. However, it makes two changes to the set of available predicates. First, it extends the network predicate with a header h, giving it the template $N^h(m)$. The header is meant to identify precisely a message within a protocol instance: it will typically contain the postulated sender and intended recipient, the name and version number of the protocol and a step locator. An attacker can alter the header at will. The second change is the introduction of predicates $R^v(m)$, which will act as *local registers* during a verification step. Similarly to the local state predicates $L^v(\_)$, the dynamically created superscript v is intended to prevent confusion.

An MSR rule application consists of two distinct phases: the left-hand side mandates a number of verification operations on incoming and retrieved messages, while the right-hand side prescribes how to construct out-going or archived messages. Both are represented succinctly in MSR, yet they can be very complex. Fine-Grained MSR replaces each MSR rule $r = (lhs \rightarrow rhs)$ with a number of *verification rules*, each corresponding to an individual verification step in *lhs*, and a single *building rule*, which produces *rhs*. Reducing *rhs* to atomic steps is not necessary since construction cannot fail once verification has succeeded. Registers are used to serialize these rules in a collection that we call *rule target*.

In order to account for failure, we must split rule application into two stages. During the *pre-screening phase*, a rule is selected based uniquely on the predicate names (including headers and superscripts) appearing in its left-hand side and in the current configuration. In particular, the arguments are not considered. We commit to the selected rule. Then, the *verification phase* checks whether the arguments have the expected form. In case of success, the next configuration is computed as in MSR. In case of failure, the clean-up clause is invoked and the entire role this rule belonged to is removed. See [3] for a formalization of these ideas.

The intruder capabilities traditionally considered for security protocol verification follow the well-known Dolev-Yao model [8, 14]: the intruder can intercept and generate network traffic, take apart and construct messages as long as it has all the elements to do so in a proper way (*e.g.*, it should know the appropriate key in order to perform a cryptographic operation). This model disallows guessing unknown values and performing operations that are considered "hard" (*e.g.*, recovering a key from a ciphertext). Let I be a memory predicate belonging to the intruder, so that $I(m)$ indicates that it knows (or has intercepted) the message m (this most simplistic setting can be considerably refined). Then, the Dolev-Yao model can be expressed by the following rules:

$$
\begin{array}{ll}
N^h(x) \rightarrow I(x) & I(x) \rightarrow N^h(x) \\
M_*(\boldsymbol{x}) \rightarrow \boldsymbol{I}(\boldsymbol{x}), M_*(\boldsymbol{x}) & \cdot \rightarrow \exists x.I(x) \\
\boldsymbol{I}(\boldsymbol{y}), I(\mathrm{op}_{\boldsymbol{y}}(\boldsymbol{x})) \rightarrow \boldsymbol{I}(\boldsymbol{x}) & \boldsymbol{I}(\boldsymbol{x}) \rightarrow I(\mathrm{op}(\boldsymbol{x})) \\
I(x) \rightarrow I(x), I(x) & I(x) \rightarrow \cdot
\end{array}
$$

The first line corresponds to network interception and injection. The second is access to public information and data generation (when allowed). The third abstractly expresses dismantling and constructing messages (of course, some combinations are disallowed). The fourth line contains administrative rules. Note that, unsurprisingly, these capabilities correspond very closely to the rules of the Fine-Grained MSR [3]. The correspondence would be even more exact if we had reduced the right-hand side to atomic constructions.

The Dolev-Yao model allows the intruder to perform "easy" operations. Once we explicitly assign cost to actions, we can introduce and reason about intermediate degrees between "easy" and "impossible", which is really what the Dolev-Yao restrictions boil down to. Indeed, we will allow attacks that involve performing "hard" operations, guessing values, and subverting principals. We will also be able to quantify "easy", "hard" and levels in between.

The *subversion* of a principal is easily modeled by another intruder memory predicate, $X(A)$. The first row of rules below represent subversion and rehabilitation of a principal A. The others stand for access to A's private data and for the intruder covering its traces.

$$
\begin{array}{ll}
\cdot \rightarrow X(A) & X(A) \rightarrow \cdot \\
X(A), M_A(\boldsymbol{x}) \rightarrow X(A), \boldsymbol{I}(\boldsymbol{x}) & X(A), \boldsymbol{I}(\boldsymbol{x}) \rightarrow X(A), M_A(\boldsymbol{x})
\end{array}
$$

We model *"hard" operations* by simply extending the set of patterns allowed in rule template $(\boldsymbol{I}(\boldsymbol{y}), I(\mathrm{op}_{\boldsymbol{y}}(\boldsymbol{x})) \rightarrow \boldsymbol{I}(\boldsymbol{x}))$ to represent non Dolev-Yao inferences. For example, taking a discrete logarithm is expressed as:

$$
I(g), I(g^x) \rightarrow I(x).
$$

Clearly there are limitations to this method as it applies only to the inversion of bijections. Other "hard" operations, such as finding hash collisions, can be modeled as guessing problems.

The trivial *guessing rule* $(\cdot \rightarrow I(x))$ is unrealistic and hard to work with from a cost accounting point of view. Therefore, following the pioneering work of Lowe [11], we require that every guess be backed up by a *verification procedure*. We express both the guess and its verification as an MSR role of the following form:

$$\exists u, v_1, v_2. \begin{bmatrix} \cdots \rightarrow G^u(x), \cdots & \left.\vphantom{\begin{matrix}a\\a\end{matrix}}\right\} \text{Guess} \\ \cdots \\ \cdots \rightarrow \cdots, V_1^{v_1}(m_1) \\ \cdots \rightarrow \cdots, V_2^{v_2}(m_2) \\ V_1^{v_1}(y), V_2^{v_2}(y), G^u(x) \rightarrow I(x) \end{bmatrix} \Big\} \text{Verification}$$

On the right, G, V_1 and V_2 are local state predicates (generically called L in Section 2) that hold the guess and two constructions (the *verifiers*) that should produce the same value if the guess is correct. See [11] for conditions required of acceptable verifiers. The exact format can vary, as illustrated below. Guessing roles are protocol specific, in general.

As a concrete example, the following role expresses the guess of a Diffie-Hellman exponent:

$$\exists u, v. \begin{bmatrix} I(g^x) \rightarrow G^u(x'), V^v(g^x, g^{x'}) \\ G^u(x), V^v(y, y) \rightarrow I(x) \end{bmatrix}$$

Note that, although this role is functionally equivalent to the discrete logarithm specification above, the exponent is explicitly guessed here rather than reverse-engineered as above.

Our final example describes the guess of the shared key k in the toy protocol informally described to the right of this text.

$$A \rightarrow B : \{n_a\}_k$$
$$B \rightarrow A : n_a$$

$$\exists u, v. \begin{bmatrix} \cdot \rightarrow \exists n. G^u(k), N^h(\{n\}_k), V^v(n) \\ G^u(k), V^v(n), N^{h'}(n) \rightarrow I(k) \end{bmatrix}$$

Here, the intruder generates a nonce n, makes a guess for k and sends the expected message to B (we ignored header-formatting issues for simplicity). This copy of n is the first verifier and is memorized in the predicate V. The second verifier is simply the response from B: if the guess was correct, they will be equal, otherwise it will either come back as a different bit-string, or be dropped by B altogether if the forgery attempt is uncovered.

4   Cost Model

Traditional approaches to protocol analysis are only interested on whether an action is applicable in a given state. Actions that are not applicable, either because they cannot succeed or because "computationally infeasible", are unobservable. In this paper, we are concerned with the cost of successful and failed applications. Cost will be measured in terms of whatever resource of interest changes as a result of attempting the action. Primary focuses are time and storage, but other parameters, such as energy, or the lowered randomness of some quantity (that may be used for side-channel attacks, for example) can also be used.

4.1   An Algebra of Cost

We will now define a generic infrastructure for expressing cost. The details of the resulting algebra shall be application specific.

We want to associate a value to each type of cost incurred by a principal. A *type*, denoted with τ, describes a resource of interest, time, space and energy are typical, but more refined types, *e.g.,* verification vs. construction time, can also be expressed. A *cost base* relates a cost type τ to a principal a. We write it as τ^a.

How much of a given cost type is incurred by a principal takes the form of a *scalar value*, which we will denote with s. Scalars can be abstract quantities (*e.g.,* Meadow's *"cheap", "medium", "expensive"*, etc. [13], or just 0 and ∞ in a Dolev-Yao setting), numbers (in $\mathbb{N}$ or $\mathbb{R}$ for example), or even complexity bounds in $\mathcal{O}$-notation. It is useful that some form of addition (written $+$) and a unit (0) be defined on scalars. These could be just free symbols, but $+$ can also be an actual operation. It is also very useful to have a comparison relation (written $<$, with the usual variants) among scalars within a cost base. Note that some forms of cost never decrease and $+$ should be monotonic with respect to $\leq$ for them. Time or energy are examples. This is the only case considered in [13]. Other costs, in particular space, do not need to be monotonic, and this restriction does not apply.

A *cost item* is a cost base τ^a together with a scalar value s. We denote it as $s\tau^a$. We extend the scalar comparison operators to cost items only when the base is the same. Such an extension rarely makes sense if the cost type is different, and should be evaluated on a case by case basis when the principals are not the same: one byte is one byte for everybody, but performing a decryption will generally take different amounts of time when hardware or implementation varies.

At this point, a *cost vector* $\mathcal{C}$ is simply a collection of cost items $s_1\tau_1^{a_1}, \ldots, s_n\tau_n^{a_n}$, which we write $\sum_i s_i\tau_i^{a_i}$. Given a cost vector $\mathcal{C}$, we write $\mathcal{C}^a$, $\mathcal{C}_\tau$, and $\mathcal{C}_\tau^a$ for its projections relative to principal a, cost type τ, and their combination, respectively. For example, $\mathcal{C}^a = \sum_{s\tau^a \in \mathcal{C}} s\tau^a$. It should be noted that a cost vector can be seen as a generalization of the notion of multiset.

4.2 Cost Assignment for Protocol Operations

In spite of their apparent simplicity, cryptographic protocols comprise a large number of operations and action classes. We will now examine them and comment on their characteristics in term of cost. Most of the issues are discussed relative to Fine-Grained MSR, and transpire also at the level of MSR. Needless to say, similar considerations apply to other specification languages.

Network: The network operations observable in MSR are receiving and sending a message. We denote their associated cost as $\kappa_{N\Rightarrow}$ and $\kappa_{\Rightarrow N}$, respectively. This generally includes time and storage components. Accounting for other transmission costs such as network latency could be easily accommodated through a simple refinement of (Fine-Grained) MSR.

Storage: Each of public (M_*), private (M_a) and local (L) storage has a temporal and a spatial component. Storage operations include allocating and recording data (*e.g.,* $\kappa_{\Rightarrow M_a}$), disposal ($\kappa_{M_a\perp}$) and look-up (κ_{M_a}). Notice in particular that the spatial component of storage disposal is negative. Note also that some values may be easier to look-up than others, and so κ_{M_a} depends on the actual predicate M.

Registers: We do not associate any cost with register management, preferring to fold it into the operations they participate in.

Constructor operations: Each constructor op has a number of operations associated with it. We consider its use as a building block of a message ($\kappa_{\Rightarrow \mathsf{op}}$) and during verification. In the latter case, we distinguish between the cost of success ($\kappa_{\mathsf{op}\sqrt{}}$) and failure ($\kappa_{\mathsf{op}\perp}$). The cost of performing Dolev-Yao and non Dolev-Yao operations is computed in the same way in our model. What will change is likely to be the magnitude of the scalar values.

Data operations: Atomic values are subject to generation (using $\exists$ in MSR), and generic values can be tested for equality. We write $\kappa_{\zeta \exists}$ and $\kappa_{\zeta =}$ respectively, where ζ represents some notion of type of a value.

Subversion: We write $\kappa_{?_a}$ for the cost of subverting principal a and $\kappa_{!_a}$ for the cost of its rehabilitation.

Guessing: The cost of a guessing attack can be modeled in two ways. At a high level of abstraction, we can associate a cost to a verification procedure ρ_G as a whole, which accounts for the cost of the expected number of guesses and verifications until one is successful. We write κ_{ρ_G} for this omnibus, MSR-oriented, cost. Alternatively and at a much lower-level level of detail, we can compile the verification procedure to Fine-Grained MSR, obtaining a role $\bar{\rho}$, assign a cost to the individual guess itself (κ_G), compute the cost of each guess and verification, $\mathcal{C}(\bar{\rho})$, as outlined below, and estimate the number of attempts it may take until a successful guess is produced. In general, this type of accounting will have the form $f(n)\,\mathcal{C}(\bar{\rho})$, where f is a function and n is a parameter such as the length of the data to be guessed.

Each of these operations, with sometimes the exception of guessing, are executed by a single principal, say a (which may also be the intruder). Each will in general involve several cost components. Therefore, κ_- corresponds to a cost vector relative to a. Guess verification can be performed locally by the intruder, or require exchange of messages with one or more principals. In the latter case, the cost vector will have appropriate components for each of the involved parties.

In general, the accuracy of a cost-based analysis directly depends on the precision of the cost associated with each basic action. For example, a classification into "*cheap*" and "*expensive*" forms the basis for a Dolev-Yao investigation, while adding an intermediate "*medium*" value already provides a setting in which one can start analyzing denial-of-service situations [13]. Moving to numerical classes adds flexibility, but non-trivial problems quickly emerge as accurate physical measurements can be difficult to gather and work with when dependent on hardware, implementation and system load. In this paper, we provide a flexible framework for taking cost into consideration, but have little to say at this stage about how to best determine the granularity and magnitude of basic costs.

4.3 Cost Calculation in MSR

The notion of cost naturally extends from individual operations to traces. First, we define the cost of a Fine-Grained MSR rule by simply adding up the cost of each operation occurring in it. There is little to do in the case of the verification rules, while building rules involve some work. Some rule have the option of failing, and therefore both a success and a failure cost is associated with them: we shall consider them as if they were different operations.

Consider now a trace $\mathcal{T} = C_0 \xrightarrow{r_1, \iota_1} \cdots \xrightarrow{r_n, \iota_n} C_{n+1}$. Let a_j be the principal executing (r_j, ι_j), and $\mathcal{C}^{a_j}(r_j) = \sum_i s_{ij} \tau_{ij}^{a_j}$ its cost. The cost of the trace is then given by

$$\mathcal{C}(\mathcal{T}) = \sum_j \mathcal{C}^{a_j}(r_j) = \sum_j \sum_i s_{ij} \tau_{ij}^{a_j}$$

The cost calculation for a trace extends naturally to the cost of a script since substitutions do not play any role when computing a cost. The presence of alternatives in an attack script forces us to define cost for them over (multi-dimensional) intervals rather than points. We have the following definition:

$$
\begin{aligned}
\mathcal{C}(\cdot) &= I_0 \\
\mathcal{C}(\mathcal{A}\,(r, \sigma)) &= \mathcal{C}(\mathcal{A}) + \mathcal{C}^{a_{[\sigma]r}}(r) \\
\mathcal{C}(!_n\,\mathcal{A}) &= n\,\mathcal{C}(\mathcal{A}) \\
\mathcal{C}(\mathcal{A}_1 + \mathcal{A}_2) &= [\min\{\mathcal{A}_1, \mathcal{A}_2\}, \max\{\mathcal{A}_1, \mathcal{A}_2\}]
\end{aligned}
$$

Here, I_0 is some fixed interval, typically $[0, 0]$. We extend scalar product and addition to intervals by applying these operations to its endpoint, *i.e.*, $n[a, b] = [na, nb]$ and $[a, b] + [c, d] = [a + c, b + d]$.

Since most tools for security protocol analysis rely, often symbolically, on traces, the infrastructure we just outlined is compatible with their underlying methodology. Indeed, systems based on explicit model checking can immediately take costs into account, while symbolic approaches need to have the cost model indirectly encoded as part of the problem description. Similar considerations applies to analysis based on theorem proving. In general, how easy it is to extend a tool with cost computation capabilities depends on how deeply the intruder model is ingrained in their implementation. The required modifications include tracking cost and allowing for non Dolev-Yao intruder actions.

Note that any tool natively supporting cost calculation (or even retrofitted to do so) can still perform traditional verification by assigning cost ∞ to non Dolev-Yao intruder actions and abandoning any attack trace as soon as its cost reaches ∞.

5   Quantitative Security Analysis

A first-class notion of cost leads to protocol analysis opportunities that lay far beyond the traditional Dolev-Yao feasibility studies. In this section, we will examine some of the possibilities related to time and space, well aware that many more lay out there, waiting for the imaginative mind to grab them. We elaborate on two non Dolev-Yao forms of verification: *threshold analysis* tries to determine what attacks are possible given a bound on the resources available to the intruder alone; *comparative analysis* studies attack opportunities when the resource bounds of all involved parties are taken into consideration. Denial-of-service attacks are a prime example.

5.1   Threshold Analysis

A rather trivial use of cost is to first ascertain that a protocol is secure relative to the Dolev-Yao model, and then compute the amount of resources it requires. This may be useful already in situations characterized by limited capacities, such as protocols implemented on smart-cards. If κ_{HW} is an inventory of the available resources, this problem is abstractly stated as "$\mathcal{C}(\mathcal{T}_{ER}) \leq \kappa_{HW}$?".

Dually, an intruder can pre-compute the cost of mounting an attack on a discovered vulnerability. This is generally not very interesting in a Dolev-Yao setting where an attack uses the same kind of operations as the protocol itself, and the intruder is implicitly assumed to have access to resources similar to honest principals. This becomes crucial when the intruder experiments with "computationally infeasible" operations, principal subversion, guessing, or a combination of these non Dolev-Yao operations. Indeed, some protocol analysis tools already allow principals to "lose keys" [12], but do not assign any special status to this operation. The intruder can then calculate the cost of a candidate attack and compare it with its available resources (dictionary attacks on passwords are the simplest instance), in symbols "$\mathcal{C}(\mathcal{A}) \leq \kappa_I$?". A protocol verification tool can similarly discard attack traces as soon as their cost exceeds a predetermined amount of intruder resources.

A protocol designer can go one step further by keeping aspects of the cost calculation as parameters. He can then determine value ranges that would require extravagant amounts of resources from an intruder in order to implement the attack (given foreseeable technology): "$\min x.\mathcal{C}(\mathcal{A}(x)) \gg \kappa_I$?". This is how key lengths and other parameters of cryptographic algorithms have traditionally been set. The approach we are promoting extends this form of safe parameter determination in that it takes into account the whole protocol rather than an isolated cryptographic primitives. This is particularly valuable as modern ciphers offer the option of variable key lengths.

5.2   Comparative Analysis

A cost infrastructure can be useful to a designer to choose a protocol among two candidates based on resource usage "$\mathcal{C}(\mathcal{T}^{P_1}) > \mathcal{C}(\mathcal{T}^{P_2})$?", or on their resilience to a certain type of attacks: "$\mathcal{C}(\mathcal{A}_1) > \mathcal{C}(\mathcal{A}_2)$?". By the same token, an attacker or law enforcement agency can evaluate attack strategies based on their cost.

Denial-of-service (DoS) attacks operate by having a possibly distributed intruder waste a server's resources with fake requests to the point where legitimate uses cannot be serviced in any useful time frame (or the server crashes). It stresses the bounds on the server's resources, typically time (or service rate) and storage capacity. A precise cost analysis, like the one proposed here, helps compute actual values for the resources used by both the intruder and the server at different stages of the protocol execution. The statement here is "$\mathcal{C}^B(\mathcal{A}) > \mathcal{C}^I(\mathcal{A})$?". Given assumptions about performance and buffer sizes, it can help determine how many requests can be handled concurrently and in particular by how many compromised hosts. The same calculation can be used to determine the amount of resources needed to withstand a given target level of attack.

Consider the abstract protocol below (left), where a client C initially contacts the server S with some message m_1, is given a challenge m_2, and receives the requested service m_4 only after it has provided an adequate response m_3 to m_2:

$$
\begin{array}{cccccccc}
 & & & C & & & S & \\
C \rightarrow S : m_1 & & s_1^C & t_{b1}^C & \xrightarrow{m_1} & t_{v1}^S & s_1^S & \\
S \rightarrow C : m_2 & & s_2^C & t_{v2}^C & \xleftarrow{m_2} & t_{b2}^S & s_2^S & \\
C \rightarrow S : m_3 & & s_3^C & t_{b3}^C & \xrightarrow{m_3} & t_{v3}^S & s_3^S\ [= -(s_2^S + s_3^S)] & \qquad T \\
S \rightarrow C : m_4 & & s_4^C & t_{v4}^C & \xleftarrow{m_4} & t_{b4}^S & s_4^S\ [= 0] &
\end{array}
$$

The exchange on the right shows the time (t_{xi}^a) and space (s_i^a) cost incurred by each principal. Let us measure time in seconds and space in bytes. We wrote t_{bi}^a for the time a spent building message m_i and $t_{vi}^{a'}$ for the time a' spent verifying it. For simplicity, we assume that the time incurred in a failed verification is also t_{vi}^a. Our approach allows for a much more precise model. It is reasonable to assume that the server will not allocate any buffer space upon sending m_4, hence $s_4^S = 0$ and that it releases any used buffer space as soon as it has verified m_3, i.e., $s_3^S = -(s_2^S + s_3^S)$. We further assume that the server will time-out after T seconds if it does not receive message m_3 from C. In this case it will deallocate the space $s_2^S + s_3^S$.

This simple protocol template is susceptible to three forms of time DoS, and one form of space DoS:

- An attacker can induce the server to waste time unsuccessfully verifying a fake message m_1. This time is at most t_{v1}^S. The server's verification rate is therefore at least $1/t_{v1}^S$, which must be matched by the intruder in order to successfully attack S. While this is easily achieved as a fake m_1 can be an arbitrary string, t_{v1}^S will often be comparable to networking overhead in a protocol designed with DoS attacks in mind.

  As a concrete example, a simple initial request containing the client's name, a timestamp, a nonce and a checksum will take under $1\,\mu s$ to verify on fast hardware. Therefore, the server can process at least 1,000,000 requests per second. Assuming that the server has a 1 Gbit/s network interface and that request packets are 50 bytes long (i.e., 400 bits), the network layer will be able to deliver 2,500,000 packets per second to the protocol.

  A dedicated attacker may match these numbers. He may also perform the attack through a number of compromised hosts, which will typically have more limited computing power and bandwidth. While an arbitrary string can be put together in $1\,\mu s$ on many home computers, typical outbound network speeds are less than 4 Mbit/s. Therefore, the attacker will need to synchronize 250 compromised hosts to overwhelm the server with a simultaneous attack.

- A time-out waiting for the reception of m_3 leads to another potential point of DoS. In this case, the server has spent $t_{v1}^S + t_{b2}^S$ while the attacker has incurred a cost t_{b1}^C. Again, this gives us a way to compare the attacker's and the server's rate.

  Continuing our example, $t_{v1}^S + t_{b2}^S$ may amount to $100\,\mu s$ as the server's response will generally involve the generation of a nonce or of cryptographic material. Therefore, the resulting rate may be 10,000 replies per second.

- Another option for time DoS is the reception of a fake message m_3 by S. Here S needs to spend $t_{v1}^S + t_{b2}^S + t_{v3}^S$ seconds, while the attacker's cost amounts to t_{b1}^C plus the minimal time it takes to produce the counterfeit m_3 (the intruder is likely to ignore m_2). This strategy wastes more server time, but it will release storage earlier unless carefully timed. Moreover, the reception of a large number of garbled message may trigger countermeasures on the server.

Looking at our example again, the verification of a fake message m_3 will typically involves substantial use of cryptography, often expensive asymmetric cryptography. We can then take $t_{v1}^S + t_{b2}^S + t_{v3}^S$ to be 10 milliseconds, which results in a rate of just 100 exchanges per second.

In all these situations, the resilience of the server is given by comparing the service rate as measured above, with the individual attack rate multiplied by the number of attackers. Our methodology can give useful ranges as it takes into account the exact structure of the messages involved, including that of the messages faked by the intruder.

- A time-out on m_3 is also the target of a space DoS. Let B be the size in bytes of the buffer where S stores received bits of m_1 and generated fragments of m_2. Then, S can serve at most $n(B) = B/(s_1^S + s_2^S)$ concurrent requests: the larger B, the larger the number of parallel attacks the system can withstand. The space allocation rate is given by $(s_1^S + s_2^S)/(t_{v1}^S + t_{b2}^S)$ bytes per second relative to an individual attacker, while the space reclamation rate is at least $(s_1^S + s_2^S)/(T + t_{v3}^S)$.

  Now, given B, we can calculate optimal values for the time-out T. First, T should be large enough for all legitimate usage pattern to complete: $T > t_{min}$. On the other hand, it should not be so large that an attacker coalition may file more than $n(B) - 1$ fake service requests while waiting for time-out on any initial exchange: $T \le (t_{v1}^S + t_{b2}^S) \times (n(B) - 1)$. We are looking for the maximum value of T satisfying these bounds.

  Concretely, if $s_1^S + s_2^S = 128$ bytes, $t_{v1}^S + t_{b2}^S = 10$ milliseconds, $t_{min} = 90s$, and the maximum number of expected parallel attacks is 10,000, we deduce that B should be at least 1.28 Mb, and that T can be about 1 minute and 40 seconds. If this value is too low, then B should be increased (which would make the system resilient to more concurrent attacks).

References

1. I. Cervesato. A specification language for crypto-protocol based on multiset rewriting, dependent types and subsorting. In G. Delzanno, S. Etalle, and M. Gabbrielli, editors, *Proceedings of the Workshop on Specification, Analysis and Validation for Emerging Technologies — SAVE'01*, pages 1–22, Paphos, Cyprus, 2001.

2. I. Cervesato. Typed MSR: Syntax and examples. In V. Gorodetski, V. Skormin, and L. Popyack, editors, *First International Workshop on Mathematical Methods, Models and Architectures for Computer Network Security — MMM'01*, pages 159–177, St. Petersburg, Russia, 2001. Springer-Verlag LNCS 2052.

3. I. Cervesato. Fine-Grained MSR Specifications for Quantitative Security Analysis. In *Fourth Workshop on Issues in the Theory of Security — WITS'04*, pages 111–127, 2004.

4. Y. Chevalier, R. Küsters, M. Rusinowitch, and M. Turuani. Deciding the Security of Protocols with Diffie-Hellman Exponentiation and Products in Exponents. In *FSTTCS 2003: Foundations of Software Technology and Theoretical Computer Science — 23rd Conference.* Springer-Verlag LNCS 2914, 2003.

5. K. Christou, I. Lee, A. Philippou, and O. Sokolsky. Modeling and analysis of power-aware systems. In *9th International Conference on Tools and Algorithms for the Construction and Analysis of Systems — TACAS 2003*, pages 409–425, Warsaw, Poland, 2003. Springer-Verlag LNCS 2619.

6. J. Clark and J. Jacob. A survey of authentication protocol literature. Technical report, Department of Computer Science, University of York, 1997. Web Draft Version 1.0 available from http://www.cs.york.ac.uk/~jac/.

7. H. Comon-Lundh and V. Shmatikov. Intruder deductions, constraint solving and insecurity decision in presence of exclusive or. In *Proceedings of the Eighteenth Annual IEEE Symposium on Logic in Computer Science (LICS 2003)*, pages 261–270. IEEE, Computer Society Press, 2003.

8. D. Dolev and A. C. Yao. On the security of public-key protocols. *IEEE Transactions on Information Theory*, 2(29):198–208, 1983.

9. C. Gunter, S. Khanna, K. Tan, and S. Venkatesh. DoS protection for reliably authenticated broadcast. In M. Reiter and D. Boneh, editors, *Proceedings of the 11th Networks and Distributed System Security Symposium — NDSS'04*, San Diego, CA, 2004.

10. A. Juels and J. Brainard. Client puzzles: a cryptographic defence against connection depletion attacks. In S. Kent, editor, *Proceedings of the 5th Networks and Distributed System Security Symposium — NDSS'99*, pages 151–165, San Diego, CA, 1999.

11. G. Lowe. Analysing protocols subject to guessing attacks. In J. Guttman, editor, *Second Workshop on Issues in the Theory of Security — WITS'02*, Portland, OR, 2002.

12. C. Meadows. The NRL Protocol Analyzer: An overview. *Journal of Logic Programming*, 26(2):113–131, 1996.

13. C. Meadows. A cost-based framework for analysis of denial of service in networks. *Journal of Computer Security*, 9(1/2):143–164, 2001.

14. R. Needham and M. Schroeder. Using encryption for authentication in large networks of computers. *Communications of the ACM*, 21(12):993–999, 1978.

15. D. Tomioka, S. Nishizaki, and R. Ikeda. Cost estimation calculus for analysing denial-of-service attack resistance. Pre-proceedings of ISSS'03, Tokyo, Japan, Nov. 2003.

16. R. Zunino and P. Degano. A note on the perfect encryption assumption in a process calculus. In I. Walukiewicz, editor, *7th International Conference on Foundations of Software Science and Computation Structures — FoSSaCS'04*, pages 514–528, Barcelona, Spain, 2004. Springer-Verlag LNCS 2987.

The Lower Bound of Attacks on Anonymity Systems – A Unicity Distance Approach

Dogan Kesdogan and Lexi Pimenidis

Aachen University of Technology,
Computer Science Department Informatik IV,
Ahornstr. 55, D-52074 Aachen, Germany

{kesdogan,lexi}@i4.informatik.rwth-aachen.de

Abstract. During the last years a couple of attacks on generic anonymity protocols emerged, like e.g. the hitting-set attack. These attacks make use of informations gained by passively monitoring anonymizing networks to disclose the communication profile of the users.

It has been proven that the longer a person, we call her Alice, communicates over an anonymizing infrastructure using the same set of peers (i.e. following a prefixed profile), the more likely it gets that a link between her and her peers can be detected. On the other hand, if she changes her peers dynamically, this is getting harder.

In this work we are going to present a method to calculate a *lower bound* of observations that is needed to identify all peer partners of Alice (i.e. total break) by assuming a prefixed personal profile of Alice. We claim in this work that this number is comparable to the well known measure 'unicity distance' in the area of cryptography.

1 Introduction

Anonymity in networks has been a hot topic ever since David Chaum's publication about Mixes to guarantee anonymous communication [25]. A Mix forwards messages on behalf of the original senders to hide their true identity. To avoid traffic analysis attacks, the messages are encrypted, stored and forwarded in a random order. Further enhancements include the deployment of multiple Mixes in a so called Mix network or Mix cascade, to avoid corrupted Mixes from learning sensitive information.

There were several proposals made, to improve the security of a basic Mix (see e.g. [2], [27], [29]). On the other hand, even the most elaborate system (e.g. pool mix) can be generalized to a simple threshold mix[1] by determining the *effective size of an anonymity set* as suggested in [15].

Never the less, the proposed protocols proved to leak informations. In the course of the time, more and more sophisticated attacks on these protocols were developed. Those allowed to recompute the sender/recipient relation which was meant to be hidden by the

---

[1] Note, that this assumption is only approximately satisfied. However, the 'level of approximation' can be determined by the user (see [15]).

anonymizing infrastructure. Attacks range from simple as the Sybil attack [30], which attacked the anonymizing infrastructure itself, to intersection attacks (e.g. the disclosure attack [1]). Note that the intersection attack is hard to thwart, since it assumes only a passive observing attacker. However, the attacker applying the disclosure attack has to solve an NP-complete problem. Thus, refinements were suggested in [3], [28] to avoid solving NP-complete problems (see also [24]).

Intersection attacks and especially disclosure attacks in general use slight variations of the same model of abstraction: traffic of data is presented as single messages which are passed as a single piece of data, containing only a sender address, a recipient address and some encrypted data, padded to a unified length. While the attackers are not strong enough to break the encryption, such that the payloads content does not give him any information, the attacker is allowed to compromise some of the mix-nodes on the network and tap all lines.

In this work we use information theory to determine the number of observations that an attacker needs to detect the profile of a victim (e.g. Alice). By determining this number we measure the anonymity independently of an attack and of a generic anonymity system.

1.1 Contributions

Our contributions in this work is new[2] and are twofold:

Anonymity Measurement We determine the number of observations by using information theory that is needed to identify the profile of Alice. We show that this number has similar features as the well known 'unicity distance' measure [16].

Risk Measurement The measurement of the anonymity is conservative[3]. Thus, this number can be used as a risk value, e.g. if Alice communicates less than the identified number or changes her profile (e.g. by using dummy messages) then she is safe.

1.2 Roadmap

Since the goal to measure anonymity is not new we present in the next section related works with the same goal and compare our approach to the others. In section 3 we give a detailed view on the used model of anonymizing networks. The main part of this work is the information theoretic investigation of the stated problem. In section we present 5 some accompanying experiments. The results will be discussed in section 6. Finally we will conclude the paper with closing remarks in section 7.

2   Related Works

It is fundamental that anonymity providing techniques can be described by the fact that a subject is only anonymous within a group of other subjects, the so called *anonymity set*. Consequently, the usage of anonymity set plays a key role in this area of investigation.

---

[2] We underpin our claim by an extensive literature research.

[3] Compare this to cryptography.

We classify the anonymity measurement approaches in two distinct classes: possibilistic and probabilistic approach. The possibilistic approach mainly define the anonymity by its anonymity set size [2]. The probabilistic approach considers the likelihood of an element of the anonymity set, i.e. the elements of the anonymity set have different probabilities. These different probabilities may be so small that some elements may be excluded from the anonymity set. If the attacker gains no information (i.e. the a priori probability is the same as the a posteriori probability) then it is defined as perfect anonymity according to Shannon [16] else as ordinary anonymity (see for more information [12]).

In the field of measuring and modelling the anonymity, following works are known to us:

- In [12] a probabilistic model is suggested according to Shannon [16], i.e. considering a priori and a posteriori probability. Unfortunately, the work gives only the formal definition, but does not demonstrates how to calculate the probabilities.
- A clear possibilistic approach is given in [2]: in open environments like the Internet a user is a member of the anonymity set if the probability that the user has initiated the action is non-zero. Following their approach, the anonymity size can be determined according the given rule as a measure of anonymity (pure possibilistic view).
- Formal languages and logics have been used to suggest metrics considering the anonymity set in [19] and [14]. However, they do not consider a probability distribution on the anonymity set. Thus, it is a possibilistic approach.
- In [13] anonymity is defined as informal continuum. This model defines six degrees from absolute privacy to provably exposed. An extension to the model can be found in [17].
- A further possibilistic approach can be found in [9] that models the attacker's inability to distinguish between observational equivalences by using model equivalence relations.
- [8] and [15] use information theory to measure the anonymity with the notion of entropy. The more evenly the probability distribution is distributed over the anonymity set the greater the uncertainty. They also define the a posteriori entropy to be the effective size of the anonymity probability distribution [15]. Hence, this approach combines the both approaches, i.e. probabilistic and possibilistic approach.
- In [1] an attack is performed by considering the anonymous system as a black box and only analyzing the anonymity sets. It is shown that repeated communications disclose all hidden peers even if the anonymity system was otherwise perfect. Enhancements to this approach are suggested in [3], [5].
- In [4] the authors extend the work of [8], [15] by using the notion of unlinkability. Their model is capable only of measuring the anonymity of an actor within its anonymity set regarding to one specific action, but measure the anonymity by unlinkability of a subset of actions within a given system. However, it is an abstract extension of the prior works without showing any concrete applications of their theory.
- In [7], [6] the approach uses covert channel analysis to measure the anonymity, i.e. how much information can be transformed to the attacker using an anonymity system.

In our approach we extend the work of [4], [8], [15], [1], [3], [5] in that sense that the point where the attacker has identified the peer partners of Alice. Hence, after this point the attacker can reconstruct all the past communications of Alice[4]. And, if she keeps her profile, all future communications are not protected. We call this total break of the anonymity system or universal break. Consequently, we do not measure anymore the anonymity only by using the anonymity set (i.e. neither the size of the anonymity set nor the probability distribution on it or both). We use anonymity sets just to describe the anonymity system. By doing this, we assume that the anonymity of a system is also highly dependent on the users profile. In short, we measure the anonymity by relating the *number of observations* of effective anonymity sets and the *likelihood of a successful attack*. If the likelihood becomes one after a number of observations, then this number measures the anonymity. Note, that there are several attacks with this goal. Here, we want to investigate the general link between the observations and the likelihood of a successful attack.

In our paper we use information theory to investigate the link between the number of observations and the likelihood of a successful attack. The reason for that is that we assume a strict behavior of Alice modelled by $X(t)$. And furthermore, if we model the communication of the others as noise $n(t)$ then we can ask ourselves what is the information leakage or information gain if the attacker observes $X(t) + n(t)$, or where is the point when the attacker can identify $X(t)$ (compare this also with [3]).

Our approach is highly related to the Shannons noisy channel model, which he has also used to model the information flow in a cryptographic system. He measured the secrecy of a cryptographic system by the so called unicity distance, i.e. the smallest amount of ciphertext needed to uniquely determine the key [16] (i.e. total break). The unicity distance has the following features (compare with [31]):

- It gives a conservative estimate of the amount of ciphertext needed to break a cipher, i.e. real systems need more ciphertext.
- It shows, that exhaustive key search will always find the key except if
  - always a randomly key is chosen for each letter.
  - the available cryptogram is shorter than the unicity distance.

In section 6 we discuss and identify a similar structure in the field of anonymity.

3   Models and Methods

The purpose of this section is to introduce mixes as an example of an anonymity technique and explain the general models of abstraction.

3.1   Mixes

As already mentioned in the introduction there are a number of anonymity techniques to prevent eavesdroppers from gaining information about a user's traffic. Since the content is usually encrypted, our focus is restricted to the traffic layer. Anyone that can

---

[4] Except the case if several peer partners occur in the same anonymity set. In this case the uncertainty is limited to these peers.

read a packet can see the origin and the destination, even if its content is unreadable. Anonymity techniques strive to prevent this.

As an example: Alice wants to post her political opinion to a web forum where oppositional members exchange information. Unfortunately she lives in a country where the government is suspected to track down oppositional members. If she would just send the encrypted message, e.g. using HTTPS, her Internet Service Provider (ISP) could notice this action and save this to a record. This could lead to a point where Alice herself could get suspected because she has exchanged data with some entity.

To avoid this, Alice could use some service like JAP [23]. For this she installs a proxy on her computer that encrypts all of her traffic and sends it to a JAP proxy (i.e. Mixes [25]). Along with her there are several other, maybe several thousand, users doing likewise. The server decrypts those packets and forwards them on behalf of the users. Any returned data will be sent to the users on the same way.

Thus, any primary evidence has now gone. What remains is that Alice sends out data to an anonymity server (e.g. Mixes) which itself does not provide any other service than untraceable packet forwarding. Because of this functionality a potential attacker is not able to link an incoming packet to an outgoing packet. Using this service, Alice is beyond any suspicion to have send any packets to the oppositional forum because any of the other users could have done it, i.e. Alice and the other persons build the so called *anonymity set*.

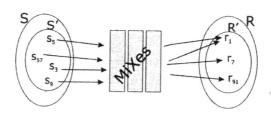

Fig. 1. Formal model of an anonymity set. In any anonymous communication (e.g. Mixes), a subset S' of all senders S sends a message to a subset R' of all recipients $\mathcal{R}$.

Mixes collect a number of packets from distinct users (anonymity set) and process them so that no single participant, except the mix itself and the sender of the packet, can link an input packet to an output packet [25]. Therefore, the *appearance* (i.e. the bit pattern) and the *order* of the incoming packets have to be changed within the mix. The change of appearance is a cryptographic operation, which is combined with a management procedure and a universal agreement to achieve anonymity:

User Protocol: All generated data packets including address information are padded to equal length (agreement), combined with a secret random number and encrypted with the public key of the mix node (see also [26]). A sequence of mixes is used to increase the reliability of the system.

Mix Protocol: A mix collects b_0 packets (called *batch*) from distinct users (identity verification), decrypts the packets with its private key, strips off the random numbers, and outputs the packets in a different order (lexicographically sorted or randomly delayed). Furthermore, any incoming packet has to be compared with formerly received packets (management: store in a local database) in order to reject any duplicates. Every mix (except the first) must include a functionality ensuring that each received packet is from a distinct user, because only the first mix can decide whether or not the packets are from distinct senders.

Applying this protocol in closed environments where all subjects participate in all anonymity sets, the mix method provides full security. The relation between the sender and the recipient is hidden from an omnipresent attacker as long as:

(a) One honest mix is in the line of the mixes which the packet passes, i.e. one that is not corrupted.
(b) The $(b_0 - 1)$ other senders do not all cooperate with the attacker.

[12] states that the mix method provides information-theoretic deterministic anonymity based on complexity-theoretic secure cryptography.

3.2 Model

In this work we consider the model that has been considered by most of the papers referred to in the introduction [2, 27, 1, 3, 28, 24]. It is generaly considered to be an abstraction from a specific type of anonymity service or implementation.

In this model, we assume that a subset S' of all senders S sends a message to a subset R' of all recipients $\mathcal{R}$, like shown in figure 1. Furthermore, in this model the adversary can easily determine anonymity sets, e.g. we assume that all network links are observable (see [25]). However, this can be assumed also in a real world scenario if the attacker is able to observe messages to and from an anonymity service. The following properties of an anonymity system are generally assumed:

– In each anonymous communication, a subset S' of all senders S sends a message to a subset R' of all recipients $\mathcal{R}$. That is, $S' \subseteq S$ and $R' \subseteq \mathcal{R}$, as Figure 1 illustrates. In a particular system, the set of all senders S can be the same as the set of all recipients $\mathcal{R}$.
– The size of the sender anonymity set is $|S'| = b_0$, where $1 \leq b_0 \ll |S|$. Note that a sender can even send multiple packets per batch.
– The size of the recipient anonymity set is $|R'| = b_1$, where $1 \leq b_1 \ll |\mathcal{R}|$ and $b_1 \leq b_0$. That is, several senders can communicate with the same recipient.
– The anonymity system provides provides perfect untraceability between incoming and outgoing packets for a single round of operation.

The typical values for $|S'|$, $|R'|$, $|S|$, and $|\mathcal{R}|$ vary from implementation to implementation and with the environment in which they operate. In [23] an implementation is presented in which $|S|$ is around $20,000$. They don't give typical values for $|S'|$, but we generally expect $|S'| < 100$.

For the sake of simplicity the following assumptions are added:

- Alice is a sender using the system to hide her m communication partners $\mathcal{P} = \{p_1, p_2, \ldots p_m\}$. She sends t messages using the system, while the attacker notes down the observations $\mathcal{O}$, the respective recipients sets $\mathcal{O} = \{R'_1, R'_2, \ldots R'_t\}$. Note that for all $R'_i \in \mathcal{O}$ there is $\mathcal{P} \cap R'_i \neq \emptyset$.

  This can be accomplished by restricting the attacker to observe only the anonymous communication of Alice. We will refer to the communication partners later on also as Alice's peers.

- The anonymizing infrastructure uses a fixed threshold mix technique. Note that other anonymity techniques can easily be reduced to this generalized model by determining the respective anonymity sets[5].

- the implementation is perfect, thus providing unlinkability in each single(!) round of the system, thwarting replay attacks, sybil attacks and other attacks trying to exploit weaknesses in the implementation and deployment.

3.3 Attacker Model

The attacker is defined to have full passive access to the network, i.e. he can read all data from the complete network. He may also corrupt all but one node and some of the participants, but may not gain full control over the network, such that he can trivially gain all required informations due to $b_0 - 1$-attack[6] or likewise methods, i.e. he is forced to use the informations he gained from wiretapping to break the system. Having access to $\mathcal{O}$, the attacker wants to reveal $\mathcal{P}$.

Note that this is consistent with the last paragraph of section 3.1.

3.4 Putting all together

Thus we consider the tupel $\mathcal{ANON} = (\mathcal{P}, \mathcal{R}, t, \mathcal{C}, \mathcal{O})$ to be a complete description of a situation during an attack in this model:

$\mathcal{P}$ Alice's set of m peers ($\mathcal{P} = \{p_1, p_2, \ldots, p_m\}$)

$\mathcal{R}$ is the complete set of possible recipients, i.e. peer partners ($\mathcal{P} \subseteq \mathcal{R}$)

t is the number of messages, Alice has sent

$\mathcal{C}$ is the list of the t peers, Alice contacted[7] with her t messages, in the order, she contacted them ($\mathcal{C} = (c_1, c_2, \ldots, c_t)$, where $c_i \in \mathcal{P}$)

$\mathcal{O}$ is the list of t observations, made by the attacker, in chronological order ($\mathcal{O} = (R'_1, R'_2, \ldots R'_t)$, where $R'_i \in (\mathcal{R}^{b_0-1} \times \mathcal{P})$ and $c_i \in R'_i$)

---

[5] This might include bringing in some error probability, but this probability can be reduced below any value $\varepsilon > p(error) \geq 0$.

[6] The commonly known name is $n - 1$-attack, we use this term in accordance to the naming of our variables.

[7] Thus this string is abbreviated with a $\mathcal{C}$.

4   Information Theoretical Approach

In order to give a measurement of the degree of anonymity provided by a system, we determine the amount of informations gained by a passive observer. By calculating entropies of sets we determine the point in time, when there is no more uncertainty about the set of peers of Alice. This uncertainty is represented by a value of entropy. The entropy $H(R)$ of the set R is defined as the uncertainty about a certain element $r_j \in R$, chosen from its set with the help of probability vector $p(r_j)$. It is generaly defined as

$$H(R) = - \sum_{r_j \in R} p(r_j) \log p(r_j) \tag{1}$$

4.1   General equation

Following the model from section 3.2 we calculate the lower bound of attacks on an anonymity system, using an approach similar to Shannon's approach in [16]. From the general equations, where H denotes the value of entropy:

$$H(U,V,W) = H(U|V,W) + H(V,W) \tag{2}$$
$$H(X,Y) = H(X|Y) + H(Y) \tag{3}$$

it follows, with an appropriate change of variables, that

$$H(C,P,O) \quad = H(C|P,O) + H(P,O) \tag{4}$$
$$H(O,P,C) \quad = H(O|P,C) + H(P,C) \tag{5}$$
$$\implies H(C|P,O) + H(P,O) = H(O|P,C) + H(P,C) \tag{6}$$

Remember that P is the set of Alice's peers, C is the list of Alice's peers in the order they were contacted and O is the list of observations made by an adversary.

Due to equation 3 it follows that

$$H(P,C) = H(C|P) + H(P) \tag{7}$$
$$\text{and: } H(P,O) = H(P|O) + H(O) \tag{8}$$

Putting formulas 6, 7 and 8 together and resolving it to $H(P|O)$, it follows that the entropy of the set of peer partners, given only the ability of a global observer, results in:

$$H(P|O) = H(O|P,C) + H(C|P) + H(P) - H(O) - H(C|P,O) \tag{9}$$

The entropies of P, O and $C|P$ are easily calculated. $H(O|P,C)$ equals the entropy of all possibilities a stream C can be disguised in a given setting $\mathcal{ANON}$ and is slightly more complicated. $H(C|P,O)$ quantifies the uncertainty that remains in decoding C given the attacker knows P.

$H(\mathcal{P})$ is the entropy about all possible sets of Alice's peer partners. If $|\mathcal{P}| = m$ is known and all hosts in $\mathcal{R}$ are equally likely, then $H(\mathcal{P}) = \log_2 \binom{|\mathcal{R}|}{m}$

$H(\mathcal{O})$ equals the a priori entropy over all possible observations, that an attacker could possibly make, thus $H(\mathcal{O}) = t\, b_0 \log_2 |\mathcal{R}|$

$H(\mathcal{C}|\mathcal{P})$ is the entropy that is contained within the string $\mathcal{C}$. Thus, if Alice chooses to contact her peers randomly one-by-one, it equals $H(\mathcal{C}) = t \log_2 m$, which is its maximum value. If Alice's traffic contains more detailed pattern, they reduce this value appropriately.

$H(\mathcal{O}|\mathcal{P},\mathcal{C})$ is the a posteriori entropy of all possibilities to express the stream $\mathcal{C}$, consisting of elements of $\mathcal{P}$, in the attacker's observation stream $\mathcal{O}$. To properly calculate this value, we need to know, for each peer partner $p \in \mathcal{P}$ on which subset $\mathcal{L}_p \subseteq \mathcal{R}^{b_0}$ we can map $p \in \mathcal{P} \mapsto \mathcal{L}_p \subseteq \mathcal{R}^{b_0}$.

We therefore need to determine the number of elements $(x_1, x_2, \ldots x_a) \in \mathcal{R}^{b_0}$ that contain p at least once. The size of the sets $\mathcal{L}_p$ can be calculated by

$$|\mathcal{L}_p| = |\mathcal{R}|^{b_0} - (|\mathcal{R}| - 1)^{b_0} \tag{10}$$

and does not depend on p. Thus: $H(\mathcal{O}|\mathcal{P},\mathcal{C}) = t \log_2 |\mathcal{L}_p|$

$H(\mathcal{C}|\mathcal{P},\mathcal{O})$ An attacker, as defined in section 3.3, has access to $\mathcal{O}$ and is interested in learning $\mathcal{P}$. Note that the knowledge of $\mathcal{C}$ leads to the disclosure of $\mathcal{P}$, while the knowledge of $\mathcal{P}$ leaves some uncertainty about $\mathcal{C}$. This is due to the fact that other people might communicate with Alice's peers as well, and do so even at the same time. So there might be observations that include more than one element of $\mathcal{P}$ and the attacker will not be able to tell, which of them was contacted by Alice in that specific observation[8].

For each single observation the remaining entropie equals the log of the average number of Alice's peers. We call the probability that there are a peers of Alice in the same batch, in addition to the one she contacted herself, $p(a)$. In the case of a uniform probability distribution[9]:

$$p(a) \quad = \binom{b-1}{a}\left(\frac{m-1}{N}\right)^a \left(\frac{N-m-1}{N}\right)^{b-a-2} \tag{11}$$

$$\Leftrightarrow \quad p(a) \quad = \binom{b-1}{a}\frac{(m-1)^a(N-m-1)^{b-a-2}}{N^{b-2}} \tag{12}$$

$$\Longrightarrow H(\mathcal{C}|\mathcal{P},\mathcal{O}) = t\sum_{a=0}^{b-1} p(a)\log(a+1) \tag{13}$$

To calculate the average number of observations needed to break the system, $H(\mathcal{P}|\mathcal{O})$ from formula 9 is set to zero, to describe the point in time t when there is no uncertainty about Alice's peers. It then needs to be resolved to t. The exact way depends on the details of the model.

---

[8] The primary target of the attacker is $\mathcal{P}$ anyway, and we consider the knowledge of $\mathcal{C}$ to be optional information.

[9] In any case there would be no contribution to this value for $a = 0$ because there would be no doubt about Alice's peer partner.

For the example values from this section follows:

$$t = \frac{\log_2 \binom{|\mathcal{R}|}{m}}{b_0 \log_2 |\mathcal{R}| - \log_2 m - \log_2 |\mathcal{C}_i| + \sum_{i=0}^{b-1} p(i) \log(i+1)} \tag{14}$$

5 Experiments

As can be seen in figure 2, we compare the resulting average lower bound with the average number of observations needed by some known attacks on a fix-threshold mix: the SHS-attack [24], the disclosure attack [1] and the statistical disclosure attack [3]. We chose as typical system parameters $|\mathcal{R}| = 20000$, $m = 20$ and $b_0 = 50$ [23]. To show the impact on changes of these three critical variables, three series are displayed. In each series two variables were kept fix, while the third is varied along some interval. The lower bound of protection was calculated by assuming a maximum amount of entropy in $H(\mathcal{C})$. This is the case, iff Alice chooses her contacts randomly out of her set of peers by a uniform probability distribution. The same applies for the other three data series, as well.

Having higher order statistics about the peers of Alice, i.e. the victim's pattern of communication, the lower bound would be smaller than in figure 2 graphs. For certain activities, like surfing in the WWW there are already studies which offer very detailed statistics [22, 21, 20].

Calculating the lower bound for more realistic scenarios, like sending emails or surfing the web is simple, using the formulas provided in section 4 and entering the respective values.

6 Discussion

Following the previous calculations we can use the derived measure twofold: as an eavesdropper we know the minimum amount of observations that are necessary to successfully break an anonymity system. Thus we can save our computational power until there is a reasonable probability of succeeding.

On the other hand, as an user of an anonymizing network, we can now estimate the risk of our communication pattern getting revealed. A user can now e.g. compute the exact amount of dummy traffic to add into the regular communication to avoid successful traffic analysis. Thus a user could possibly maintain *perfect anonymity* even within an open environment.

The large differences between the values for the average lower bound and the best attack in figure 2 does not necessarily mean that there are yet better attacks to be discovered. As discussed in [16], the information theoretical approach does result in very conservative estimations which are often way lower than practical bounds of systems.

These results should not be applied to real systems without more detailed considerations. This is especially due to the abstraction of the model in this paper. Since modelling all details available in a deployed anonymizing network tends to be to tedious, there always remains a certain chance that some of the parameters not available to the model leak some information.

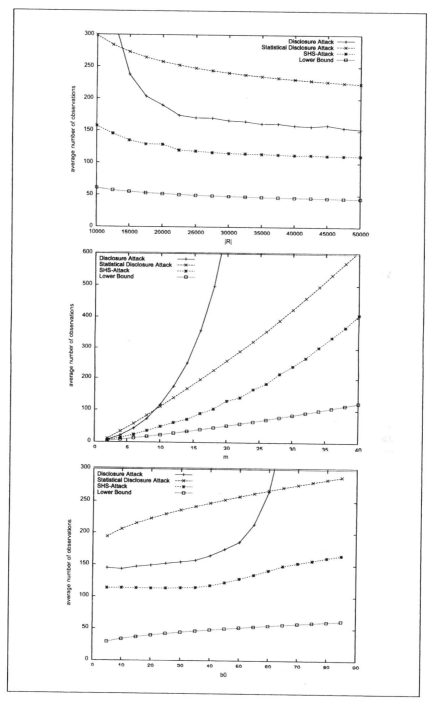

Fig. 2. Lower bound of protection of anonymity systems compared to the average number of observations needed by typical known attacks.

Finally, the lower bound of attacks have similar structure compared to the unicity distance:

- The lower bound gives a conservative estimate of the amount of observations needed to break (i.e. total break) a given anonymity system, i.e. real anonymity systems need more observations.
- It shows, that if there is a profile of a user (i.e. Alice) then this profile will always be identified except if
  - Alice changes randomly her behavior.
  - the available observations are less than the calculated lower bound.

However, the word 'break' has different meaning in both areas. Even though the peer partners of Alice are identified, the attacker can not identify the concrete peer partner of Alice for an actual communication, if within the anonymity set other peer partners occur.

7   Conclusion

In this work we listed ways of measuring the anonymity of a system and described in detail the model of anonymizing networks that was used in the most important publications on anonymity research of the last years.

Our contribution to this area is a calculation to find the average lower-bound of attacks on this systems using information theoretic measures. Thus it provides a tool to measure anonymity that can be used to determine the risk of using an anonymizing network infrastructure. We also compared these values to the amount of information needed by real attacks and discussed further outcomings. Future work will include finding concrete values for the entropies for specific types of anonymity systems.

We expect to get new results mostly from more detailed or refined models. Future research will thus focus on finding additional suitable parameters for modelling anonymizing infrastructures. For instance, we have focused here on total break, but one or two peer partners of Alice may be linked to her with high probability before the identified lower bound (partial break). Thus, it will also be a future issue to provide a theory and calculate lower bound numbers for partial break.

References

1. D. Kesdogan, D. Agrawal, and S. Penz: Limits of anonymity in open environments, in Information Hiding workshop (IH 2002), ser. LNCS, F. A. P. Petitcolas, Ed., vol. 2578. Noordwijkerhout, The Netherlands: Springer-Verlag, 7-9 October 2002, pp. 5369.
2. D. Kesdogan, J. Egner, and R. Büschkes: Stop-and-go-mixes providing probabilistic anonymity in an open system. Information Hiding 1998, LNCS 1525, Springer-Verlag Berlin 1998, pp. 83-98.
3. G. Danezis: Statistical disclosure attacks, in Security and Privacy in the Age of Uncertainty, (SEC2003), Gritzalis, Vimercati, Samarati, and Katsikas, Eds., IFIP TC11. Athens: Kluwer, May 2003, pp. 421426.
4. S. Steinbrecher, S. Köpsell: Modelling Unlinkability, in Proceedings of Privacy Enhancing Technologies workshop (PET 2003), ser. LNCS, May 2003.

5. N. Mathewson and R. Dingledine: Practical traffic analysis: Extending and resisting statis-
    tical disclosure, in Proceedings of Privacy Enhancing Technologies workshop (PET 2004),
    ser. LNCS, May 2004.
6. I. S. Moskowitz, R. E. Newman, D. P. Crepeau, and A. R. Miller: Covert channels and
    anonymizing networks, in Workshop on Privacy in the Electronic Society (WPES 2003),
    Washington, DC, USA, October 2003.
7. I. S. Moskowitz, R. E. Newman, and P. F. Syverson: Quasi-anonymous channels, in Com-
    munication, Network, and Information Security (CNIS 2003), New York, USA, 10-12 De-
    cember 2003.
8. C. Diaz, S. Seys, J. Claessens, and B. Preneel: Towards measuring anonymity. Privacy En-
    hancing Technologies 2002, LNCS 2482, Springer-Verlag Berlin.
9. D. Hughes and V. Shmatikov: Information hiding, anonymity and privacy: A modular ap-
    proach. To appear in Journal of Computer Security, 2003.
10. M. Köhntopp and A. Pfitzmann: Anonymity, unobservability, and pseudonymity - a proposal
    for terminology. Draft v0.12., June 2001.
11. M.G. Reed, P.F. Syverson, and D. Goldschlag: Anonymous connections and onion routing.
    IEEE Journal on Selected Areas in Communication, Special Issue on Copyright and Privacy
    Protection, 1998.
12. A. Pfitzmann: Dienstintegrierende Kommunikationsnetze mit teilnehmerüberprüfbarem
    Datenschutz. IFB 234, Springer-Verlag, Heidelberg 1990 (in German).
13. M. K. Reiter and A. D. Rubin: Crowds: Anonymity for web transactions. ACM Transactions
    on Information and System Security 1(1), November 1998, pp. 66-92.
14. S. Schneider, A. Sidiropoulos: CSP and anonymity. ESORICS 1996, LNCS 1146, Springer-
    Verlag Berlin 1996, pp. 198-218.
15. A. Serjantov, G. Danezis: Towards an information-theoretic metric for anonymity. Privacy
    Enhancing Technologies 2002, LNCS 2482, Springer-Verlag Berlin.
16. C. E. Shannon: Communication theory of secrecy systems. The Bell System Technical Jour-
    nal 28/4 (1949), pp. 656-715.
17. V. Shmatikov: Probabilistic analysis of anonymity. Proc. 15th IEEE Computer Security
    Foundations Workshop (CSFW) 2002, pp 119-128.
18. S. G. Stubblebine, P. F. Syverson, and D. M. Goldschlag: Unlinkable serial transactions:
    Protocols and applications. ACM Transactions on Information and System Security, Vol. 2,
    No. 4, Nov.1999, pp. 354-389.
19. P. F. Syverson and S. G. Stubblebine: Group principals and the formalization of anonymity.
    FM'99 - Formal Methods, Vol. I, LNCS 1708,, Springer-Verlag 1999pp. 814-833.
20. Minos N. Garofalakis, Rajeev Rastogi, and Kyuseak Shim: Sequential pattern mining with
    regular expression constraints. 1999.
21. Bamshad Mobasher, Namit Jain, Eui-Hong Han, and Jaideep Srivastava. Web mining: Pattern
    discovery from world wide web transactions. 1996.
22. Lara D. Catledge and James E. Pitkow. Characterizing browsing strategies in the world wide
    web. 1995.
23. Oliver Berthold, Hannes Federrath, and Stefan Köpsell. Web MIXes: A system for anony-
    mous and unobservable Internet access. In H. Federrath, editor, Proceedings of Designing
    Privacy Enhancing Technol ogies: Workshop on Design Issues in Anonymity and Unobserv-
    ability, pages 115-129. SpringerVerlag, LNCS 2009, July 2000.
24. Dogan Kesdogan and Lexi Pimenidis. The Hitting Set Attack on Anonymity Protocols. In
    Proceedings of Information Hiding, 7th International Workshop. Springer Verlag, 2004.
25. David L. Chaum. Untraceable Electronic Mail, Return Addresses, and Digital Pseudonyms.
    Communications of the ACM, 24(2):84 - 88, Feb 1981.
26. B. Pfitzmann and A. Pfitzmann. How to break the direct RSA-implementation of mixes.
    pages 373 - 381. Eurocrypt '89, LNCS 434. Springer-Verlag, Berlin, 1990.

27. Marc Rennhard and Bernhard Plattner. Introducing MorphMix: Peer-to-Peer based Anonymous Internet Usage with Collusion Detection. In Proceedings of the Workshop on Privacy in the Electronic Society (WPES 2002), Washington, DC, USA, November 2002.
28. George Danezis. The traffic analysis of continuous-time mixes. In David Martin and Andrei Serjantov, editors, Privacy Enhancing Technologies (PET 2004), May 2004.
29. George Danezis, Roger Dingledine, and Nick Mathewson. Mixminion: Design of a Type III Anonymous Remailer Protocol. In Proceedings of the 2003 IEEE Symposium on Security and Privacy, May 2003.
30. John Douceur. The Sybil Attack. In Proceedings of the 1st International Peer To Peer Systems Workshop (IPTPS 2002), March 2002.
31. D. E. R. Denning. Cryptography and Data Security.Addison-Wesley Pub (Sd) (June 1, 1982), ISBN: 0201101505.

Intersection Attacks on Web-Mixes: Bringing the Theory into Praxis

Dogan Kesdogan, Lexi Pimenidis, and Tobias Kölsch

Aachen University of Technology,
Computer Science Department Informatik IV,
Ahornstr. 55, D-52074 Aachen, Germany

{kesdogan,lexi,koelsch}@i4.informatik.rwth-aachen.de

Abstract. In the past, different intersection attacks on Chaum Mixes have been proposed and shown to work well in simulation environments. In this work we describe intersection attacks that have been performed on data from anonymized proxy log files. This approach creates all new problems that arise in real systems, where real-world users do not behave like those in the idealized model. E.g. the attack algorithm has to cope with a fixed number of observations. From the performed first experiments on the "dirty" real world data we get valuable insight into theory and practice of real anonymizers.

1 Introduction

Today's networks do not protect the traffic information, i.e. addresses of the senders and recipients are open to an adversary. Having such information it is easy to build communication profiles, i.e. who has communicated with whom, when, how long, from which location etc. This is considered as an invasion of privacy. Therefore, a number of anonymity techniques were suggested to thwart such attacks. In this work we investigate protection strength of anonymity techniques, i.e. the ability of building profiles even though strong anonymity techniques are applied.

The present work is one step on the way to develop a general anonymity system that serves all people and protects all their traffic against strong attackers. The goal is to find general weaknesses of presented techniques, to be able to circumvent them. Most practicable rerouting techniques can be represented by the model presented in Section 2.1. As a result the attacks performed on the model represent a upper bound of the security of those systems.

Today we have the situation that a generally secure system does not exist. There are a number of anonymity techniques that might be able to generally protect a user's traffic, but most of them are theoretical concepts and only a few working systems can be found. To evaluate the strength of these anonymity techniques most works use theoretical models and simulations based on a variety of assumptions. However, the results from these models can be generalized to the real world only to some extent, as we will show.

In [MD04,KP04,KAP02] the anonymity systems security is analyzed in simulations that assume a uniform probability distribution of the communication partners. Poisson distributed traffic is assumed in [Dan04]. Further works that analyze anonymity based on simulated traffic are [SS03,LRWW04].

In [DSD04] Diaz et al. analyze the security provided by two practical mix designs with the help of a simulation that is based on log files. As opposed to our work their work does measure the size of the anonymity set, whereas we try to give a probability of a successful compromise. Additional differences include that Diaz' work is focused on email messages, while we observe web surfing.

Another publication that handles traffic analysis on more than simulated data is [MD05]. Murdoch and Danezis show how to reduce the anonymity provided by a real system, i.e. Tor. While our work doesn't break a specific existing anonymity system, we're attacking mixes instead of onion routers. We also make use of passive global adversary, while [MD05] uses an active local attacker.

1.1 Contributions

Our contributions in this work come from our first simulation results of experiments with real data (i.e. 80 Gigabyte squid logs). These contributions are:

Experiments: Due to lack of real anonymity systems most investigations in this area use theoretic models to evaluate anonymity systems. In this work we show how to overcome this drawback by using today's traffic (squid logs). We emulate a "real" anonymity system by using Web data as good as possible.

Protection limit: We investigate the protection limit of anonymity system in a real environment and compare it to the theoretical results. By this we also give an upper bound on the protection most systems can provide.

Simulations versus "real" system: It is indeed a very difficult problem for the theory to model the users in a rigorous manner. So attack results on Simulated traffic do not have to reflect results on real traffic. By evaluating the "real" traffic we:

- gain information on how the user behavior differs from typical model assumptions which enables us to refine the models for better theory;
- deduce valuable insights on how to build practical anonymity systems that are better suited to real users needs.

2   The Basic Setting: From Mix to Anonymity Set

The purpose of this section is to introduce mixes as an example of an anonymity technique and explain the general model of abstraction we use for our attacks, i.e. the anonymity set. It is important to note, that the mixes are only an example. The presented abstraction applies to most anonymity techniques, also independently of the kind of traffic being transmitted. Being an abstraction it does not take into account specific improvements that could result from regarding implementation specific characteristics of some special techniques. On the other hand, attacks performed at this level of abstraction can be performed on any anonymity technique, that generates anonymity sets. So we investigate the maximum level of security any such system can provide.

2.1 Mixes

As mentioned in the introduction there are a number of anonymity techniques to prevent eavesdroppers from gaining information about a user's traffic. Since the content can be encrypted, our focus is restricted to the traffic layer. Anyone who can read a packet can see its origin and the destination, even if the content is unreadable. Anonymity techniques strive to prevent this.

Mixes, as proposed in [Cha81], collect a number of packets from distinct users (the anonymity set) and process them so that no single participant, except the mix itself and the sender of the packet, can link an input packet to an output packet. To achieve this, the *appearance* (i.e. the bit pattern) and the *order* of the incoming packets have to be changed within the mix. To increase the security of the system, the packets can be sent through various mixes instead of through just one. The change of appearance of the packets is a cryptographic operation, which is combined with a universal agreement and a management procedure to achieve anonymity:

- On the user side all generated data packets including address information are padded to equal length (the universal agreement), combined with a secret random number and encrypted with the public key of the mix node (see also [PP90]). If a sequence of mixes is used to increase the security of the system, the packets have to be encrypted for each mix in the reverse order they go through them. Then the packets are sent to the first mix.
- A mix collects b_0 packets (called *batch*) from users, decrypts the packets with its private key, strips off the random numbers, and outputs the packets in a different order. Furthermore, all incoming packets have to be compared with formerly received packets (management: store in a local database) in order to reject any duplicates.

Applying this protocol in closed environments where all subjects participate in all anonymity sets, the mix method provides full protection. The relation between the sender and the recipient is hidden from an omnipresent attacker as long as:

(a) One honest mix is in the line of the mixes which the packet passes.
(b) The $(b_0 - 1)$ other senders do not all cooperate with the attacker.

[Pfi90] states that the mix method provides information-theoretic deterministic anonymity based on complexity-theoretic secure cryptography.

2.2 Model

In this work we consider the model that has been considered by most publications (notably [KEB98,RP02,KAP02,Dan03,Dan04,KP04]). It is generally considered to be an abstraction from a specific type of anonymity service or implementation.

In this model, we assume that a subset S' of all senders S sends a message to a subset R' of all recipients $\mathcal{R}$, like shown in Figure 1. Furthermore, in this model the adversary can easily determine anonymity sets, e.g. we assume that all network links are observable (see [Cha81]). However, this can be assumed also in a real world scenario if the attacker is able to observe messages to and from an anonymity service. The following properties of an anonymity system are generally assumed:

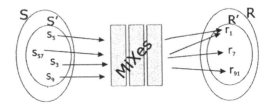

Fig. 1. Formal model of the anonymity set. In any anonymous communication (e.g. mixes), a subset S' of all senders S sends a message to a subset R' of all recipients $\mathcal{R}$. S' is then called the anonymity set.

- In each anonymous communication, a subset S' of all senders S sends a message to a subset R' of all recipients $\mathcal{R}$. That is, $S' \subseteq S$ and $R' \subseteq \mathcal{R}$, as Figure 1 illustrates. In a particular system, the set of all senders S can be the same as the set of all recipients $\mathcal{R}$.
- The size of the sender anonymity set is $|S'| = b_0$, where $1 \leq b_0 \ll |S|$. Note that in this model a sender can send multiple packets per batch.
- The size of the recipient anonymity set is $|R'| = b_1$, where $1 \leq b_1 \ll |\mathcal{R}|$ and $b_1 \leq b_0$. That is, several senders can communicate with the same recipient.

The anonymity system provides perfect untraceability between incoming and outgoing packets for a single round of operation. The typical values for $|S'|$, $|R'|$, $|S|$, and $|\mathcal{R}|$ vary from implementation to implementation and with the environment in which they operate. [BFK00] presents an implementation in which $|S|$ is around $20,000$. They do not give typical values for $|S'|$, but we generally expect $|S'| \leq 30$.

For the sake of simplicity the following assumptions are added:

- Alice is a sender using the system to hide her m communication partners $\mathcal{P} = (p_1, p_2, \ldots p_m)$. During the attack, she sends t messages using the system. The attacker notes down the observations $\mathcal{O}$, the respective recipients sets
  $\mathcal{O} = \{R'_1, R'_2, \ldots R'_t\}$. We assume that for all $R'_i \in \mathcal{O}$ there is $\mathcal{P} \cap R'_i \neq \emptyset$.
  This can be accomplished by restricting the attacker to observe only the anonymous communication of Alice. We will refer to the communication partners later on also as Alice's peers.
- The model anonymizing infrastructure uses a mix with a fixed size of the anonymity set b. Note that other anonymity techniques can easily be reduced to this generalized model by determining the respective anonymity sets[1].

3 Attacks

Here we regard intersection attacks. They belong to the family of contextual attacks according to Raymond [Ray01]. The basic idea of the intersection attacks is that the

---

[1] this might include bringing in some error probability, but this probability can be reduced below any arbitrary $\varepsilon > 0$

attacker can determine the peer partners of a user through repeated observations. These attacks are based on the assumption that users typically communicate with only a small number of parties, i.e. the communication of the users is not random.

The attacker is defined to have full passive access to the network, i.e. he can read all data from the complete network. He may also corrupt all but one mix node. However, he is forced to use the informations he gained from wiretapping to break the system.

3.1 Disclosure Attack

The disclosure attack [KAP02] is based on the concept of set intersections and consists of two phases: the learning and the attacking phase. If Alice has m peers, the attacker looks for m disjunct observations in the learning phase. Thus he can be sure that each observation contains exactly one of Alice's peers. Those sets are successively reduced in the attacking phase, until all other peers have been removed from these sets and only the peer partners remain.

- *Learning Phase*: The attacker tries to learn one observation for each peer of his victim. One precondition of this attack is for the attacker to know the number of his victim's peers, m. He can find this observations by noting down anonymity sets, which he can link to the user, until he has m mutual disjunctive observations $(R_1, \ldots, R_m)$, i.e. $\forall i \neq j$ holds $R_i \cap R_j = \emptyset$.
- *Attacking Phase*: Once the attacker has completed the first stage, he can shrink the size of the sets R_i. Iff a new observation R_{new} has a non-empty intersection with exactly one R_i, the attacker knows that this observation has to contain the same peer as R_i. He can thus replace R_i with $R_i \cap R_{new}$, whose size is smaller or equal to the size of R_i and still contains the same peer partner.
  If all sets R_i consist of a single element only, the attacker found the peer partners of his victim. Iff an attacker does not have enough observations to complete the second phase, he isn't able to identify all peers. Only the peers from sets R_i with $|R_i| = 1$ have been identified then.

3.2 Statistical Disclosure Attack

Danezis describes in [Dan03] a variation of the above disclosure attack. One of the main differences is that the statistical disclosure attack does not always identify the peer partners correctly, i.e. has a certain error probability. The concept bases on signal recognition, where the observer tries to reconstruct the target's peers with the help of the observations he made.

The statistical disclosure attack has up to now only been simulated [MD04] or analytically analyzed [DS04]. One of the preconditions of the original form is that the traffic pattern base on a uniform distribution. The longer an attacker observes this system, the clearer will it become that a certain set of elements appear with a higher frequency. This set is equal to the set of the victim's peer partners and can be found out by simple statistical means.

An advantage of this attack is that the attacker doesn't necessarily need to know the number of his victim's peer partners. But it lacks some relevance in practice because users don't tend to communicate according to uniform distributions. On the other hand, an attacker can normalize other distributions and achieve again uniform probabilities [Rat04].

3.3 Statistical Hitting-Set Attack

The statistical hitting set attack is based on set intersections, as the disclosure attack. In the Hitting Set attack the observations represent hyper-edges of a graph. To identify the user's peer partners is equivalent to determine a unique minimal hitting set of the hyper-graph. A detailed description can be found in [KP04].

The statistical variant of this attack makes heavy use of heuristics to cut down the searching space from an NP-complete space to some fixed constant. Given, the attacker knows the number of a user's peer partners, m, he can build a fixed set of most probable solutions to this problem and tests them for validity. If only a single solution suffices the condition, namely to be a hitting set for the observations made, it is most likely the set of peer partners. Note that due to the heuristic approach, the solution is also prone to some error probability.

In our paper we use these attacks to show the probability that, given a passive adversary with the ability to observe the respective anonymity sets, an existing anonymity system can be broken. This applies to all implemented anonymity systems, as e.g. JAP[BFK00] or Mixminion[DDM03].

4 Experimental Environment

To evaluate the attacks, presented in Section 3, under realistic conditions either traffic of real users or appropriate log-files of user traffic has to be used for the attacks. The data source for our experiments are log files from the RWTH Aachen web proxy server that relays large parts of the outgoing traffic. The proxy is used by CIP-pool terminals, researchers, student dormitories, dial-in users and even by other universities (e.g. University of Cologne). As many users are hidden behind different network address translation gateways, many source IPs do not identify a single person but rather an abstract entity accessing webpages. We call these compound users.

The files contain nearly two million entries per day during the semester. To be usable for our experiments, these logs had to be preprocessed to emulate the behavior of a large scale anonymizing network. However, first we stripped off all information from the log entries except for the sender and the receiver of the log files, to simplify the further processing.

A large problem that was encountered is that some popular websites have multiple names and IP-addresses for load-balancing purposes. E.g. *www1.gmx.net* and *www2.gmx.net* are both webservers of the same email service. This increases the number of a user's peer hosts, but not the number of his peer partners. The mapping of different URLs back to one provider was done by comparing the server name with DNS entries.

Another problem came from the large compound sources, as the University of Cologne, that hide many users behind one IP. To cast a more realistic image, we excluded the largest of them in some experiments. It also showed that the results of the experiments varied largely depending on the user. To get a better understanding of the results, the participating entities were classified. This was done using a hierarchical cluster analysis for the users in the two-dimensional space defined by the properties *number of requests* and *number of peer partners*. The analysis was refined subsequently until the grouping that can be seen in Figure 2 was obtained.

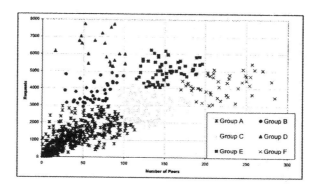

Fig. 2. Grouping of Victims according to their access habits.

In a further preprocessing step the operation of a mix was simulated using the log data. More precisely the anonymity sets that a global observer would see are generated. This is done by creating one batch for each user request and joining it with the $b_0 - 1$ requests that follow in the log file. The real peer partners for the specific target are saved in a separate file.

For each user, we fixed the time of the attack to seven days and ran our analysis on the resulting set of observations. This was done for four different weeks to get more representative results.

5   Identifying the Number of Peer Partners

In this section we show how to determine the number of a user's peer partners. The knowledge of this is a precondition to a successful run of the Disclosure Attack and the Hitting Set Attack. To this end, we make use of results that are related to the hitting set attack as presented in [KP04]. As has been shown, the breaking of an anonymity system can be solved with the help of a *minimal hitting set* problem.

An estimation of the number of a user's peer partners can be computed using a simple greedy algorithm on the associated minimal hitting set problem: the element with the highest frequency is repeatedly chosen. We call this set $\mathcal{G} = \{g_1, g_2, \ldots g_{\tilde{m}}\}$ with the size $|\mathcal{G}| = \tilde{m}$. Note that this value is larger or equal to the size of the true minimal hitting set in case the observations permit deanonymization.

The experiment was performed by taking the logging information of one week for different users. The anonymization was performed as presented in Section 4.

Interesting enough, the estimations $\tilde{m}$ were often a bit smaller than the real value m. This can be explained by the nature of the specific test procedure: we ran the tests on observations that partially did not qualify to reveal a user's peer partners to an attacker. This is because we took data from a fixed time frame, i.e. observations from the network of one week. It is thus possible that there were not enough observations to get the minimal hitting set of m.

Calculating the differences from the estimation $\tilde{m}$ and the real value m, we found that the difference grew with larger values of b, the size of the anonymity set. Thus, we tried the following formula to compensate the difference of the estimated value $\tilde{m}_u$ and the real value m_u of each user u:

$$m_u \simeq \tilde{m}_u{}^{\alpha(b)} \tag{1}$$

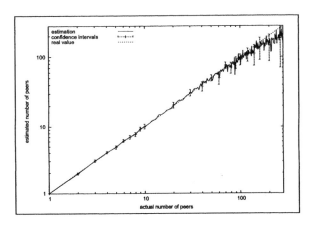

Fig. 3. Overall quality of estimating the number of a user's peer partners

The value of $\alpha(b)$ was calculated to fit best, depending on b. The resulting values can be seen in Table 1, where we show the value depending on the size of the anonymity set b.

As we estimated the parameter $\alpha(b)$ empirically on some reference data, we evaluated the resulting parameters on an independent set of data to make sure the values are generally applicable. The results of the verification are presented in Figure 3, where we display the corrected average estimation of a user's peer partners depending on the number of of peers he contacted during the time of observation. The intervals shown represent the 95% confidence intervals.

As can be clearly seen in Table 1, the corrected estimated value has an average error of less than 2.5% on all simulated systems. Still, the average deviation of the estimation can be as large as 20%. Note that the quality of the estimation, the size of the error and the deviation don't depend on the number of a user's peer partners m.

Size of anonymity set	$\alpha(b)$	average error	average deviation
5	1.03	0.33%	7.3%
10	1.06	0.35%	11.5%
15	1.09	1.10%	14.4%
20	1.11	1.64%	17.0%
25	1.13	1.27%	19.5%
30	1.15	2.14%	21.7%

Table 1. Average error on estimated number of peer partners

Given these numbers, it is safe to assume for the next sections that an attacker either knows the number of a user's peer partners or can estimate it sufficiently well to apply further methods of traffic analysis.

6 Identifying the Peer Partners

In this section we present the results that have been achieved with the three different attacks on the preprocessed proxy data.

In a first experiment the targets were chosen equally distributed from all user groups, this includes the aforementioned compound users. About 300 targets were chosen representatively out of all groups. For each selected target the traffic of a one week period was taken. His traffic was anonymized as described earlier in Section 4. The experiments have been performed for different sizes of anonymity sets b_0 and using different attacks, notably the *Disclosure Attack*, the *Statistical Disclosure Attack*, and the *Hitting Set Attack*. The results are displayed in Figure 4. A maximal batch size of 30 was chosen, as real time traffic is handled and the delays of the anonymizing infrastructure should not impose high delays. This would lead to users not using the system.

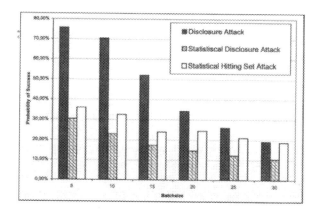

Fig. 4. Success of different attack techniques for different anonymity sets.

As can be seen the Disclosure Attack generally performs best. This is especially true for small batch sizes. However, its performance decreases rapidly with increasing batch sizes. The Statistical Disclosure Attack performs worse independent of the batch size. This shows that the approach is not that well suited for deanonymization of real data. The Statistical Hitting Set Attack performs significantly worse than the Disclosure Attack, especially for small batch sizes. But it is noteworthy that its performance does not decrease as much as the other attacks when the batch size increases. For $b = 30$ the results of the Disclosure Attack and the Hitting Set Attack are almost the same. This comes from the way the Disclosure Attack works. The training depends on m mutually disjunctive observations. However, this condition is hard to satisfy for large b_0. This problem is also known as the clique problem and is NP-complete.

In the next experiment the compound users have not been regarded as targets. This simplification is acceptable since a global observer as defined could resolve the different users who hide behind the one compound IP found in the proxy logs. In this experiment we examined, how the Disclosure Attack performs for the different user groups that have been shown in Figure 2. The anonymity sets are created as in the previous experiment. The attacks were performed on 3 different periods of the log files. Also the attack length has been varied randomly between one and four weeks. The results depending on the user category and on the batch size can be seen in Figure 5.

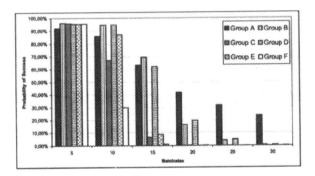

Fig. 5. Success on different types on users

Note that the general results are better than those presented in the earlier graphic. This is because compound users, which are difficult to deanonymize, have not been regarded. It can be seen that at a batch sizes of 5 the results are similarly good for all user types. The linkability of sources and targets using the Disclosure Attack can be regarded as good. In fact they reflect the image given by the simulation results of earlier publications [KAP02,KP04]. However, when batch size increases, the linkability on the real data rapidly decreases.

It is notable that the recognition rate does not decrease equally fast for all types of users. While users from the groups A, B, and D can be deanonymized moderately well at a batch size of 15, the anonymity of peers of the groups C, E, and F is protected well by the mix. As the batch size increases the members of group A are the only ones that can somewhat be deanonymized. The reason for this can be found when looking at aforementioned simulation results. In earlier simulative evaluations of Pimenidis and Penz the number of necessary observations for deanonymization increased about quadratically with the number of peers m. If a target with many different peer partners is chosen, it is likely that there are not enough observations for a successful deanonymization. As can be seen in Figure 2, the groups C, E, and F are those with a large amount of different peer partners. The groups A, B, and D are those with few different peers.

Regarding this, it still strikes that the actual results on real data are worse than those of the simulations from the initial publications [KAP02,Dan03,KP04]. As was presented earlier, the recognition errors come from the lack of observations. However, even if a high number of observations were present, the results would still stay behind those of the simulations. This is because the access frequencies to homepages vary highly. Where the experiments usually assume an equal distribution of peer frequencies, real users regularly visit some pages, while others are visited just a very few times. In the proxy logs about 60% of the pages are accessed less then 10 times by one user. But as the experiments in [KP04] show that for an m of 20 an average of 35 observations are necessary for successful deanonymization using the Disclosure Attack. So, if the last access by the user to one of those rare peers has occurred without this peer being identifiable, there will be no chance to identify him later on. To present the high variability of user access numbers, Table 2 presents the mean number of accesses for specific domains together with the average difference from these values. It can be seen that the mean difference is even larger than the mean number of accesses. This comes from the high amount of pages that are accessed very few times and from some few pages that are accessed often by a single user.

Group	A	B	C	D	E	F
Mean	35.2	72.8	17.6	67.5	32.5	20.3
Mean Diff.	41.9	92.7	19.6	86.3	38.6	22.6

Table 2. Mean and mean difference from mean of accesses to the web pages for the different types of users.

This high variance constitutes a large obstacle for the performance of the presented passive attacks on mixes as can be seen in the experimental results. Some adaption of the existing algorithms will be necessary such that these methods cope better with the tasks, for which they are designed in realistic environments.

7   Conclusions

Results from attacks on mixed real world data have been presented. For this the logs of our university's main proxy have been used. As many attacks rely on the knowledge of the number of a target's peers, a method to approximate this number has been presented and shown to work quite well. One of the results of this work is that attacks in real world environments are more difficult than in simulations. This is shown to come from the structure of real user behavior in the Internet. Real access patterns are far less regular than those usually assumed in simulations. To further analyze this, the users have been automatically clustered into different groups. It is shown that users with few different peers can be attacked relatively successfully. To provide this group with adequate protection batch sizes significantly larger than 30 are necessary, whereas the identification of the other users peers was only successful in less than 1% of the experiments with a batch size of 30.

In future we plan to refine our models of user behavior. From this more effective attack and protection mechanisms should be developed. One possibility for attacks could be approximative algorithms that are specifically designed for different kinds of IP traffic. Furthermore we plan to develop traffic models that imitate the user behavior the best possible. The results from Section 6 also suggest that low overhead dummy traffic methods can be created to effectively increase the protection of user against strong attackers.

Acknowledgements: Thanks to Oliver Rattay for providing us with very useful feedback and information. This work took great advantage of his extensive analysis.

References

[BFK00]   Oliver Berthold, Hannes Federrath, and Stefan Köpsell. Web MIXes: A system for anonymous and unobservable Internet access. In H. Federrath, editor, *Proceedings of Designing Privacy Enhancing Technologies: Workshop on Design Issues in Anonymity and Unobservability*, pages 115–129. Springer-Verlag, LNCS 2009, July 2000.

[Cha81]   David L. Chaum. Untraceable Electronic Mail, Return Addresses, and Digital Pseudonyms. *Communications of the ACM*, 24(2):84 – 88, Feb 1981.

[Dan03]   George Danezis. Statistical disclosure attacks: Traffic confirmation in open environments. In Gritzalis, Vimercati, Samarati, and Katsikas, editors, *Proceedings of Security and Privacy in the Age of Uncertainty, (SEC2003)*, pages 421–426, Athens, May 2003. IFIP TC11, Kluwer.

[Dan04]   George Danezis. The traffic analysis of continuous-time mixes. In David Martin and Andrei Serjantov, editors, *Privacy Enhancing Technologies (PET 2004)*, May 2004.

[DDM03]   George Danezis, Roger Dingledine, and Nick Mathewson. Mixminion: Design of a Type III Anonymous Remailer Protocol. In *Proceedings of the 2003 IEEE Symposium on Security and Privacy*, May 2003.

[DS04]   George Danezis and Andrei Serjantov. Statistical Disclosure or Intersection Attacks on Anonymity Systems. Proceedings of the 6th Information Hiding Workshop (IH2004), LNCS, Toronto, 2004.

[DSD04]   Claudia Díaz, Len Sassaman, and Evelyne Dewitte. Comparison between two practical mix designs. In *Proceedings of 9th European Symposium on Research in Computer Security (ESORICS)*, LNCS, France, September 2004.

[KAP02]   Dogan Kesdogan, Dakshi Agrawal, and Stefan Penz. Limits of Anonymity in Open Environments. In *Information Hiding, 5th International Workshop*. Springer Verlag, 2002.

[KEB98]   Dogan Kesdogan, Jan Egner, and Roland Büschkes. Stop-and-Go-Mixes Providing Anonymity in an Open System. In D. Aucsmith, editor, *Information Hiding 98 - Second International Workshop*, pages 83 – 98. Springer Verlag, 1998.

[KP04]   Dogan Kesdogan and Lexi Pimenidis. The Hitting Set Attack on Anonymity Protocols. In *Proceedings of Information Hiding, 7th International Workshop*. Springer Verlag, 2004.

[LRWW04]   Brian N. Levine, Michael K. Reiter, Chenxi Wang, and Matthew K. Wright. Timing attacks in low-latency mix-based systems. In Ari Juels, editor, *Proceedings of Financial Cryptography (FC '04)*. Springer-Verlag, LNCS 3110, February 2004.

[MD04]   Nick Mathewson and Roger Dingledine. Practical traffic analysis: Extending and resisting statistical disclosure. In *Proceedings of Privacy Enhancing Technologies workshop (PET 2004)*, LNCS, May 2004.

[MD05]   Steven J. Murdoch and George Danezis. Low-cost Traffic Analysis of Tor. Oakland, California, USA, May 2005. IEEE Symposium on Security and Privacy.

[Pfi90]   A. Pfitzmann. Dienstintegrierende Kommunikationsnetze mit teilnehmerüberprüfbarem Datenschutz. IFB 234, Springer-Verlag, Heidelberg 1990, 1990. (in German).

[PP90]   B. Pfitzmann and A. Pfitzmann. How to break the direct rsa-implementation of mixes. pages 373 – 381. Eurocrypt '89, LNCS 434. Springer-Verlag, Berlin, 1990.

[Rat04]   Oliver Rattay. *Sicherheitsbewertung von Anonymisierungsverfahren im World Wide Web (in german)*. Diploma thesis, Lehrstuhl für Informatik IV, RWTH Aachen, Germany, September 2004.

[Ray01]   Jean-François Raymond. Traffic analysis: Protocols, attacks, design issues and open problems. In H. Federrath, editor, *Designing Privacy Enhancing Technologies: Proceedings of International Workshop on Design Issues in Anonymity and Unobservability*, volume 2009 of *LNCS*, pages 10–29. Springer-Verlag, 2001.

[RP02]   Marc Rennhard and Bernhard Plattner. Introducing MorphMix: Peer-to-Peer based Anonymous Internet Usage with Collusion Detection. In *Proceedings of the Workshop on Privacy in the Electronic Society (WPES 2002)*, Washington, DC, USA, November 2002.

[SS03]   Andrei Serjantov and Peter Sewell. Passive attack analysis for connection-based anonymity systems. In *Proceedings of ESORICS 2003: European Symposium on Research in Computer Security (Gjøvik), LNCS 2808*, pages 116–131, October 2003.

Using Guesswork as a Measure for Confidentiality of Selectively Encrypted Messages

Reine Lundin, Stefan Lindskog, Anna Brunstrom, and Simone Fischer-Hübner

Department of Computer Science
Karlstad University, Sweden
{Reine.Lundin,Stefan.Lindskog,Anna.Brunstrom,
Simone.Fischer-Huebner}@kau.se

Abstract. In this paper, we start to investigate the security implications of selective encryption. We do this by using the measure guesswork, which gives us the expected number of guesses that an attacker must perform in an optimal brute force attack to reveal an encrypted message. The characteristics of the proposed measure are investigated for zero-order languages. We also introduce the concept of reduction chains to describe how the message (or rather search) space changes for an attacker with different levels of encryption.

1 Introduction

Security has traditionally been thought of as a system or network attribute that is the result of the joint endeavors of the designers, maintainers, and users, among others. Even though security would never reach a 100% level, the aim was typically as much security as possible, given the actual boundary conditions. With the advent of, e.g., many low-power computing and communication devices it has become desirable to trade security against other system parameters, such as performance and energy consumption. Thus, in many situations, tunable or selectable security, rather than maximum security, is desirable.

Today's standard and widely used encryption algorithms (RSA and AES) are assumed to be almost impossible to break with the remark that we in the future could discover existing flaws in the algorithms. Hence the only (simple) way to attack messages encrypted with those algorithms is to use a brute force attack on the key space. Furthermore, if the key space is larger than 128 bits for the AES encryption algorithm and 1024 bits for the RSA encryption algorithm, we today consider encrypted messages to be computationally secure. That is, the cost of breaking encrypted messages exceeds the value or the useful lifetime of the encrypted information. The question that now arises is: Using selective encryption, how much and which parts of a message can we leave unencrypted and still have a message space that is harder to perform a brute force attack on than the corresponding key space? If we can find an answer to the question above, then it is possible to find out how to selectively encrypt messages while still making them computationally secure.

In this paper, we start to investigate the answer to the question above by adopting the measure guesswork, so that it can also be used for selective encryption. This is done by using simple artificial languages and the concept of reduction chains, which describes how the message (search) space changes for the attacker with different levels of encryption.

The remainder of the paper is organized as follows. In Section 2 we give a note on measures in computer security. In Section 3 we present the general model of selective encryption and give examples of previous work in the area and investigate application scenarios where selective encryption could be used to gain performance. In Section 4 we investigate the measure guesswork, how it can be transformed for selective encryption and introduce the concept of reduction chains. Finally, in Section 5 we discuss conclusions and future work.

2   A Note on Security Measures

Computer security is traditionally and most frequently defined by the three attributes: confidentiality, integrity, and availability. These are often collectively known as the "CIA" [22]. Confidentiality is the prevention of unauthorized disclosure of information, integrity is the prevention of unauthorized modification of information, and availability is the prevention of unauthorized withholding of information or resources.

Recently, there has been an interest in using probabilistic methods for quantifying operational security. A promising attempt to quantify security is described in [14], in which game theory is used as a method for modeling and computing the probabilities of expected behaviors of attackers. A game theoretical method is also used in [8] to analyze the security of computer networks. Although not pursued in this paper, we also believe that it might be possible to use game theory as a confidentiality measure for selective encryption.

A key problem with security is that it is hard to quantify. Today, neither security nor its attributes are easily measurable. An alternative is to define indirect measures that can be used as an approximation for security or one of its attributes. Examples of indirect measures for confidentiality of encrypted messages are entropy, unicity distance and guesswork. Entropy is the classical measure of uncertainty that originally was suggested by Shannon [16]. He defined it as the average amount of information from a random variable. The higher the entropy of a random variable is, the harder it is to guess or be certain about its value on the average. The highest value of the entropy is obtained when the variable has a uniform distribution. In [16] Shannon also used entropy to define the concept of unicity distance. The unicity distance approximates the minimum amount of cipher text needed for which it is reasonably likely that there is only one meaningful decryption. Hence, cipher texts that are (much) shorter than the unicity distance are assumed to have a higher level of confidentiality, since it is more likely that they could have several meaningful decryptions. Guesswork [12], on the other hand, measures the expected number of guesses that an attacker must perform in an optimal brute force attack to reveal an encrypted message. In [12], the author also show that entropy is inappropriate as a measure of work in cipher attacks, due to the asymptotic equipartition property. In this paper, we hence propose the use of guesswork as a confidentiality measure for selective encryption.

3 Selective Encryption

In this section we describe the general model of selective encryption and define the encryption level, the amount of selectively encrypted data in a message. We also present examples of previous work in the area and give examples of two application scenarios where selective encryption can be used to gain performance or lower energy consumption.

3.1 General Model

For selective encryption the idea is to only encrypt chosen units of a message while leaving the remaining units unencrypted or encrypted with a weaker encryption algorithm. We assume, in this paper, that the units are equally sized and that the remaining units are unencrypted. In Fig. 1, we show a selectively encrypted message M having five encrypted units (gray) and three unencrypted units (white).

Fig. 1. Example of a selectively encrypted message.

The fraction of encrypted units in a message naturally defines the encryption level, how much of the message is encrypted, as follows.

Definition 1. *Let M be a selectively encrypted message, consisting of n equally sized units. Then the encryption level, EL of M, is defined as the ratio*

$$EL = \frac{n_e}{n} \qquad (1)$$

where n_e is the number of encrypted units in M.

Since the number of encrypted units satisfy the inequality $0 \leq n_e \leq n$, we always have that $0 \leq EL \leq 1$. Note that definition 1 also works for units of unequal size, if the number n_e (and n) is transformed to an appropriate smaller quantity, for example bytes or bits.

3.2   Previous Work on Selective Encryption

The concept of selective encryption was independently introduced by Spanos and Maples [19], Li et al. [5], and Meyer and Gadegast [9] in 1995 and 1996 for the purpose of reducing the amount of encrypted MPEG data in a video sequence while at the same time providing an acceptable security level. Spanos and Maples proposed that only the I-frames in an MPEG video stream need to be encrypted. Li et al. proposed a protection hierarchy that allows the choice of encrypting (1) only I-frames, (2) I- and P-frames, or (3) all I-, B-, and P-frames in any video sequence. Meyer and Gadegast proposed four levels of encryption—from header only encryption to complete encryption. Selective encryption methods for MPEG video are presented and discussed in [1, 4, 17, 21]. In addition, Sony recently announced that they use a scalable approach based on selective encryption in their Passage technology [18] aimed for digital CATV networks.

Selective encryption has also been used to protect image data. In [13], a selective bit plane encryption is proposed for JPEG images. The authors claim that encrypting the most significant bit plane only is not sufficiently secure. However, they show that a sufficient confidentiality level could in many cases be achieved by encrypting only two bit planes, whereas encrypting four bit planes provides a high degree of confidentiality. Two types of simple cipher-only attacks are used to assess this. The first attack is referred to as a replacement attack and the second to as a reconstruction attack. In the case of the replacement attack, a constant value was used to replace the encrypted data. The idea of the reconstruction attack, on the other hand, is to reconstruct data with the aid of the unencrypted remaining data.

Van Droogenbroeck and Benedett [2] suggest two different methods for selectively encrypting compressed and uncompressed images. In [15], Servetti and De Martin propose a selective encryption scheme for speech compressed with the ITU-T G.729 8 kb/s speech encoding standard. The authors claim that their scheme offers effective content protection and can also easily be adapted to other speech coding standards. Goodman and Chandrakasan [3] propose a scalable encryption scheme intended to maximize the battery lifetime of a wireless video camera. Their scheme is based on a stream cipher that allows varying levels of encryption for data streams with varying priorities.

Recently, a generic SCTP-based tunable encryption service which uses a selective encryption approach that can be used on different contents and by various applications is suggested in [6]. The aim of the service is to protect data transfers in networking environments, by offering various encryption levels that can be tuned and controlled by applications. Support for selective encryption has also recently been integrated directly into several multimedia applications, e.g., Nautilus [11] and Speak Freely [20].

Note that all references given above are mainly focused on performance issues when using selective encryption. The security implications are either only briefly mentioned or analyzed in a very rudimentary way, such as in [13]. Our purpose with this paper is therefore to investigate the security implication of selectively encrypted messages using a generic approach.

3.3   Application Scenarios

A key issue for selective encryption is typically to reduce the computational overhead produced by encryption and decryption of messages. Selective encryption is thus especially suitable for multimedia applications in which a large amount of data is transferred with soft real-time requirements, such as video on demand (VoD), video conferencing, and live pay-per-view (PPV) TV. Furthermore, in both current and future networking environments heterogeneous devices with varying computational resources are used. Some devices, such as servers and desktop computers, are often very powerful, while others, such as various types of hand-held devices, have limited processing power and memory, limited batteries, etc. Thus, since encryption puts a heavy burden on the processor it has become desirable to trade security against other parameters such as latency, throughput, and energy consumption.

As pointed out by Lookabaugh and Sicker [7], selective encryption can also be used to enable new system functionality. Imagine for example a live PPV event that should be accessible by heterogeneous terminals with two different encryption systems based on different encryption algorithms, e.g., DES and AES. Every piece of data must then be encrypted and transferred twice. However, encrypting only parts of the data, say 20%, and leaving the rest unencrypted implies that 80% of the data is common for all devices independently of which encryption system they use. As compared to fully encrypting two streams, this will result in a 40% bandwidth reduction and an 80% computational reduction for encryption at the sender. At the receiver side, an 80% computational reduction for decryption will be achieved at each receiver.

4   Guesswork as a Measure of Confidentiality

In this section, we first present the assumptions on the attacker's environment. Then we examine some properties of languages and describe the concept of guesswork, which is a measure telling us how many guesses an attacker, using an optimal strategy in a brute force attack must do on average to find the correct message. For a more comprehensive and detailed discussion on guesswork see [12]. Finally, we investigate how guesswork can be adopted to also include selective encryption and examine some of its properties and security implications for zero-order languages.

4.1 Scope

In the following we assume that the attacker performs an optimal brute force attack on the message space, and not on the key space as is usually done. An optimal brute force attack, in this context, means that the attacker is supposed to know the probability distribution of the message space and can hence guess at messages in nonincreasing probability order starting with the most probable message. We will later define this in a more formal way. It is also best to assume that the attacker has complete knowledge of the size of the encrypted part of the selectively encrypted message, since this restricts the size of the message space. Furthermore we assume that the attacker knows when the correct message is found in the guessing process of the attack.

4.2 Languages

Let Σ be our alphabet, which is a finite nonempty set of symbols. Then a message or string M over Σ is a finite sequence of symbols drawn from that alphabet, with size

$|M| \in \mathbb{N}$. The set of all messages over an alphabet Σ is called the transitive closure and is denoted Σ^*. Every set $L \subset \Sigma^*$ is called a language and hence, by definition Σ^* is also a language, the largest language with respect to the alphabet Σ.

When an attacker knows the language L of a message $M \in L$ he will reduce his message (search) space from Σ^* to L, and we write this as $\Sigma^* \rightarrow L$. If he also knows the size of the message he will even further reduce his message space. To describe this reduction we will use the concept of n-languages, which are defined as follows.

Definition 2. *Let L be a language, then the set*

$$L^n = \{M \in L; |M| = n\} \tag{2}$$

is called a n-language.

The transitive closure of an n-language will be denoted Σ^n. From definition 2 we immediately see that $L^n \subset L$ since if $M \in L^n$ then $M \in L$, hence all n-languages are also languages. We also have that a language is the union of its n-languages

$$L = \bigcup_{n=0}^{k} L^n \tag{3}$$

where k is an arbitrary large nonnegative integer. Furthermore, since we have that $L^i \cap L^j = \emptyset$ if $i \neq j$, the size of a language, which is the number of strings in the language, is the sum of the sizes of its n-languages.

$$|L| = \sum_{n=0}^{k} |L^n| \tag{4}$$

For example, suppose that we have the alphabet $\Sigma = \{A, B\}$ and the language $L = \{\epsilon, A, B, A^2, B^2, \ldots, A^k, B^k\}$ constructed from messages that only contain the same symbols, where ϵ is the empty message. Then the n-languages are $L^0 = \{\epsilon\}$, $L^1 = \{A, B\}$, $L^2 = \{A^2, B^2\}$, $\ldots$, $L^k = \{A^k, B^k\}$ and hence we see that the n-languages are disjoint and that the union of them construct the entire language according to (3). From (4) we get that $|L| = 1 + 2k$.

To describe in a formal way the reduction of the message space for the attacker, let u be the size of the equally sized units of a message. Then the size of the encrypted part of the message is $n_e u$ and the attacker's message space changes with the number of encrypted units[1] as $L^{|M|} \rightarrow L^{n_e u}$. From this, we can now define the reduction chain R of selectively encrypted messages as follows.

Definition 3. *Let L be a language, n_e the number of encrypted units and u the size of the equally sized units of a selectively encrypted message. Then a reduction chain R is defined as follows*

$$R = L^{nu} \rightarrow L^{(n-1)u} \rightarrow \ldots \rightarrow L^u \rightarrow L^0 \tag{5}$$

---

[1] Omitting the order of languages, which make it possible to penetrate into encrypted units and even more reduce the message space.

Note, that for a given message there often exist several reduction chains from $L^{|M|} \rightarrow L^0$ depending on the distribution of the encrypted units. For example, a message of size two units will give rise to two reduction chains since an encryption level of 50% includes two possibilities, encrypting the first unit or encrypting the second unit.

A language L (or L^n) can be approximated by simpler artificial languages L_ω [16], where ω denotes the order of the approximation. The basic idea is shown in the following list.

1. L_0, zero-order approximation, symbols are independent and equally probable.

2. L_1, first-order approximation, symbols are independent but with probabilities as in L.

3. L_2, second-order approximation, symbols are dependent on one preceding symbol (digrams) as in L.

4. L_3, third-order approximation, symbols are dependent on two preceding symbols (trigrams) as in L.

The essential thing here is that symbols in a language normally have different probabilities and that they often depend on each other. Thus messages in a language will also occur with different probabilities, a property which we shall use in the next section. An exception occurs for the zero-order languages where all messages have equal probability. For example, the language Σ_0^2 with $\Sigma = \{A, B\}$ consist of four strings AA, AB, BA and BB, each with probability $\frac{1}{4}$.

4.3   Guesswork and α-work-factor

Let x be an L-valued random variable with probability distribution p. That is, the variable x attains messages in L with probability $p(x)$. We may then arrange the messages in L in a nonincreasing order according to p as

$$p_1 \geq p_2 \geq \ldots \geq p_{|L|} \qquad (6)$$

where $p_i = p(x_i)$ is the probability of message i. For example, if we have the language

Σ_1^2 with $p(A) = \frac{1}{3}$ and $p(B) = \frac{2}{3}$, then $p(AA) = \frac{1}{9}$, $p(AB) = p(BA) = \frac{2}{9}$ and $p(BB) = \frac{4}{9}$. Hence, the order of the messages will be BB, AB, BA and AA, where the order of AB and BA is irrelevant.

We order the messages in this way since it is best to assume that an attacker conducting a brute force attack has complete knowledge of the distribution p. This means that an attacker can arrange the messages according to (6) and start testing them in a nonincreasing order. The crack package [10] for UNIX passwords orders the passwords in a similar way.

The expected number of guesses (work) an adversary must do to discover the value of an L-valued random variable x is called the guesswork of x (see [12]).

Definition 4. *Let x be an L-valued random variable whose probabilities are arranged according to (6). Then the guesswork is defined as*

$$W(x) = \sum_{i=1}^{|L|} i p_i \tag{7}$$

By using the fact that the guesswork can be seen as a sum of rectangular areas with base p_i and height i, we now create a step function called the α-work-factor to describe how $W(x)$ changes with p_i (see [12]).

Definition 5. *Let x be an L-valued random variable whose probabilities are arranged according to (6). Then the α-work-factor is defined as*

$$wf_\alpha(x) = min\left\{ k; \sum_{i=1}^{k} p_i \geq \alpha \right\} \tag{8}$$

That is, the α-work-factor tells us how many guesses or how much work an adversary must do to be certain within probability α to discover the value of x. Note that if $\alpha = 1$ then $wf_\alpha(x) = |L|$, the whole language (message space).

Suppose we have the language Σ_1^1, with $p(A) = 0.75$ and $p(B) = 0.25$. Then the guesswork W(x) = p(A)+2p(B) = 1.25 and the corresponding α-work-factor is plotted in Fig. 2. Note that the guesswork is equal to the area below the α-work-factor function.

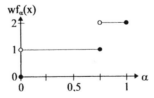

Fig. 2. α-work-factor when $p(A) = 0.75$ and $p(B) = 0.25$.

Since $wf_\alpha(x)$ is by definition the step function to $W(x)$ we have

$$W(x) = \int_0^1 wf_\alpha(x) d\alpha \tag{9}$$

4.4   Measure for Confidentiality

To find a measure of confidentiality for selectively encrypted messages, we start by investigating how the guesswork changes for the reduction chain $R = \Sigma_0^n \rightarrow \Sigma_0^{(n-1)} \rightarrow \cdots \rightarrow \Sigma_0^1 \rightarrow \Sigma_0^0$. That is, we examine how the guesswork changes with the number of encrypted units for the zero-order languages, when the unit size is one.

In Fig. 3 we have plotted the α-work-factor for the reducing chain $\Sigma_0^2 \rightarrow \Sigma_0^1 \rightarrow \Sigma_0^0$. Note that, since the area below the α-work-factor function represents the guesswork we also see how the guesswork changes with the number of encrypted units; $W(x) = \frac{5}{2}$ when $n_e = 2$, $W(x) = \frac{3}{2}$ when $n_e = 1$ and $W(x) = 1$ when $n_e = 0$.

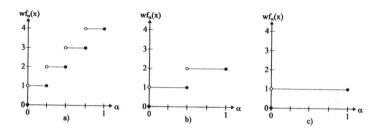

Fig. 3. α-work-factor for reduction chain $\Sigma_0^2 \rightarrow \Sigma_0^1 \rightarrow \Sigma_0^0$.

To easily calculate the guesswork for the zero-order languages, note that the number of strings in $\Sigma_0^{n_e}$ are $|\Sigma|^{n_e}$ and that each string occur with probability $|\Sigma|^{-n_e}$, thus we get

$$W_{n_e}(x) = \sum_{i=1}^{|\Sigma|^{n_e}} i|\Sigma|^{-n_e} \qquad (10)$$
$$= \frac{|\Sigma|^{n_e} + 1}{2}$$

We use the subscript n_e since it is a parameter affecting the guesswork.

By simple calculus it is easy to show that the function 10 is an increasing function by the number of encrypted units.

$$W_{n_e+1}(x) - W_{n_e}(x) = \frac{|\Sigma|^{n_e+1} + 1}{2} - \frac{|\Sigma|^{n_e} + 1}{2} \qquad (11)$$
$$= \frac{|\Sigma|^{n_e}(|\Sigma| - 1)}{2}$$

Hence, since $|\Sigma| > 0$ the statement holds.

To illustrate the asymptotic behaviour of (10), we have in Fig. 4 plotted the $\log_2$ of the function as stars when $|\Sigma| = 2$. The base of the logarithm is taken to be two since this gives us the doubling rate between two adjacent integers. The two continuous lines, which in reality should be plotted as points, show the $\log_2$ of the corresponding α-work-factor functions $wf_{0.5}(x)$, the lower line, and $wf_1(x)$, the upper line. They represents the number of trials an attacker must do to be certain within 50% and 100% to discover the correct message. More generally, the attacker must perform $wf_\alpha(x) = \lceil \alpha |\Sigma|^{n_e} \rceil$ guesses to be certain within probability α to discover the correct message.

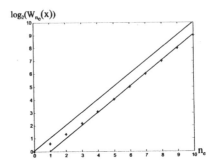

$\log_2(W_{n_e}(x))$

Fig. 4. $\log_2(W_{n_e}(x))$ when $|\Sigma| = 2$, including $\log_2(wf_{0.5}(x))$ and $\log_2(wf_1(x))$.

From Fig. 4 we also see that it looks like the function $\log_2(W_{n_e}(x))$ asymptotically narrows the function $\log_2(wf_{0.5}(x))$, as the number of encrypted units increases. To show the asymptotic behavior we calculate the limit of the difference between the two functions.

$$\lim_{n_e \to \infty} |\log_2(W_{n_e}(x)) - \log_2(wf_\alpha(x))| = \lim_{n_e \to \infty} \left| \log_2 \frac{|\Sigma|^{n_e} + 1}{2 \lceil \alpha |\Sigma|^{n_e} \rceil} \right| \quad (12)$$

$$= \log_2 \frac{1}{2\alpha}$$

Thus if $\alpha = 0.5$ the limit is zero and hence $\log_2(W_{n_e}(x)) \to \log_2(wf_{0.5}(x))$ when $n_e \to \infty$. The interpretation of this, is that for zero-order languages the expected number of guesses needed to discover the secret message tends to one half the size of the message space as the number of encrypted units increases, which is as expected.

Since (10) is also dependent on the number of symbols in the language, we have in Fig. 5 plotted the log_2 of it, when $|\Sigma| = 2$, $|\Sigma| = 4$ and $|\Sigma| = 8$. Two curves $W_{n1_e}(x) = \frac{|\Sigma_1|^{n1_e}+1}{2}$ and $W_{n2_e}(x) = \frac{|\Sigma_2|^{n2_e}+1}{2}$ will thus end up with the same value of the guesswork if $|\Sigma_1|^{n1_e} = |\Sigma_2|^{n2_e}$. Hence, by comparing the value of the guesswork for the key space (uniform distribution) with key length k bits and the message spaces of zero-order, we get that the message spaces are harder to break according to the guesswork if $2^k \le |\Sigma|^{n_e}$.

5   Conclusions and Future Work

By using the measure guesswork, we have in this paper started to investigate the security implications of using selective encryption. We have for zero-order languages investigated some properties of the measure and identified when the message space is harder to break than the key space, using an optimal brute force attack.

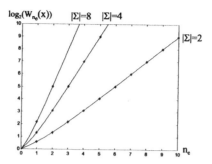

Fig. 5. $\log_2(W_{n_e}(x))$ when $|\Sigma| = 2$, $|\Sigma| = 4$ and $|\Sigma| = 8$.

Until now we have only investigated how the guesswork behaves for selective encryption of zero-order languages. To understand the full impact of the security implications of selective encryption, higher order languages must be studied. When using higher order languages the size and distribution of the encrypted units will also become important. The presented theory does not include entropy. The relation between entropy and guesswork for different orders of languages is something we will also investigate in our future work.

References

1. H. Cheng and X. Li. Partial encryption of compressed images and videos. *IEEE Transactions in Signal Processing*, 48(8):2439–2451, August 2000.
2. M. Van Droogenbroeck and R. Benedett. Techniques for a selective encryption of uncompressed and compressed images. In *Proceedings of Advanced Concepts for Intelligent Vision Systems (ACIVS'02)*, pages 90–97, Ghent, Belgium, September 9–11, 2002.
3. J. Goodman and A. P. Chandrakasan. Low power scalable encryption for wireless systems. *Wireless Networks*, 4(1):55–70, 1998.
4. T. Kunkelmann and U. Horn. Video encryption based on data partitioning and scalable coding: A comparison. In T. Plagemann and V. Goebel, editors, *Proceedings of the 5th Interactive Distributed Multimedia Systems and Telecommunication Services (IDMS'98)*, volume 1483 of *Lecture Notes in Computer Science*, pages 95–106, Oslo, Norway, September 8–11, 1998. Springer-Verlag.
5. Y. Li, Z. Chen, S. M. Tan, and R. H. Campbell. Security enhanced MPEG player. In *Proceedings of the 1996 International Workshop on Multimedia Software Development (MMSD'96)*, pages 169–176, Berlin, Germany, March 25–26 1996.
6. S. Lindskog and A. Brunstrom. Design and implementation of a tunable encryption service for networked applications. In *Proceedings of the First IEEE/CREATE-NET Workshop on Security and QoS in Communications Networks (SecQoS 2005)*, September 9, 2005. To appear.
7. T. Lookabaugh and D. C. Sicker. Selective encryption for consumer applications. *IEEE Communications Magazine*, 42(5):124–129, May 2004.
8. K.-w. Lye and J. Wing. Game strategies in network security. In *Proceedings of Foundations of Computer Security*, Copenhagen, Denmark, July 25–26, 2002.

9. J. Meyer and F. Gadegast. Security mechanisms for multimedia data with the example MPEG-I video, 1995. http://www.gadegast.de/frank/doc/secmeng.pdf.

10. Alec D. E. Muffett. Crack: A sensible password checker for UNIX, 1992.

11. Nautilus secure phone homepage. http://nautilus.berlios.de/, June 9, 2004.

12. J. O. Pliam. *Ciphers and their Products: Group Theory in Private Key Cryptography*. PhD thesis, University of Minnesota, Minnesota, USA, 1999.

13. M. Podesser, H. P. Schmidt, and A. Uhl. Selective bitplane encryption for secure transmission of image data in mobile environments. In *Proceedings of the 5th IEEE Nordic Signal Processing Symposium (NORSIG '02)*, Tromsø/Trondheim, Norway, October 4–6, 2002.

14. K. Sallhammar and S. J. Knapskog. Using game theory in stochastic models for quantifying security. In *Proceedings of the Ninth Nordic Workshop on Secure IT Systems (NordSec 2004)*, Espoo, Finland, November 4–5, 2004.

15. A. Servetti and J. C. De Martin. Perception-based selective encryption of G.729 speech. In *Proceedings of the 2002 IEEE Internatinal Conference on Acoustics, Speech, and Signal Processing*, volume 1, pages 621–624, Orlando, Florida, USA, May 13–17, 2002.

16. C. E. Shannon. Communication theory of secrecy systems. *Bell Systems Technical Journal*, 28:656–715, October 1949.

17. C. Shi and B. Bhargava. An efficient MPEG video encryption algorithm. In *Proceedings of the Workshop on Security in Large-Scale Distributed Systems*, pages 381–386, West Lafayette, Indiana, USA, October 20–22, 1998.

18. Sony Electronics. Passage: Freedom to choose, February 10 2003. http://www.sonypassage.com/features.htm.

19. G. A. Spanos and T. B. Maples. Performance study of a selective encryption scheme for security of networked, real-time video. In *Proceedings of the 4th International Conference on Computer Communications and Networks (ICCCN '95)*, pages 72–78, Las Vegas, Nevada, USA, September 1995.

20. Speak Freely homepage. http://www.speakfreely.org/, June 9, 2004.

21. L. Tang. Methods for encrypting and decrypting MPEG video data efficiently. In *Proceedings of the ACM Multimedia 1996*, pages 219–229, Boston, Massachusetts, USA, November 1996.

22. U.S. Department of Defense. Trusted computer system evaluation criteria (TCSEC). DoD 5200.28-STD, December 1985.

Measuring Inference Exposure in Outsourced Encrypted Databases

E. Damiani, S. De Capitani di Vimercati, S. Foresti, P. Samarati, M. Viviani

Università deli Studi di Milano
Dipartimento di Technologie dell'Informazione
Via Bramante, 65 – 26013 Crema (CR) – Italia
{damiani,decapita,foresti,samarati,viviani}@dti.unimi.it

Abstract. Database outsourcing is becoming increasingly popular introducing a new paradigm, called *database-as-a-service*, where an encrypted client's database is stored at an external service provider. Existing proposals for querying encrypted databases are based on the association, with each encrypted tuple, of additional indexing information obtained from the plaintext values of attributes that can be used in the queries. However, the relationship between indexes and data should not open the door to inference and linking attacks that can compromise the protection granted by encryption.

In this paper, we present a simple yet robust indexing technique and investigate quantitative measures to model inference exposure. We present different techniques to compute an aggregate measure from the inference exposure associated with each single index. Our approach can take into account the importance of plaintext attributes associated with indexes and/or can allow the user to weight the inference exposure values supplied in relation to their relative ordering.

1 Introduction

In most organizations databases hold sensitive information that has to be protected from unauthorized accesses. As the size of these databases is increasing very quickly, organizations may choose to add data storage to their systems at a high rate or to outsource data to external providers. The main advantage of outsourcing is related to the costs of in-house versus outsourced hosting: outsourcing provides significant cost savings and service benefits, and promises higher availability and more effective disaster protection than in-house operations. However, database outsourcing is not free from problems: since sensitive data are not under the direct control of their owner, data confidentiality and even integrity may be put at risk. These problems are traditionally addressed by means of encryption [5]. By encrypting the information, the client is guaranteed that it alone can access the data. However, since decryption must be executed only client-side for security reasons, the remote DBMS cannot execute any query because it has not access to plaintext data. Therefore, the whole relation involved in a query would be sent back to the client for query execution, thus nullifying the advantages of outsourcing.

A first proposal toward the solution of this problem was presented in [3, 4, 9–11] where the authors proposed storing, together with the encrypted database, additional indexing information. The scenario just described, called *database-as-a-service* (DAS), involves mainly three entities (see Figure 1):

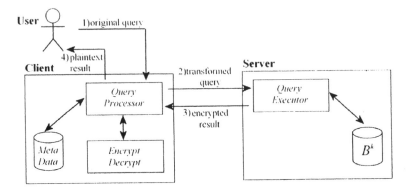

Fig. 1. DAS Scenario

- *User*: human entity that presents requests (queries) to the system (1);
- *Client*: front-end that transforms the user queries into queries on the encrypted data stored on the server (2) and decrypts the result of a query (4);
- *Server*: an organization that receives the encrypted data from a data owner, executes queries submitted by clients, and returns the encrypted results to them (3).

Two conflicting requirements need to be taken into consideration in the index construction: on one side, the indexing information should be related with the data well enough to provide for an effective query execution mechanism; on the other side, the relationship between indexes and data should not open the door to inference and linking attacks that can compromise the protection granted by encryption [6]. To balance query execution efficiency and data protection from inference, it is important to provide indexing techniques able to balance these two requirements.

In this paper, after a brief explanation of data organization in the DAS scenario, we investigate quantitative measures to model inference exposure. We present different techniques to compute an aggregate measure from the inference exposure associated with each single index. The proposed techniques allow us to compute the inference exposure associated with a whole relation. The remainder of this paper is organized as follows. Section 2 describes the DAS scenario. Section 3 describes the abstract models used to compute the exposure coefficient in different scenarios. Section 4 illustrates different aggregation operators that can be used to combine the exposure coefficients associated with single indexes. Finally, Section 5 concludes the paper.

2 Data Organization

We consider a relational DBMS where data are organized in relations (e.g., see relation Employees in Figure 2(a)); the underlined attributes represent the primary key of the

Employees

Id	Name	Age	Marital Status	Job
A1	Alice	30	Married	Manager
A2	Bob	26	Married	Director
B1	Alice	30	Married	Employee
B3	Carol	26	Single	Manager
B2	David	21	Single	Employee
A3	Alice	40	Divorced	Employee
B4	Bob	30	Single	Manager

(a)

Employees^k

Count	Etuple	I_1	I_2	I_3	I_4	I_5
1	r*tso/yui+	π	α	δ	μ	λ
2	hai4de-0q1	π	β	ϵ	μ	λ
3	nag+q8*L	ρ	α	δ	μ	γ
4	K/ehim*13-	σ	α	ϵ	η	λ
5	3gia*ni+aL	π	β	ϵ	η	γ
6	F0/rab1DW*	ρ	α	ϵ	μ	γ
7	Bid2*k1-l0	σ	β	δ	η	λ

(b)

Fig. 2. An example of plaintext (a) and encrypted (b) relation

relations. In principle, database encryption may be performed at different levels of granularity: relation level, attribute level, tuple level, and element level. Both relation level and attribute level imply the communication to the user of the whole relation involved in a query. On the other hand, encrypting at element level would require an excessive workload for clients in encrypting/decrypting data. For balancing the client workload and query execution efficiency, we assume that the database is encrypted at tuple level. The main effort of current research in this scenario is the design of a mechanism that makes it possible to directly query an encrypted database [9]. The existing proposals are based on the use of indexing information associated with each relation in the encrypted database [4, 11]. Such indexes can be used by the server to select the data to be returned in response to a query. More precisely, the server stores an encrypted relation with an index for each attribute on which a query can include a condition. Each plaintext relation is represented in the encrypted database as a relation with an attribute for the encrypted tuple and as many attributes as indexes to be supported. Formally, each relation r_i over schema $R_i(A_{i1}, A_{i2}, \ldots, A_{in})$ in a plaintext database DB is mapped onto a relation r_i^k over schema $R_i^k(\underline{\text{Count}}, \text{Etuple}, I_1, I_2, \ldots, I_n)$ in the encrypted database DB^k where, Count is the primary key; Etuple is an attribute for the encrypted tuple whose value is obtained using an encryption function E_k (k is the key); I_i is the index associated with the i-th attribute.[1] For instance, given relation Employees in Figure 2(a), the corresponding encrypted relation Employees^k is represented in Figure 2(b). As it is visible from this figure, the encrypted relation has the same number of rows as the original one. Let us now discuss how to represent indexing information. A trivial approach to indexing would be to use the plaintext value of each cell. This approach is obviously not suitable as plaintext data would be disclosed. An alternative approach providing the same fine-grained selection capability without disclosing plaintext values is to use the individual encrypted values as index. Therefore, for each cell the outcome of an invertible encryption function over the cell value is used. Formally, for each tuple t in r_i, there exists a tuple t' in r_i^k where, $j = 1, \ldots, n, t'[I_j] = E_k(t[A_{ij}])$. This solution has the advantage of preserving plaintext distinguishability, together with precision and efficiency in query execution, as all the tuples returned belong to the query set of the original query. As a drawback, however, encrypted values reproduce exactly

---

[1] For the sake of simplicity, we assume that each attribute of the original relation has an index in the encrypted one.

	Direct encryption	Hashing
Freq + DB^k	Quotient table	Multiple subset sum problem
DB + DB^k	RCV-graph	RCV line graph

Fig. 3. Abstract models supporting computation of exposure in the four attack scenarios

the plaintext values distribution with respect to values' *cardinality* (i.e., the number of distinct values of the attribute) and frequencies.

A third alternative approach is to use as index the result of a *secure hash function* over the attribute values rather than straightforwardly encrypting the attribute values; this way, the attribute values' distribution can be *flattened* by the hash function. A flexible characteristic of a hash function is the cardinality of its co-domain B, which allows us to adapt it to the granularity of the represented data. When B is small compared with the cardinality of the attribute, the hash function can be interpreted as a mechanism that distributes tuples in $\mid B \mid$ *buckets*; a good hash function (and a secure hash has to be good) distributes uniformly the values in the buckets. For instance, the Employees relation in Figure 2(a) can be indexed considering two buckets, α and β, for attribute Name, and Alice and Carol can be mapped onto α and Bob and David cam be mapped onto β (see Figure 2(b)).[2] With respect to direct encryption, hash-based indexing provides more protection as different plaintext values are mapped onto the same index (see Section 3). By contrast, when hashing is used, the query results will often include spurious tuples (all those belonging to the same bucket of the index) that will have to be removed by the front end receiving it.

As indexes constructed using hash or encryption functions do not preserve the domain order of the original attributes, they cannot support range queries. To this purpose, a fourth indexing approach based on *B+-trees* has been proposed in [4]. In the following sections, we will describe how to compute the inference exposure coefficient when a direct encryption method or an hash based method are used to compute the indexes.

3   Exposure Coefficient Measures

As discussed in Section 1, it is important to be able to evaluate quantitatively the level of exposure associated with the publication of certain indexes and to determine the proper balance between index efficiency and protection. To this purpose, two different scenarios can be considered that differ in the assumption about the attacker's prior knowledge [4]. In the first scenario, called **Freq+DB^k**, the attacker is aware of the exact (or approximate) distribution of plaintext values in the original database in addition to knowing the encrypted database. In the second scenario, called **DB+DB^k**, the attacker has both the encrypted and the plaintext database. Note however that the computation of the exposure coefficient $\mathcal{E}$ depends also on the method adopted for indexing the database, that is, direct encryption or hashing. Figure 3 summarizes the abstract models that we used to obtain an indication of the exposure that characterizes generic databases.

---

[2] Here, the result of the hash function is represented as a Greek letter.

We now briefly describe the rationale behind these abstract models (we refer the reader to [2, 4] for a complete description of these models).

3.1 Direct Encryption Exposure

In the **Freq+DB^k** scenario, although the attacker does not know which index corresponds to which plaintext attribute, she can determine the actual correspondence by comparing their occurrence profiles. Intuitively, values with the same number of occurrences are indistinguishable to the attacker. The exposure of an encrypted relation to indexing inference can then be thought of in terms of an equivalence relation where indexes (and plaintext values) with the same number of occurrences belong to the same equivalence class. The measure of exposure for a single cell in the table is then equal to the inverse of the cardinality of the equivalence class to which it belongs. Consequently, the probability of disclosing a specific association (a tuple is a specific association) is the product of the inverse of the cardinalities of its cells. The exposure of the whole relation can then be estimated as the average exposure of each tuple as follows:

$$\mathcal{E} = \frac{1}{n} \sum_{i=1}^{n} \prod_{j=1}^{k} \mathrm{IC}_{i,j}$$

Here, i ranges over the tuples and j ranges over the columns, and $\mathrm{IC}_{i,j}$ denotes the exposure of value j in tuple i. The exposure coefficient can be computed in $O(n \cdot k)$, where n is the number of tuples and k is the number of attributes.

In the **DB+DB^k** scenario, the model of the attack is based on the definition of *RCV-graphs*. Given a relational table, the corresponding 3-colored undirected graph $G = (V, E)$, called the *RCV-graph* (i.e., the row-column-value–graph), is a graph where the set V of vertexes contains one vertex for each attribute, one vertex for each tuple, and one vertex for each distinct value in each of the attributes; if the same value appears in different attributes, a distinct vertex is introduced for every attribute in which the value appears. The set E of edges contains both edges connecting each vertex representing a value with the vertex representing the column in which the value appears and edges connecting each vertex representing a value with the vertexes representing tuples in which the value appears. This graph has an important property, that is, the RCV-graph built starting from a plaintext table is identical to the RCV-graph built starting from the corresponding encrypted table. The identification of the correspondence between plaintext and index values requires then to establish a correspondence between the encrypted vertex labels and the plaintext values. This correspondence is strongly related to the presence of automorphisms in the RCV-graph. We used the *Nauty* algorithm [13] to produce a concise representation of all the automorphisms. The automorphisms over a graph constitutes a group that, for undirected graphs, can be described by the coarsest *equitable partition* [13] of the vertexes, where each element of the partition (each subset appearing in the partition) contains vertexes that can be considered interchangeable in an automorphism. The Nauty algorithm starts, for the group definition, from a partition on the vertexes that can be immediately derived grouping all the vertexes with the same color and connected by the same number of edges. This partition is then iteratively refined. From the structure of the partition $(C_1 \ldots C_i)$, it derives that the vertexes appearing in the generic partition element C_j are equivalently substitutable in all the automorphisms, as they have exactly the same characteristics. From this observation, it derives that the probability p_i of a correct identification of a vertex $v_i \in C_j$ is equal to the inverse of the cardinality of C_j. Then, given $|C_j|$ vertexes in the partition element C_j, n elements in the equitable partition, and a total number m of vertexes, the exposure coefficient of the table is:

$$\mathcal{E} = \sum_{i=1}^{m} p_i/m = \sum_{j=1}^{n} \sum_{v_i \in C_j} p_i/m = \sum_{j=1}^{n} \sum_{v_i \in C_j} 1/(|C_j| \ m) = \sum_{j=1}^{n} 1/m = n/m$$

The exposure coefficient can be computed in $O(n^2 \log n)$, where n is the number of vertexes in the RCV-graph.

3.2   Hashing Exposure

It is important to note that collisions due to hashing increase protection from inference. The hash function is then characterized by a *collision factor* denoting the number of attribute values that on average collide on the same index value. As an example, consider the relation in Figure 2. Here, Alice and Carol are mapped on the same value α. The abstract models used for the computation of the inference exposure consider separately each attribute of the table; the inference exposure for the whole table can be obtained by aggregating the values associated with each single attribute (see Section 4). Note that while direct encryption indexing methods preserve the association of values of attributes within the tuples, the hash based methods do not preserve this association and therefore a potential intruder cannot use such information. Consequently, the exposure index computation is performed at attribute level and then each single value is aggregated to derive the exposure associated with the whole table.

In the **Freq+DB^k** scenario, the goal of the attacker is to find a mapping from plaintext values to indexing values that satisfies the constraints given by the attacker's prior knowledge which is represented by the occurrences of each plaintext value and each hashed one. The exposure coefficient is then computed as follows. We first enumerate the different mappings by using an adaptation of Pisinger's algorithm for the subset sum problem. We then compute the exposure coefficient for each mapping and we take the average of these exposure coefficients. The exposure coefficient can be computed in $O(n^k)$, where n and k are values related to the number of different items in the index domain and their frequency in the encrypted table.

In the **DB+DB^k** scenario, the exposure coefficient is computed by extending the RCV-graph described in the previous Section. As before, identifying the correct correspondence between plaintext and hash values requires finding a matching between each vertex of the plaintext RCV-graph and a vertex of the corresponding encrypted RCV-graph. When collisions occur, the two graphs are not identical, as different vertexes of the plaintext RCV-graph may collapse to the same encrypted RCV-graph vertex. We can observe that the number of edges connecting row vertexes to value vertexes in the plaintext and encrypted RCV-graph is the same. Therefore, the problem can be viewed as finding a correct matching between the edges of the plaintext RCV-graph and the edges of the encrypted RCV-graph. Following this observation, we compute the exposure coefficient as the average of the exposure coefficients associated with an attribute in correspondence of each matching. The exposure coefficient can be computed in $O(n!n)$, where n is the number of nodes in the graph.

4   Exposure Coefficient Measures based on Aggregation Operators

The *aggregation operators* are mathematical objects that have the function of combining a set of numbers into a unique representative (or meaningful) number. As specified in the previous Section, we are interested in computing the exposure coefficient associated with a whole table when indexes have been obtained by applying an hash-based method. To this purpose, it is possible to use one of the many operators that satisfy the definition of aggregation operator [14]. Formally, an aggregation operator is defined as follows.

Definition 1. *An operator $A : \cup_{n \in \mathbb{N}} [0, 1]^n \to [0, 1]$ is an* aggregation operator *on the unit interval if the following conditions hold:*

identity property: $A(x) = x;$[3]
boundary conditions: $A(0, \ldots, 0) = 0$ *and* $A(1, \ldots, 1) = 1;$
monotonicity: $A(x_1, \ldots, x_n) \leq A(y_1, \ldots, y_n)$ *if* $(x_i \leq y_i) \, \forall i = 1, \ldots, n.$

Note that additional properties (*mathematical* and *behavioral*) may also be added [7, 8]. Although many aggregation operators satisfy these properties [18], we consider the *Weighted Mean* (WM) [1, 16] and the *Ordered Weighted Averaging operator* (OWA) [19]. These two operators combine the input values according to a single set of weights. Therefore, to apply these operators, we first need to associate a weight (or set of weights) with each attribute of a relational table. The determination of these weights is usually done in an heuristic way (after trial and error) or asking an expert to supply them. We now describe the use of these operators more in details.

4.1   Weighted Mean

The Weighted Mean allows the system to compute an aggregate value from the ones corresponding to the exposure coefficient associated with each single index of a given table. This operator can take into consideration the risk connected to the disclosure of an attribute due to the inference from the corresponding index. The formal definition of a Weighted Mean operator is as follows.

Definition 2. *Let* $\mathbf{p} = [p_1 \; p_2 \; \ldots \; p_n]$ *be a weighting vector of dimension n such that* $i = 1, \ldots, n, p_i \in [0, 1]$ *and* $\sum_{i=1}^{n} p_i = 1$. *A mapping* $f_{\mathrm{WM}} : \mathbb{R}^n \to \mathbb{R}$ *is a Weighted Mean (WM) operator of dimension n if:*

$$f_{\mathrm{WM}}(a_1, a_2, \ldots, a_n) = \sum_{i=1}^{n} p_i a_i. \tag{1}$$

---

[3] This property is required when the argument of the aggregation operator is an unary vector.

The weighting vector **p** is here used to reflect the *sensitivity* of the attributes in the original table. More precisely, an attribute is considered more "sensitive" than another attribute when its disclosure puts more at risk the outsourced database. As above-mentioned, there are several ways to choose the weights and we assume that a domain expert provides a vector depending on the context. This vector multiplied by the values of the exposure coefficients permits the evaluation of the robustness of the indexing method: a higher protection of the most sensitive attributes (a low exposure coefficient for the connected index) leads to a lower global exposure coefficient value; on the contrary, a lower protection of the most sensitive attributes leads to a higher global exposure coefficient value. The main advantage of using a weighted mean with respect to the classical mean is that it allows to make a distinction among the attributes of a table. For instance, if the exposure coefficients associated with the indexes computed from the more sensitive attributes are low, we would expect a low global exposure co-efficient. Vice versa, if the exposure coefficients associated with the indexes computed from the more sensitive attributes are high, we would expect a high global exposure coefficient. If we use the classical mean operator, it is possible that a similar global exposure coefficient is obtained in both situations because it considers the attributes equivalent.

Example 1. Consider the relations in Figure 2 and suppose that the most sensitive attribute is Name followed by Age, Marital Status, Job, and Id. A possible weighting vector reflecting the sensitivity of the attributes is, for example, $\mathbf{p} = [.05\ .40\ .30\ .15\ .10]$ that represents the weights associated with attributes Id, Name, Age, Marital Status, and Job, respectively. Suppose now that the exposure coefficient associated with each index is computed as discussed in Section 3.2: $\mathcal{E}_I = [1/7!\ 1/36\ 1/36\ 1/8\ 1/8]$. According to the WM definition, the global exposure coefficient is:

$$\mathcal{E} = \left(\frac{1}{7!}\right)(.05) + \left(\frac{1}{36}\right)(.40) + \left(\frac{1}{36}\right)(.30) + \left(\frac{1}{8}\right)(.15) + \left(\frac{1}{8}\right)(.10) \cong .0507$$

If the exposure coefficients associated with the indexes are $\mathcal{E}_I = [1/7!\ 1/8\ 1/8\ 1/36\ 1/36]$, we would obtain $\mathcal{E} \cong .0944$ and we can conclude that the protection is worse than the first case because sensitive attributes are less protected.

It is important to note that the primary key of a table is always well protected because its values are indistinguishable. For this reason, in the above example, the weight associated with the primary key Id is very low.

4.2   Ordered Weighted Averaging Operator

The OWA operator allows the user to weight the input values in relation to their relative ordering. In this way, a system can give more importance to a subset of the input values than to another subset. The OWA operator is formally defined as follows.

Definition 3. *Let* $\mathbf{w} = [w_1\ w_2\ \dots\ w_n]$ *be a weighting vector of dimension n such that* $i = 1, \dots, n, w_i \in [0, 1]$ *and* $\sum_{i=1}^{n} w_i = 1$. *A mapping* $f_{OWA} : \mathbb{R}^n \to \mathbb{R}$ *is an*

Ordered Weighted Averaging (OWA) *operator of dimension* n *if*:

$$f_{\text{OWA}}(a_1, a_2, ..., a_n) = \sum_{i=1}^{n} w_i a_{\sigma(i)}, \qquad (2)$$

where $\{\sigma(1), \sigma(2), ..., \sigma(n)\}$ *is a permutation of* $\{1, 2, ..., n\}$ *such that* $\forall i = 2, ..., n,$
$a_{\sigma(i-1)} \geq a_{\sigma(i)}.$

The exposure coefficient associated with an index reflects how the corresponding attribute is protected. An higher exposure coefficient (always a value between 0 and 1) indicates that a particular attribute has a low protection and vice versa. Using an OWA operator, it is therefore possible to highlight this fact by choosing an appropriate weighting vector **w**. In particular, there are two strategies that the data owner may adopt:

- *maximal protection*: a table is considered protected only if all attributes are well protected (low exposure coefficient). Even a single not well protected attribute may cause a poor evaluation of the hash function adopted. In this case, it is necessary that the highest exposure coefficients have an higher weight to amplify their contribution to the final result (**w** has to be decreasing).
- *minimal protection*: a table is considered protected even if just one of its attributes is well protected. In this case, it is necessary that the lowest exposure coefficients have an higher weight (**w** has to be increasing).

There are also many other intermediate strategies between these two ones, depending on the policy that the data owner has decided to adopt.

In summary, by comparing these two aggregation operators (WM and OWA), it is easy to see that in the WM operator the weights measure the importance of the attributes independently from the corresponding exposure coefficients. On the other hand, in the OWA operator weights measure the importance of the exposure coefficients (in relation to other values), independently from the attributes with which they are associated.

Example 2. Consider the relations in Figure 2 and the exposure coefficients $\mathcal{E}_I = [1/7!\ 1/36\ 1/36\ 1/8\ 1/8]$ associated with attributes Id, Name, Age, Marital Status, and Job, respectively. We first order these coefficients thus obtaining the permutation: $\mathcal{E}_{I\sigma} = \{1/8, 1/8, 1/36, 1/36, 1/7!\}$. If the data owner wants to apply the maximal protection strategy, she has to define a decreasing weighting vector such as **w** $= [.30\ .30\ .20\ .15\ .05]$. In this case the exposure coefficient for the whole table is:

$$\mathcal{E} = \left(\frac{1}{8}\right)(.30) + \left(\frac{1}{8}\right)(.30) + \left(\frac{1}{36}\right)(.20) + \left(\frac{1}{36}\right)(.15) + \left(\frac{1}{7!}\right)(.05) \cong .0848$$

On the contrary, if the data owner wants to apply the minimal protection strategy she has to choose an increasing weighting vector such as **w** $= [.05\ .15\ .20\ .30\ .30]$. In this case, the exposure coefficient for the whole table is: $\mathcal{E} \cong .03894$ and is lower than the previous one because the low values in $\mathcal{E}_{I\sigma}$ have high weights.

5   Conclusions and Future Work

We presented different measures for evaluating the robustness of indexing techniques against inference attacks in the DAS scenario. Issues to be investigated will include the analysis of more complex operators for the computation of the exposure coefficient of a whole table such as non linear operators and the WOWA operator.

Acknowledgments

This work was supported in part by the European Union within the PRIME Project in the FP6/IST Programme under contract IST-2002-507591 and by the Italian MIUR within the KIWI and MAPS projects.

References

1. Aczél, J.: On Weighted Synthesis of Judgments. Aequationes Math. **27** (1984) 288–307
2. Ceselli, A., Damiani, E., De Capitani di Vimercati, S., Jajodia, S., Paraboschi, S., Samarati, P.: Modeling and Assessing Inference Exposure in Encrypted Databases. ACM Transactions on Information and System Security (TISSEC) **8(1)** (February 2005) 119–152
3. Damiani, E., De Capitani di Vimercati, S., Finetti, M., Paraboschi, S., Samarati, P., Jajodia, S.: Implementation of a Storage Mechanism for Untrusted DBMSs. In Proc. of the Second International IEEE Security in Storage Workshop, Washington DC, USA (May 2003)
4. Damiani, E., De Capitani di Vimercati, S., Jajodia, S., Paraboschi, S., Samarati, P.: Balancing Confidentiality and Efficiency in Untrusted Relational DBMSs. In Proc. of the 10th ACM Conference on Computer and Communications Security, Washington, DC, USA (October 2003)
5. Davida, G.I., Wells, D.L., Kam, J.B.: A Database Encryption System with Subkeys. ACM Transactions on Database Systems **6(2)** (June 1981) 312–328
6. Denning, D.E.: Cryptography and Data Security. Addison-Wesley (1982)
7. Fodor, J., Marichal, J.L., Roubens, M.: Characterization of the Ordered Weighted Averaging Operators. IEEE Transactions on Fuzzy Systems **3(2)** (1995) 236–240
8. Grabisch, M.: Fuzzy Integral in Multicriteria Decision Making. Fuzzy Sets and Systems **69** (1995) 279–298
9. Hacigümüs, H., Iyer, B., Mehrotra, S.: Providing Database as a Service. In Proc. of the 18th International Conference on Data Engineering, San Jose, California, USA (February 2002)
10. Hacigümüs, H., Iyer, B., Mehrotra, S.: Ensuring Integrity of Encrypted Databases in Database as a Service Model. In Proc. of the IFIP Conference on Data and Applications Security, Estes Park Colorado (August 2003)
11. Hacigümüs, H., Iyer, B., Mehrotra, S., Li, C.: Executing SQL over Encrypted Data in the Database-Service-Provider Model. In Proc. of the ACM SIGMOD'2002, Madison, Wisconsin, USA (June 2002)
12. Hore, B., Mehrotra, S., Tsudik, G.: A Privacy-Preserving Index for Range Queries. In Proc. of the 30th Very Large DataBase Conference, Toronto, Canada (2004)
13. McKay, B.D.: Practical Graph Isomorphism. Congressus Numerantium, **30** (1981) 45–87
14. Mesiar, R., Komorníková, M.: Aggregation Operators. In Proc. of the XI Conference on Applied Mathematics "PRIM' 96", Budva, Serbia and Montenegro (1996).

15. Mykletun, E., Narasimha, M., Tsudik, G.: Authentication and Integrity in Outsourced Database. In Proc. of the 11th Annual Network and Distributed System Security Symposium, San Diego, California, USA (February 2004)
16. Torra, V.: The Weighted OWA Operator. International Journal of Intelligent Systems **12(2)** (1997) 153–166
17. Torra, V.: On the Learning of Weights in some Aggregation Operators: the Weighted Mean and the OWA Operators. Mathware and Soft Computing **6** (1999) 249–265
18. Xu, Z.S., Da, Q.L.: An Overview of Operators for Aggregating Information. Iternational Journal of Intelligent Systems **18** (2003) 953–969
19. Yager, R.: On Ordered Weighted Averaging Aggregation Operators in Multicriteria Decision Making. IEEE Transactions on Systems, Man and Cybernetics **18(1)** (1988) 183–190

Author Index